IMAGES
of America

UKRAINIANS OF WESTERN PENNSYLVANIA

I0805884

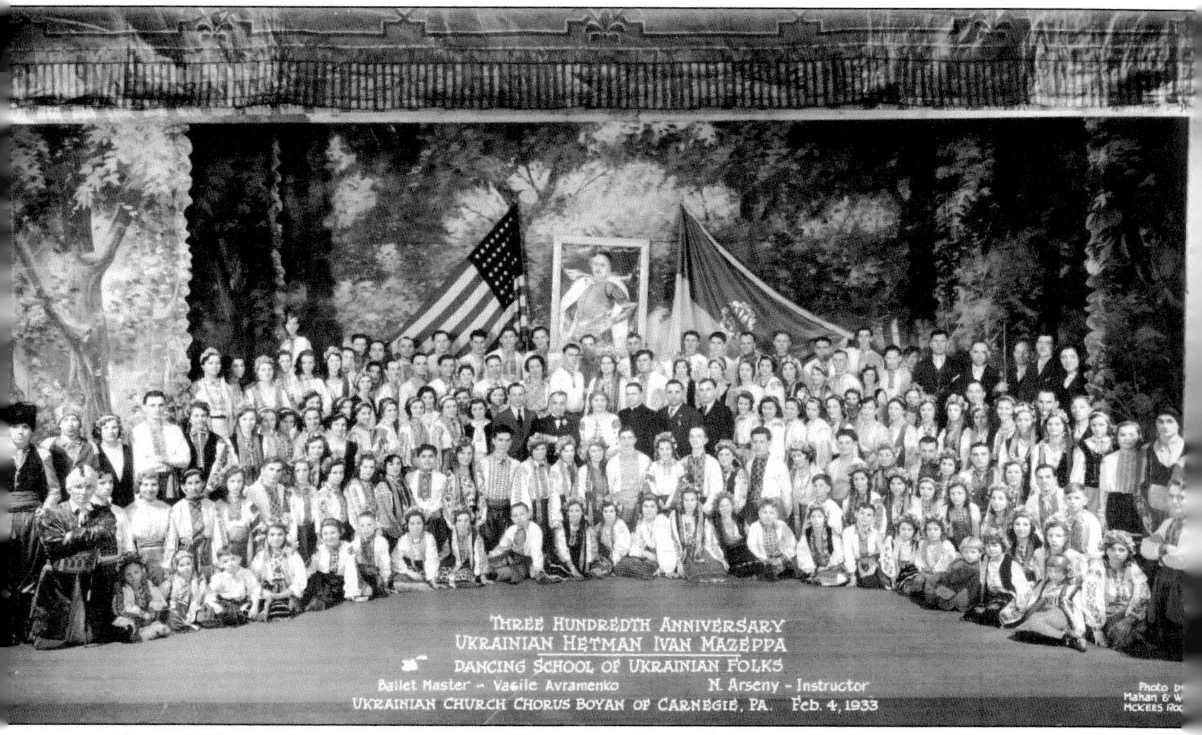

THE 300TH ANNIVERSARY OF HETMAN IVAN MAZEPPA'S BIRTH. Ukrainians from throughout western Pennsylvania gather on February 4, 1933, for a celebration surrounding the 300th anniversary of Hetman Ivan Mazeppa's (also known as Mazepa) birth. Hetman Mazepa was the leader of the Zaporozhian Kozaks (Cossacks) and benefactor of the Ukrainian people, best known to Americans via works by Victor Hugo, Franz Liszt, and Lord Byron dedicated to his historical role and personal characteristics of bravery and valor.

On the cover: Please see above. (Courtesy of Museum and Archives of SS. Peter and Paul Ukrainian Orthodox Greek Catholic Church, Carnegie.)

IMAGES
of America

UKRAINIANS OF WESTERN PENNSYLVANIA

Stephen P. Haluszczak

ARCADIA
PUBLISHING

Copyright © 2009 by Stephen P. Haluszczak
ISBN 978-0-7385-6495-1

Published by Arcadia Publishing
Charleston, South Carolina

Printed in the United States of America

Library of Congress Control Number: 2008938223

For all general information contact Arcadia Publishing at:
Telephone 843-853-2070
Fax 843-853-0044
E-mail sales@arcadiapublishing.com
For customer service and orders:
Toll-Free 1-888-313-2665

Visit us on the Internet at www.arcadiapublishing.com

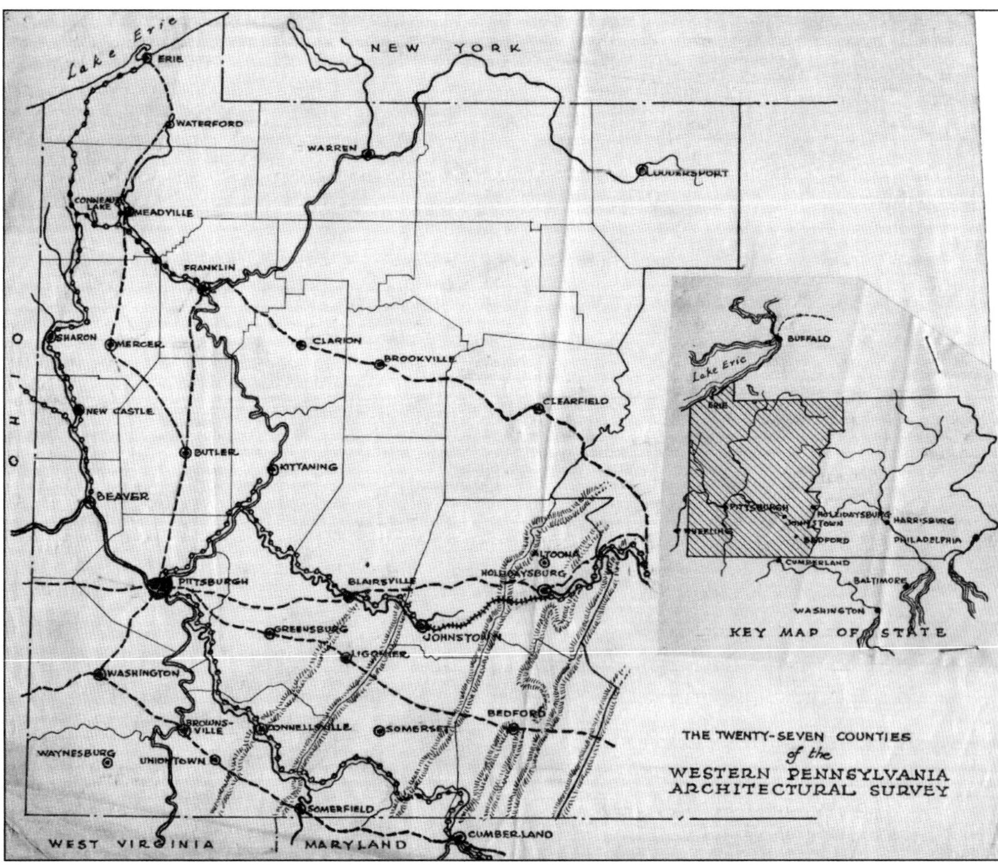

WESTERN PENNSYLVANIA. This architectural survey shows the 27 counties that constitute western Pennsylvania. (Courtesy of Library and Archives Division, Senator John Heinz History Center.)

Contents

ACKNOWLEDGMENTS

I dedicate this book to my parents, Paul Haluszczak and Marlene Kapeluck Haluszczak, who among so many things have given me the gift of identity and the love of heritage.

It has been a genuine honor for me to write this book—truly a community project. Without the assistance of western Pennsylvania Ukrainians and other friends, its writing would not have been possible.

My heartfelt thanks to Ralph Ashworth for suggesting that I apply to write this book and for prodding me when I hesitated; Janice Auth for suggesting I write "Tour Ukrainian Pittsburgh" in 2007—a publication of the Ukrainian Cultural and Humanitarian Institute and a precursor to this project; the Ukrainian Selfreliance of Western Pennsylvania Federal Credit Union and its manager Yaroslaw Hodowanec for invaluable logistical and technical support; my proofreaders and advisors: Oksana Byczkalo, Kateryna Dowbenko, Marlene Haluszczak, Yaroslaw Hodowanec, Melanie Hutskow, Nickolas C. Kotow, Tam Malloy, Ty Malloy, Lesya Protynyak, and Fr. Steve Repa; Lt. Col. Stephen P. Hallick-Holutiak Jr. (U.S. Army, retired) for advice and research about Ukrainians in western Pennsylvania; Dr. Alexander Lushnycky for advice and support; Michael Komichak for promotion; Melanie Hutskow for administrative help; and for assistance in gathering photographs: Bishop Robert Moskal of the Ukrainian Catholic Church of America, Bishop Daniel Zelinsky of the Ukrainian Orthodox Church of the United States of America, Fr. Andrew Gall, Fr. John Haluszczak, Fr. Ihor Hohosha, Fr. Michael Kochis, Fr. Dea. Dennis Lapushansky, Fr. Paisius McGrath, Fr. Valerian Michlic, Fr. Tim Tomson, American-Ukrainian Citizens Club of Wilmerding, Annita Andrick, Dr. Ihor Bemko, Bohdan Bohonok, Oksana Byczkalo, Stephanie Fedora, Paula and John Howe, Carol Hubenthal, Michael Jula, Michael Kapeluck, Dana Krupnyk, Dr. Myron Kuropas, David Lamont, Susan Leis, Marie Lidgett, John Alan Makar, Eva Malesnick, Natalia Tokar Milligan, Ethan and Natalie Nixon, Gina Peirce, Helen Proch, Karen Sheptak, Emily Stecko, Oksana Trytjak, Taris Vrcek, Marika Zaliszczuk, and Lauren Zebelsky.

I am indebted to the elders of the community and all Ukrainians of western Pennsylvania who have passed into eternal memory for building such an interesting community. And I thank my Lord and Savior Jesus Christ for blessing me with the ability and strength to complete this project.

Finally, I thank my editor Erin Vosgien for her professionalism, her trust and belief in me, and her always-prompt replies. Arcadia Publishing made this project a pleasure to develop.

Abbreviations for courtesy lines are as follows: Library and Archives of Very Reverend Stephen Hallick-Holutiak (LAVRSHH); Museum and Archives of SS. Peter and Paul Ukrainian Orthodox Greek Catholic Church, Carnegie (MASPPUOGCCC); Ukrainian Catholic Diocese of St. Josaphat in Parma (UCDSJP); Ukrainian Cultural and Humanitarian Institute (UCHI); Ukrainian Orthodox Church of the United State of America (UOCUSA); and Ukrainian Selfreliance of Western Pennsylvania Federal Credit Union (USWPFCU).

INTRODUCTION

Western Pennsylvania is a region blessed with abundant natural resources, including coal, oil, natural gas, and lumber. In the late 1800s, these resources combined with the region's geographical location to produce one of the most powerful industrial centers the world has ever known. It was the home of business titans such as Andrew Carnegie and Henry Clay Frick, as well as the United Steel Workers. At the height of its industrial might, a dozen steel plants lined the Monongahela River, "coal patch" towns were everywhere, and a multitude of jobs beckoned immigrants from far and wide. Many of the immigrants who came were Ukrainians.

Who are the Ukrainians? The earliest known people to inhabit the territory of Ukraine were the Trypillians (around 6000–1500 BC). Various nomadic peoples including the Cimmerians, Sarmatians, and Scythians migrated to what today is Ukraine between 1500 and 200 BC The Ukrainian people's direct ancestors, the Slavs, moved to contemporary Ukrainian territory starting in the fourth century. The kingdom of Kyivan-Rus' existed from around 880 AD until the mid-13th century, thriving as a commercial city located on the main route of trade between the northern parts of Europe and the Byzantine Empire.

The Kyivan state was overrun by Mongol and Tatar hordes, initiating a period of decline in importance as a trading center and creating long-term political instability. At this time, many Kyivan-Ukrainians moved west into the politically stable kingdom of Galicia-Volhyn—now western Ukraine. This state lost its independence in 1340 with Galicia falling under Polish rule and Volhyn under Lithuanian rule. With the subsequent union of Poland and Lithuania, these Ukrainian lands came under the rule of the Polish Commonwealth. The Ukrainian people eventually became serfs—peasant farm laborers, who were literally the property of landowners.

The Ukrainians organized social and military brotherhoods known as the *kozaky*, which safeguarded the Ukrainian language, religion, culture, and identity. Living freely in the frontier regions of the Ukrainian steppes, they organized their life under democratically elected hetmans (leaders). The kozaky united with Ukrainian peasants in revolts against the harsh rule of the Polish kings and in 1648 established a Kozak state named Ukraine—a term in use for centuries, which some translate as "borderland."

After a military treaty with Russian czar Peter the Great, which Russia interpreted as one of union rather than protection, Ukraine allied itself with Poland and Lithuania in 1658 in order to rid itself of Russian rule. Although victorious over Russia in 1659, Ukraine was divided in half between Poland and Russia along the Dnipro River just eight years later. After several unsuccessful attempts to regain Ukrainian independence and decades of resistance to foreign rule, the kozaky ceased to exist by 1781.

The Russian Empire passed edicts and laws outlawing the use of the Ukrainian language, as well as other expressions of the Ukrainian identity. Ukrainians lived as serfs until 1848 in western Ukrainian regions and until 1861 in central Ukraine. During the mid-1800s, a reawakening of nationalities was sweeping Europe. The advancing cause of national self-determination continued into World War I as delineated by U.S. president Woodrow Wilson's "Fourteen Points" foreign policy.

Within this context of struggle, it is estimated that 268,311 Ukrainians settled in the United States just between 1899 and 1930—almost half of them in Pennsylvania. Ninety percent of them remained in the United States and most settled in industrial centers and mining communities, taking jobs as manual laborers. The very first of the Ukrainians settled in northeastern Pennsylvania, and soon after began to migrate into western Pennsylvania.

Most Ukrainian immigrants to western Pennsylvania arrived before World War I and worked in the coal mines and steel mills that were scattered throughout the region. Hailing from a region of Europe abundant with natural resources but with a poorly educated populace living in poverty, these early immigrants struggled with a foreign language, the lack of a social support network from an established ethnic community, and harsh working conditions. Yet it was they who built the foundations upon which the future Ukrainian community would stand and thrive—the many churches, organizations, and insurance fraternals, which would have a long-term impact.

Those claiming Ukrainian heritage include a diverse group of people, including the Boykos, Hutsuls, Lemkos, Bukovinians, as well as those from central and eastern parts of Ukraine. The political and linguistic experiences of the earliest Ukrainian immigrants differed somewhat as they hailed from lands controlled by others—the Austro-Hungarian Empire, the Russian Empire, Poland, and Rumania. They found common ground in their roots from Kyivan-Rus', their Eastern-rite Christian heritage, similar traditions, and a common tongue, which they referred to as speaking *po-nashomu*, meaning "in our own way."

One

Here and There
Ukrainians Everywhere

Ukrainian immigration to western Pennsylvania has progressed in a way that mirrored the political developments in Europe and has taken place in four waves: 1878 to 1914; the 1920s; 1948 through the 1950s; and 1992 to the present. At the time most Ukrainians arrived in western Pennsylvania, Ukraine did not yet exist as a sovereign political nation, and they were known by many different regional and provincial names. The fact that until 1914 the United States registered immigrants by nation of origin and not nationality added confusion causing many Ukrainians to be listed as Poles, Russians, and Austrians. Most of these early Ukrainian immigrants identified themselves by the Latin term *Ruthenian* but also used the terms *Rusyns*, *Rusnaks*, or even *Galicians*. Some whose ethnic identity was so closely connected to their religious identity identified themselves as *Greek Catholic*, and were registered as Greek. Adding to the confusion, Americans erroneously translated the terms *Rus'ka* and *Rusyn* as "Russian." Many Americans, therefore, considered them to be Russians. The term *Ukrainian* came into general usage upon the declaration of the Ukrainian National Republic in 1918.

This first group of Ukrainians settled in and around coal and steel towns scattered throughout western Pennsylvania. Preceding the era of mass vehicle ownership, these communities remained somewhat isolated from one another. By 1920, western Pennsylvania had 20 Ukrainian churches.

The 1920s saw a second wave of Ukrainian immigration—a set of people better-educated and more ethnically conscious. Ukrainian dance troupes, choral groups, and newspapers were organized, and being better standardized, the language began to flourish. In 1934, western Pennsylvanian communities that sustained formal Ukrainian organizations numbered 115.

The third wave was composed of those Ukrainians displaced by World War II. It was even better educated and arguably the most nationally conscious. This group built community structures and enhanced the Ukrainian political consciousness. The fourth wave began arriving in the early 1990s and, like the first wave, the group has come to the area in search of economic opportunity and stability. As the economy of the Pittsburgh region has shifted from its heavy dependence on manufacturing, however, the number of new immigrants has not been large.

Throughout the years, each of these established Ukrainian communities has sponsored Ukrainian activities independently. Often, they collaborated through acting troupes, choirs, and sports leagues and worked together to sponsor cultural events or protests about events taking place in Eastern Europe. While attempts have been made to coordinate activities more closely, a strong central Ukrainian community organization has never materialized. These diverse, far-flung communities share much in common, however, that constitutes a unique western Pennsylvania Ukrainian experience.

Today an estimated 100,000 western Pennsylvanians trace their heritage to Ukraine. A drive through the region will present many opportunities to spot traces of Ukrainian settlement. Such a trip will show that in western Pennsylvania, Ukrainians are here, there, and everywhere.

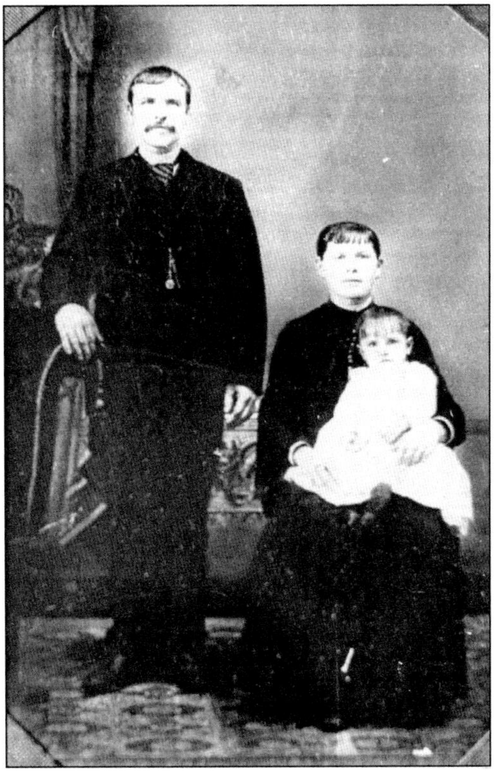

PITTSBURGH'S FIRST UKRAINIAN. The first known Ukrainian immigrants to the city of Pittsburgh were Andrew Andrejczyn and his brother Theofil, their cousin Fedir Andrejczyn, and Wasyl Vojtovych. Only Andrew made Pittsburgh his home—the others returned to their families in Europe after having achieved their primary goal in coming to America, which was to make some money in the land of opportunity. Andrew was 20 years old when he arrived in Pittsburgh and lived as a boarder with a Polish family on the city's South Side. Having saved enough money, he sent for a Ukrainian bride when he was 29. Although they had never met previously, he proposed marriage via correspondence, she accepted, and they were married. Their first child, Mary, was born on July 7, 1888, and she is considered the first Ukrainian child to have been born in the city. This photograph was taken in 1890. (Courtesy of Dr. Aleksander Lushnycky.)

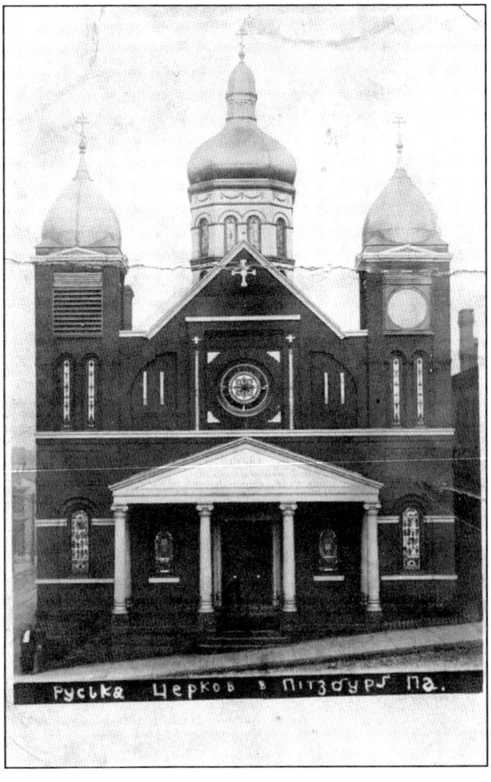

ST. JOHN THE BAPTIST UKRAINIAN CATHOLIC CHURCH, SOUTH SIDE PITTSBURGH. St. John's is pictured as it appeared in the early 1900s before expansion. Founded in 1891, it is considered the mother of all Ukrainian churches in western Pennsylvania, and for quite a time, Ukrainians from throughout the area traveled for miles to attend holy day services or to have weddings or baptisms performed here in their cherished Eastern Rite. (Courtesy of Steve Pituch.)

OFF TO THE MINES. Bituminous coal seams are located throughout western Pennsylvania, and "coal patch" towns sprang up wherever coal could be mined. This coal miner from Nanty Glo is dressed for a day's work. (Courtesy of Irene Nestor.)

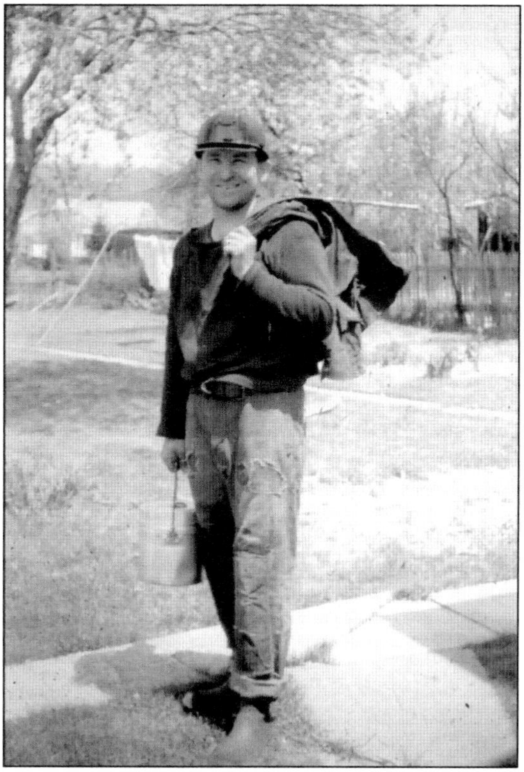

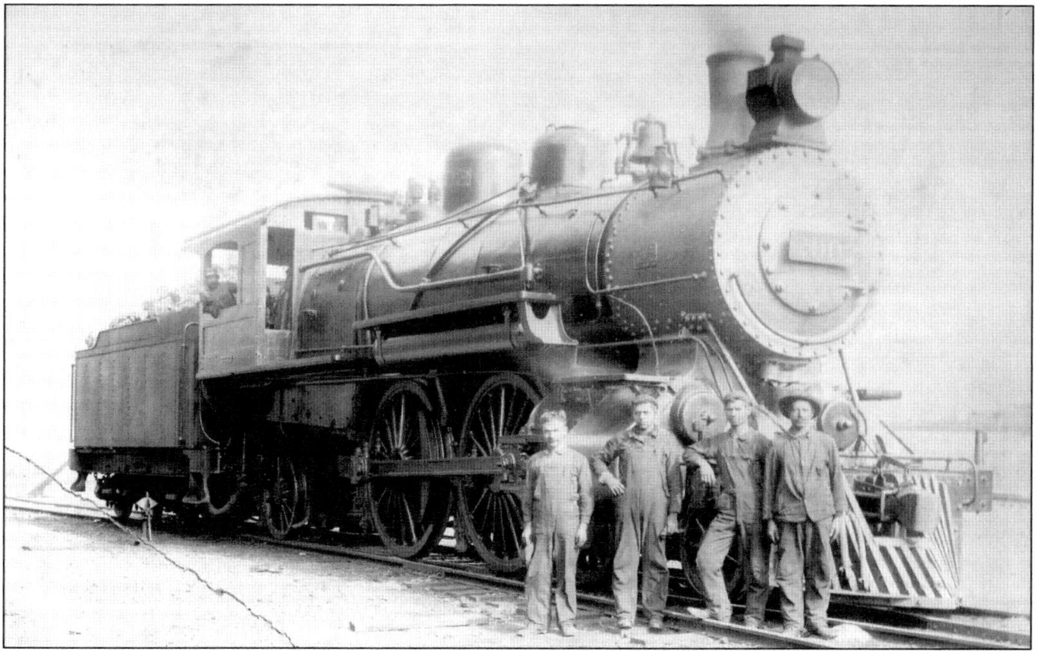

WORKING ON THE RAILROAD. Another of the major industries in western Pennsylvania that attracted immigrants was the railroads. Here four Ukrainian immigrants pose in front of a Wabash Railroad locomotive at Rook Station in Green Tree around 1910. (Courtesy of Thomas N. Sally.)

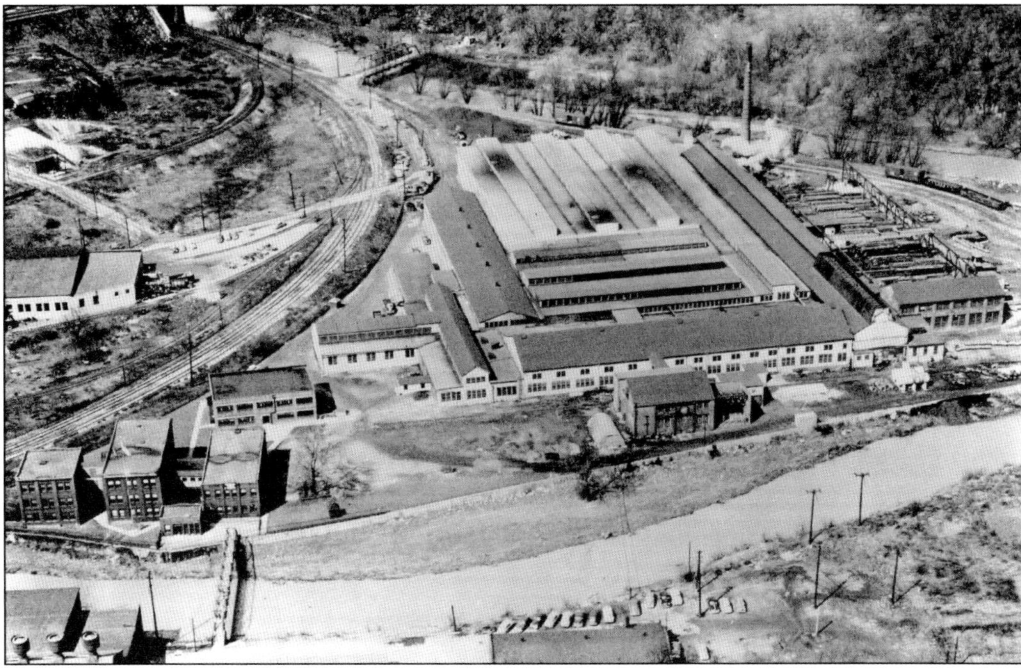

THE STEEL CITY. The city of Pittsburgh was long known as the steel city, and steel mills marked the landscape of towns throughout western Pennsylvania. This 1952 photograph shows the Columbia Steel plant located in Scott Township, which employed many Ukrainians in the southwestern part of Allegheny County. (Courtesy of MASPPUOGCCC.)

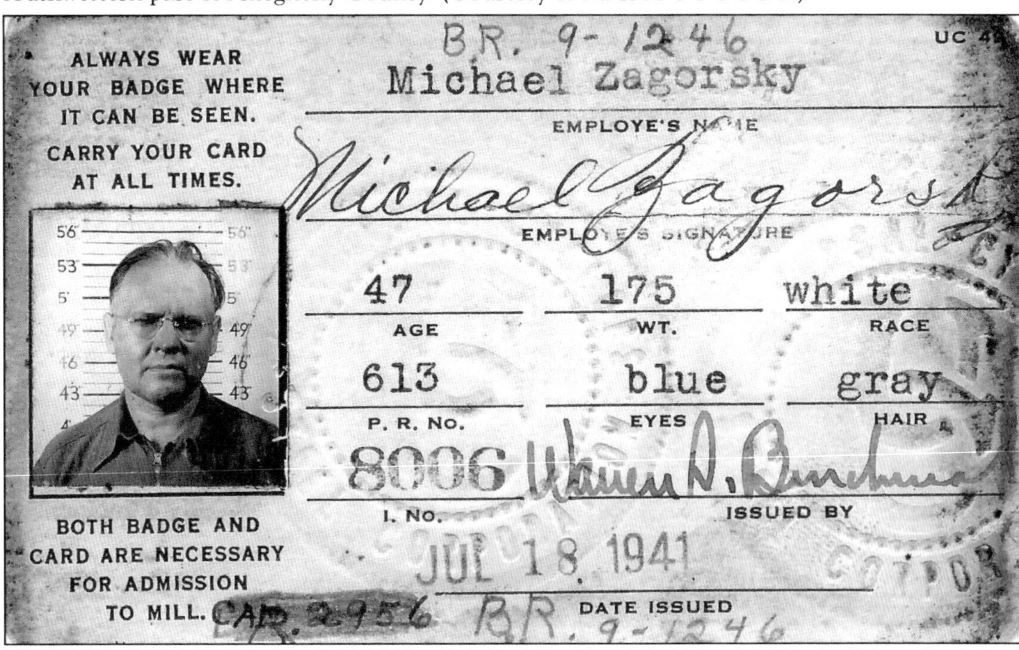

A BADGE OF HONOR. This is a typical badge worn by a worker in the many steel mills in western Pennsylvania. Pittsburgh as the center of the region, earned the nickname "Arsenal of the World" during World War I and billions of dollars flowed to the city and region during World War II to convert factories for use in the war effort. (Courtesy of Mark F. Popivchak.)

CITY LANDSCAPE. Arriving before mass ownership of the automobile, the earliest Ukrainian immigrants lived close to their work and took public transportation if it was available. Often those living in smaller towns and villages walked several miles per day to and from work, stores, and church. Stairways can be found throughout cities and towns of western Pennsylvania traversing the region's hilly topography. This scene from Ford City shows St. Mary Ukrainian Catholic Church in the background. (Courtesy of Pat Morovich.)

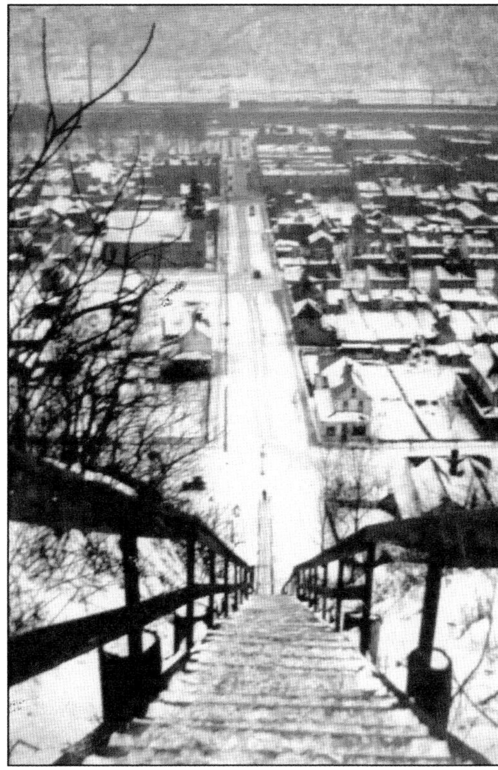

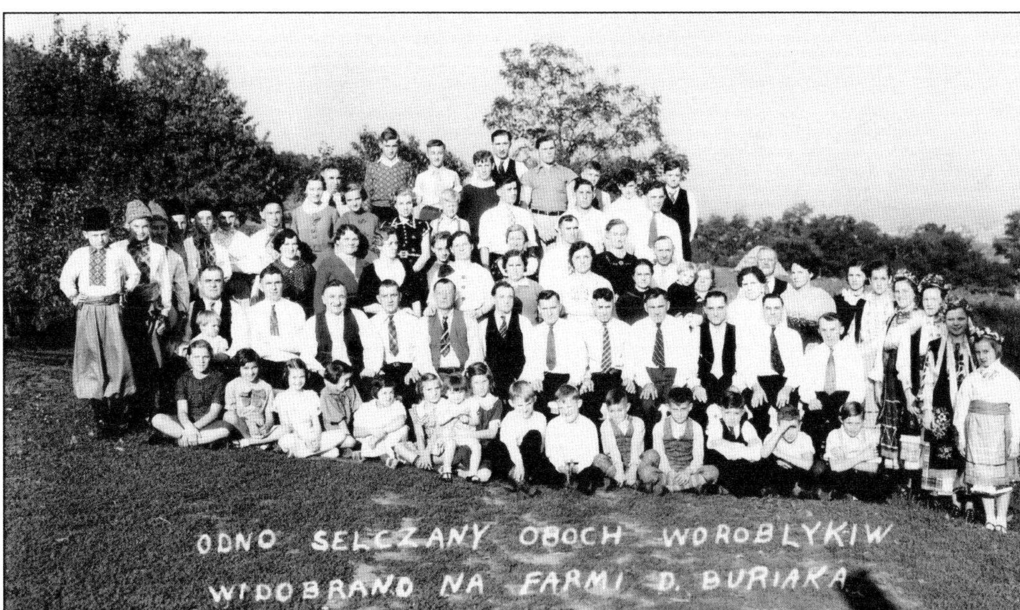

TOGETHER AGAIN ACROSS THE SEA. Former residents of the two villages of Voroblyk gather for a picnic on the farm of the Buriak family. It has been common practice for one resident of a village to settle in America and for family and friends to follow and settle near them in western Pennsylvania, depending on each other for support in finding jobs and adjusting to life in a new country. (Courtesy of Pat Morovich.)

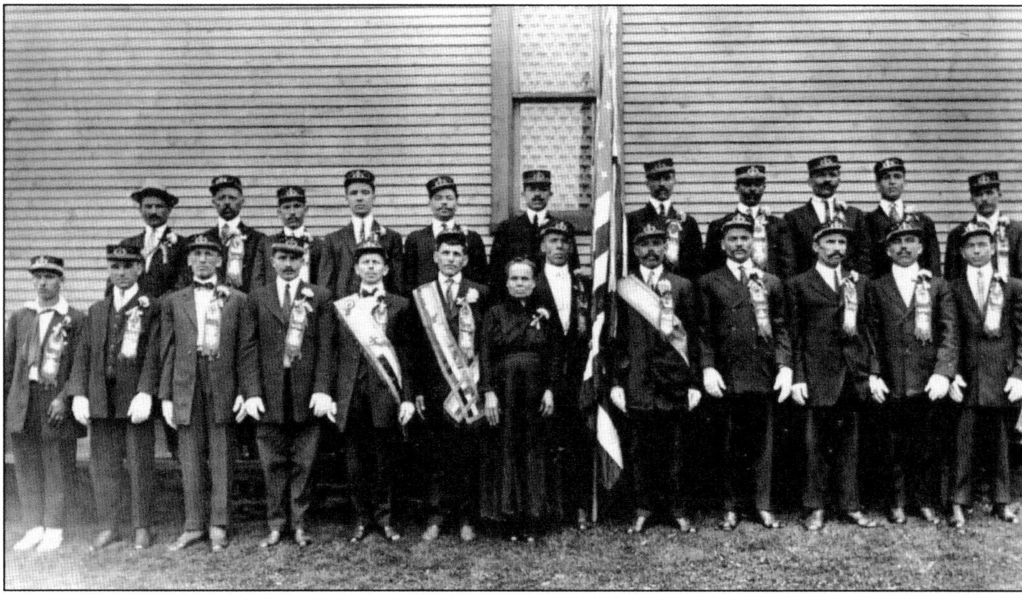

THE UKRAINIAN NATIONAL ASSOCIATION. The Ukrainian National Association (UNA) was the first of the four major Ukrainian insurance fraternals, which were founded to provide insurance products for members in the days before OSHA and workers' compensation. Originally named the Ruthenian National Soyuz, the name was changed officially in 1914. In this 1911 photograph, members of the St. Nicholas Lodge Branch 255 gather in front of Holy Family Church in West Newton. (Courtesy of Helen Kallenborn.)

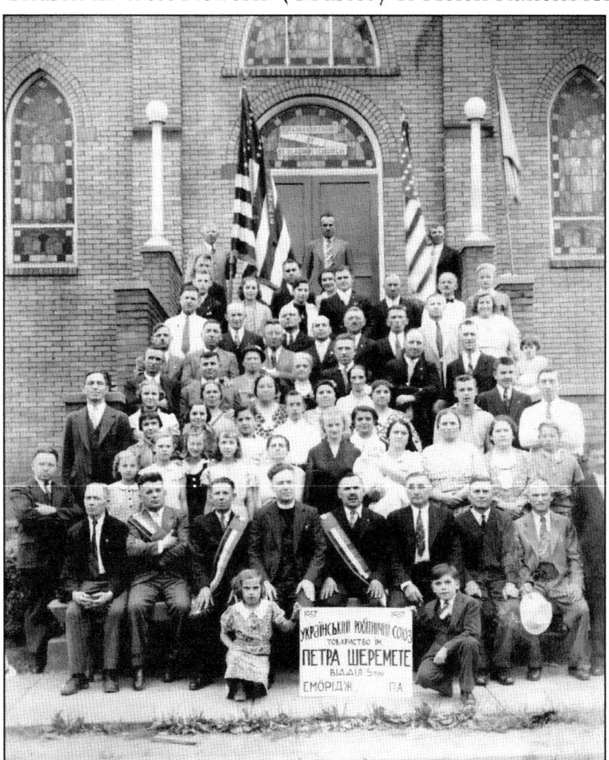

UKRAINIAN WORKINGMEN'S ASSOCIATION. Members of the Ambridge Ukrainian Workingmen's Association (UWA) branch pose on the steps of St. Vladimir Ukrainian Orthodox Church in 1937. Founded in 1911, the UWA was the second of the four Ukrainian insurance fraternals and also published *Narodna Volya*, the "people's will." Its name was later changed to the Ukrainian Fraternal Association. (Courtesy of St. Vladimir Ukrainian Orthodox Church.)

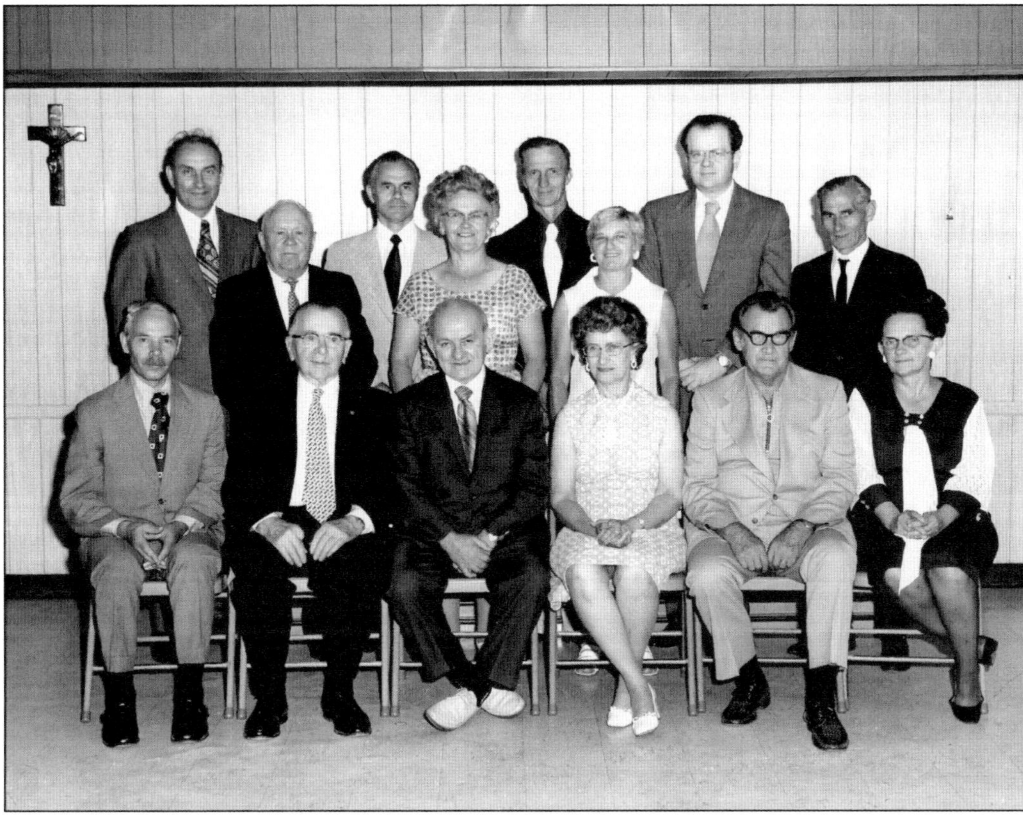

The Providence Association of Ukrainian Catholics. The third major Ukrainian fraternal insurance association in the United States, Providence (or *Provydinnya* in Ukrainian) was started in 1912 by Bishop Soter Ortynsky as a firm supporter of the Ukrainian Catholic Church and to provide financial aid to Ukrainians living in the United States. This photograph shows western Pennsylvania branch secretaries in 1974. (Courtesy of USWPFCU.)

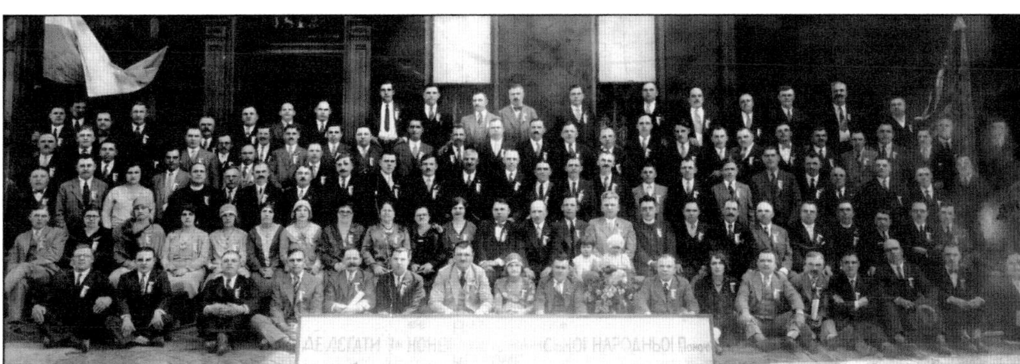

Ukrainian National Aid Association. The Ukrainian National Aid Association (UNAA) was founded in Pittsburgh in 1914 for the purpose of assisting Ukrainian immigrants in adjusting to their new life in America and published the newspaper *Narodne Slovo,* the "Ukrainian people's word." This photograph of its seventh national convention was taken in 1930. (Courtesy of Marianne Carmack.)

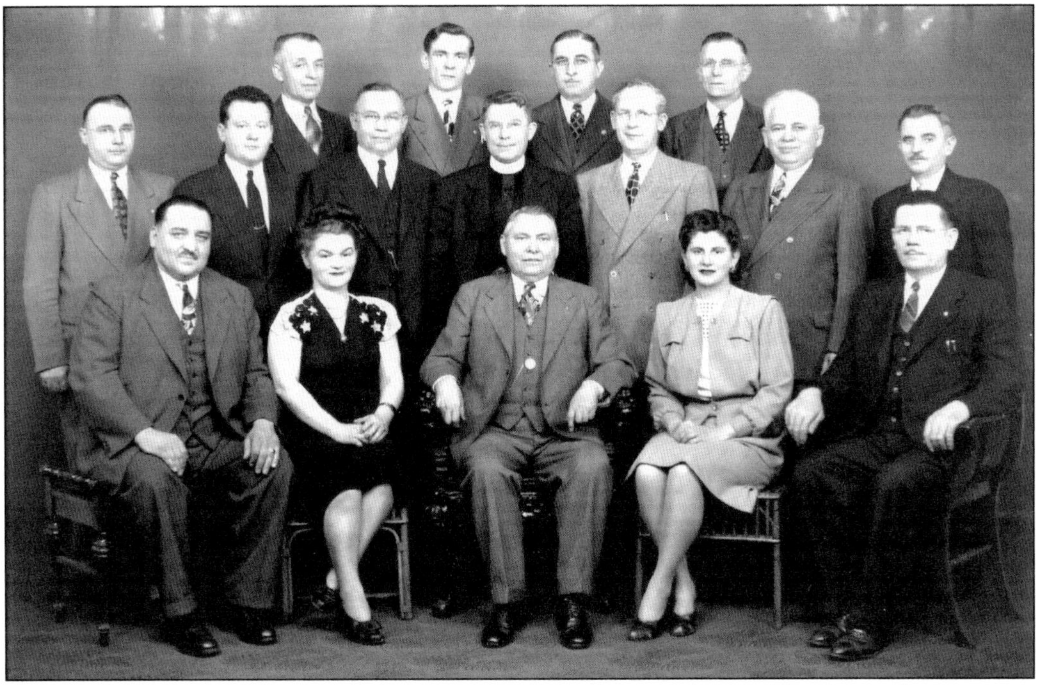

UNAA EXECUTIVE BOARD. The UNAA's main office was located on Second Avenue in downtown Pittsburgh until the 1980s. This photograph is from 1942, and long-term president Wasyl Shabatura is seated in the center of the first row. (Courtesy of Daria Mazur.)

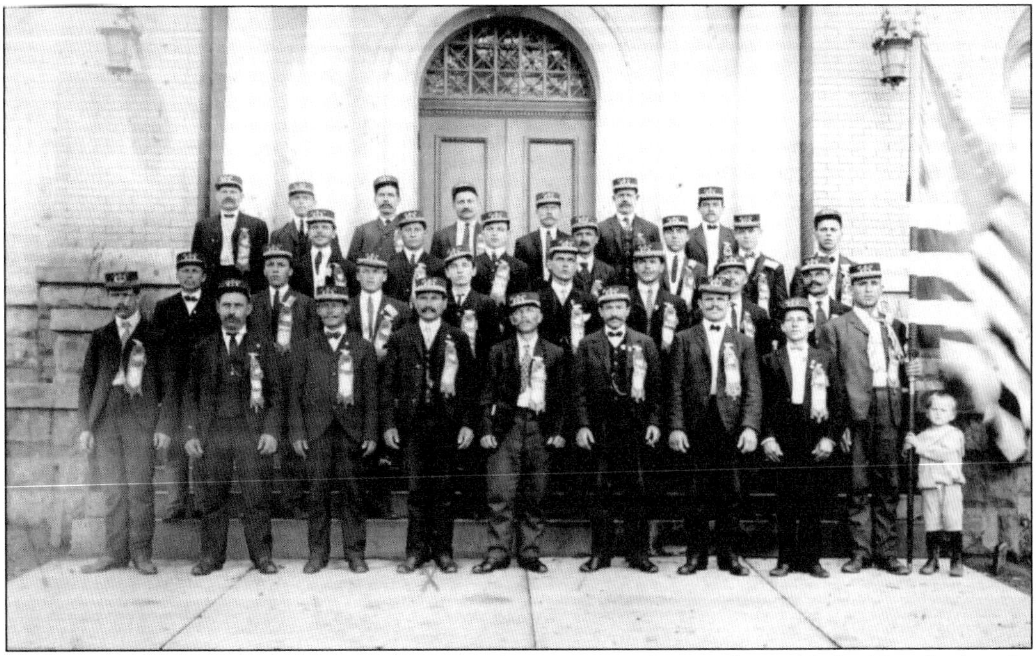

BROTHERHOOD OF ST. JOHN THE BAPTIST. The insurance fraternals established brotherhoods, which then organized many of the Ukrainian churches in the area. This 1905 photograph shows members in front of the Andrew Carnegie Free Library in Carnegie, a short distance from the church they founded. (Courtesy of MASPPUOGCCC.)

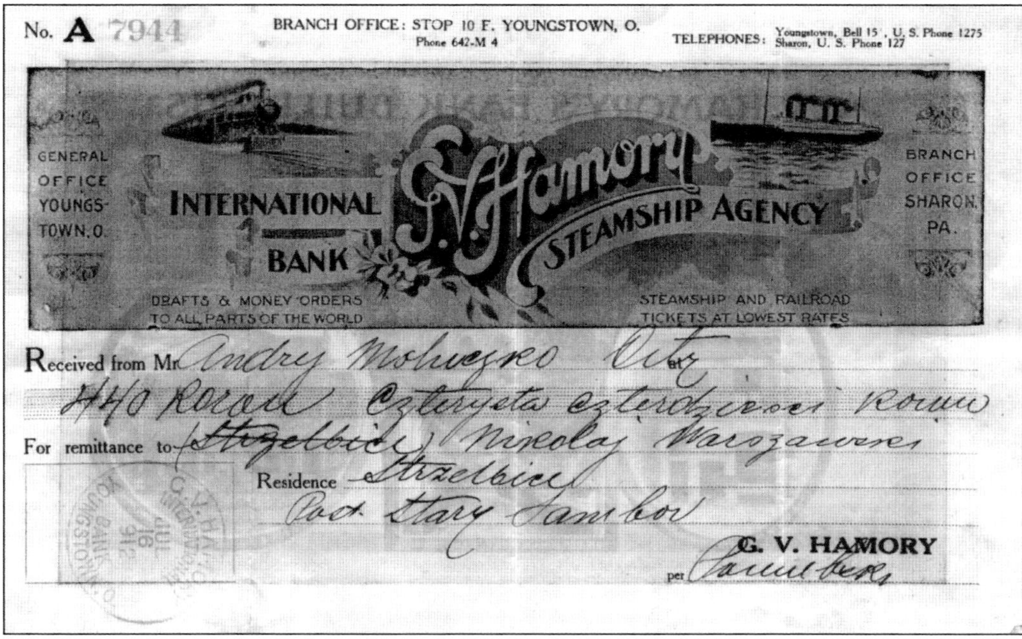

No. A 7944

BRANCH OFFICE: STOP 10 F. YOUNGSTOWN, O.
Phone 642-M 4

TELEPHONES: Youngstown, Bell 15, U. S. Phone 1275
Sharon, U. S. Phone 127

GENERAL OFFICE YOUNGSTOWN, O.

INTERNATIONAL BANK

G. V. Hamory

STEAMSHIP AGENCY

BRANCH OFFICE SHARON, PA.

DRAFTS & MONEY ORDERS TO ALL PARTS OF THE WORLD

STEAMSHIP AND RAILROAD TICKETS AT LOWEST RATES

Received from Mr. Andry [illegible]

440 Koron Czterysta czterdzieści Koron

For remittance to Strzelbice Mikolaj Warszawski

Residence Strzelbice Pod. Stary Sambor

G. V. HAMORY

per

TRAVELING TO THE LAND OF OPPORTUNITY. During early waves of immigration, the way to America was via steamship, and family members would save for years in order to purchase a ticket for a loved one to join them. (Courtesy of Margaret A. Klimko.)

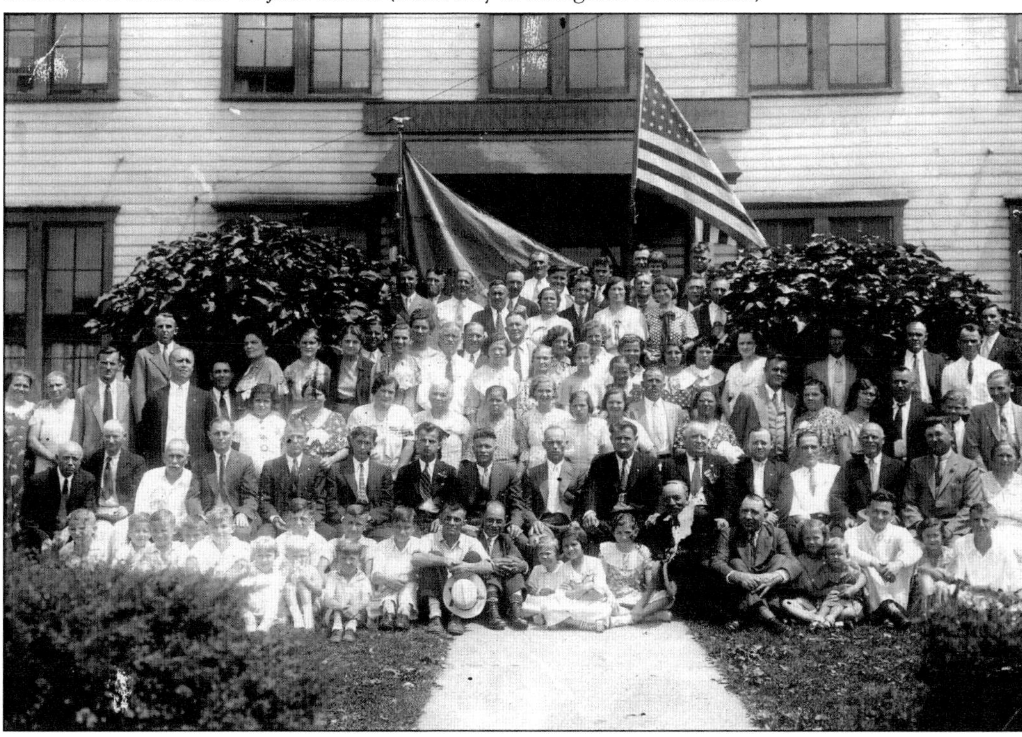

THE UKRAINIAN HOME. The fraternal lodges or branches became centers of Ukrainian community life sponsoring many educational and social activities. Many of these branches raised funds to build a "Ukrainian Home" such as this one in Ford City. (Courtesy of Pat Morovich.)

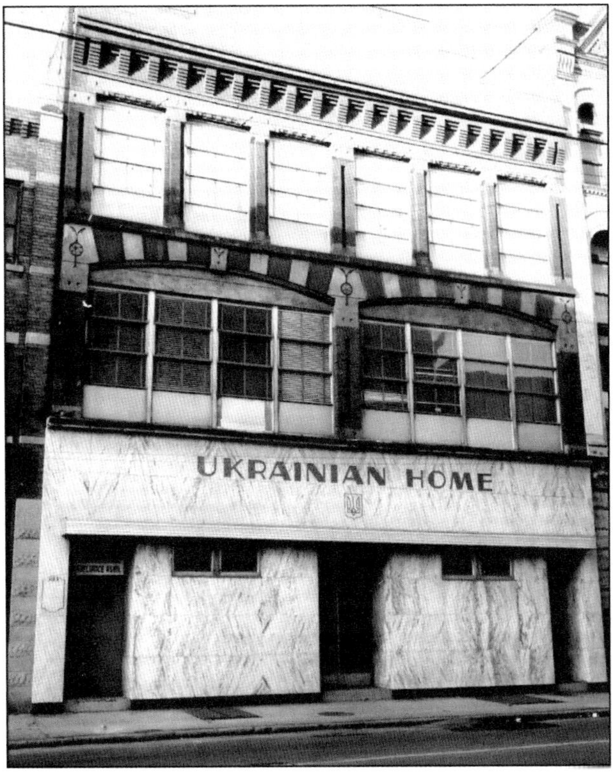

PITTSBURGH UKRAINIAN HOME. The Ukrainian Beneficial Union was founded in 1916 as a mutual aid society to provide financial assistance to needy members and as a social center. It was located in different spots on Pittsburgh's South Side until moving to this location on Carson Street in 1962. Although it closed in 1987, it was home to the Ukrainian Selfreliance of Western Pennsylvania Federal Credit Union for 13 years, various dance groups, a Ukrainian library, and countless community meetings. (Courtesy of Dr. Alexander Lushnycky.)

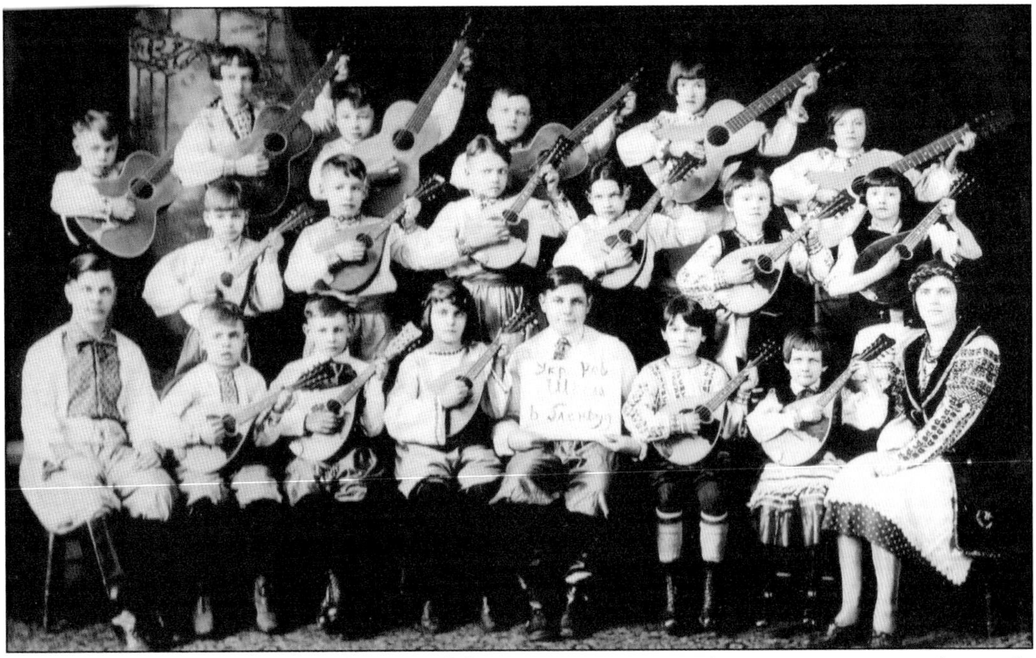

PLAYING THE MANDOLIN. The mandolin was a very popular instrument in the early 20th century, and Ukrainian groups adopted this fad and formed their own mandolin orchestras. This 1916 photograph shows a group that formed in Pittsburgh's Glenwood section. (Courtesy of MASPPUOGCCC.)

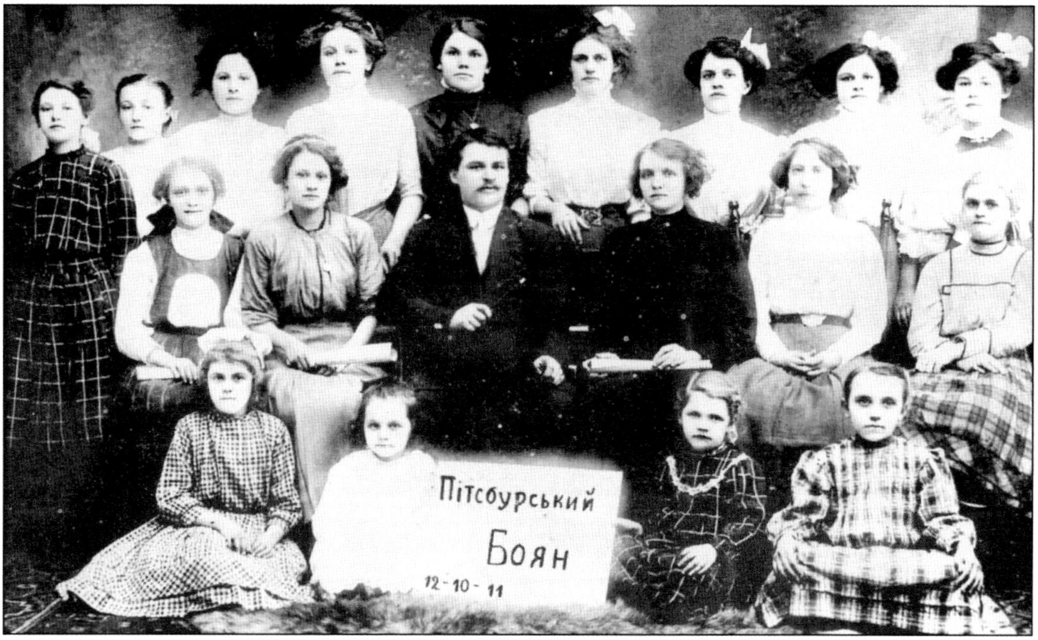

BOYAN. The word *boyan* is an ancient Ukrainian word meaning "singer" and was adopted by many Ukrainian singing groups throughout the United States in the early 1900s. This photograph was taken in 1911 in Pittsburgh's South Side neighborhood. (Courtesy of St. John the Baptist Ukrainian Catholic Church.)

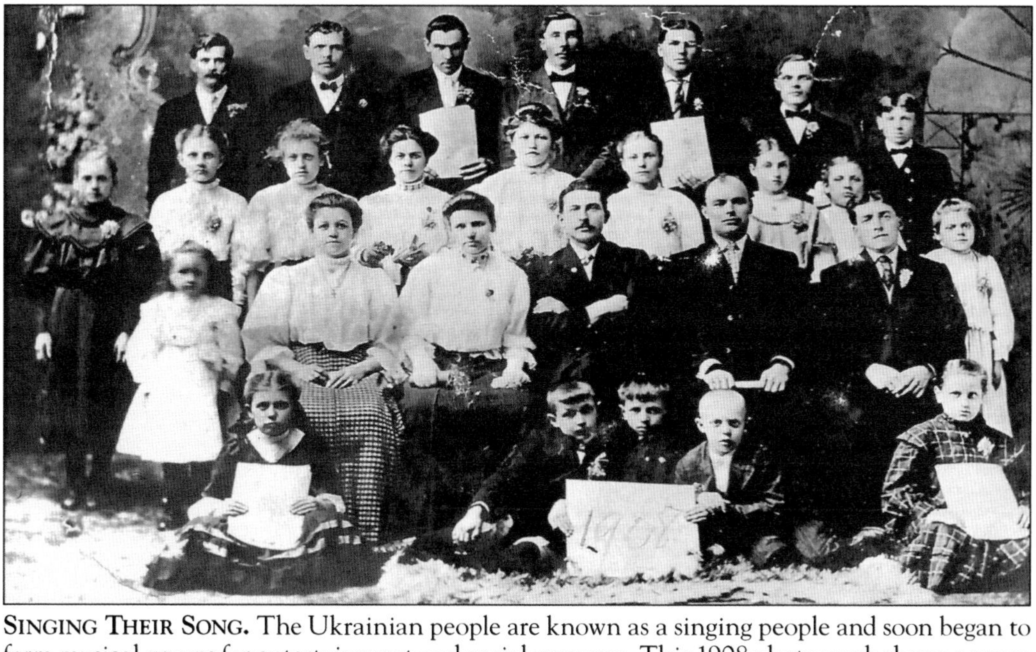

SINGING THEIR SONG. The Ukrainian people are known as a singing people and soon began to form musical groups for entertainment and social purposes. This 1908 photograph shows a group called the Bandurists. (Courtesy of MASPPUOGCCC.)

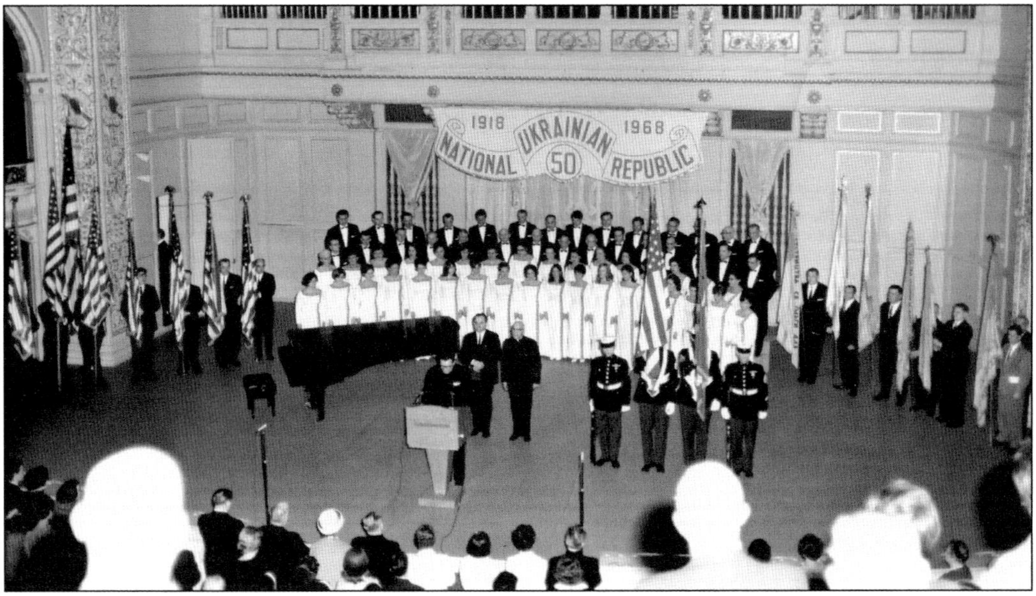

Ukrainian Independence. On January 22, 1918, the Ukrainian National Republic (UNR) was established. This photograph shows the western Pennsylvania Ukrainian community commemorating the 50th anniversary of the declaration of the UNR at Soldiers and Sailors Memorial Hall in Oakland. The UNR abolished capital punishment, offered land to peasants, and guaranteed the rights of the major minorities by creating subcabinet level posts for Jewish, Polish, and Russian affairs. (Courtesy of Michael Komichak.)

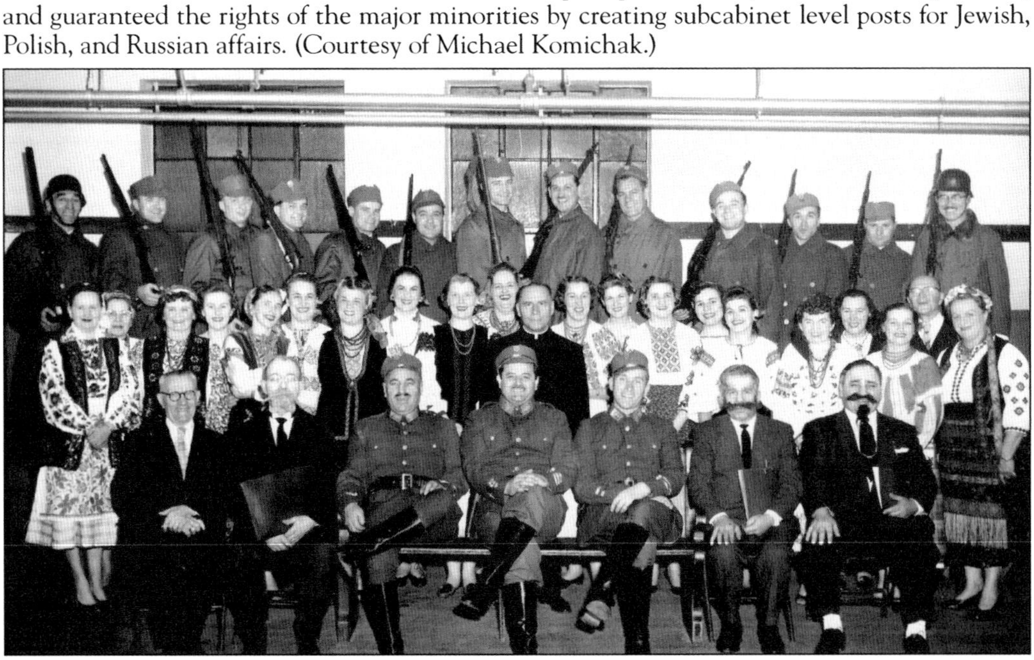

Commemorating the Republic of Western Ukraine. Established on November 1, 1918, Ukrainian leaders from Galicia and Bukovina met in L'viv and established the Republic of Western Ukraine (ZUNR), and on January 21, 1919, the Council of Khust the sub-Carpathian Mountain region of Ukraine voted to unite with ZUNR. After the German army withdrawal from Ukraine following the armistice, ZUNR formally joined the UNR and the Ukrainian nation was united for the first time in centuries. (Courtesy of Oksana Byczkalo.)

LIVING CONDITIONS. Due to rapid industrialization and weak sanitary regulations, deaths from diseases like the flu were common in western Pennsylvania during the early days of Ukrainian immigration to the region. Rivers were polluted, the air was so filled with soot that streetlights were still lit at noon, and the city of Pittsburgh was referred to as the "Smoky City." This photograph, taken in 1947, shows a young boy standing next to the grave of his maternal grandmother, who died from the flu in 1923. (Courtesy of LAVRSHH.)

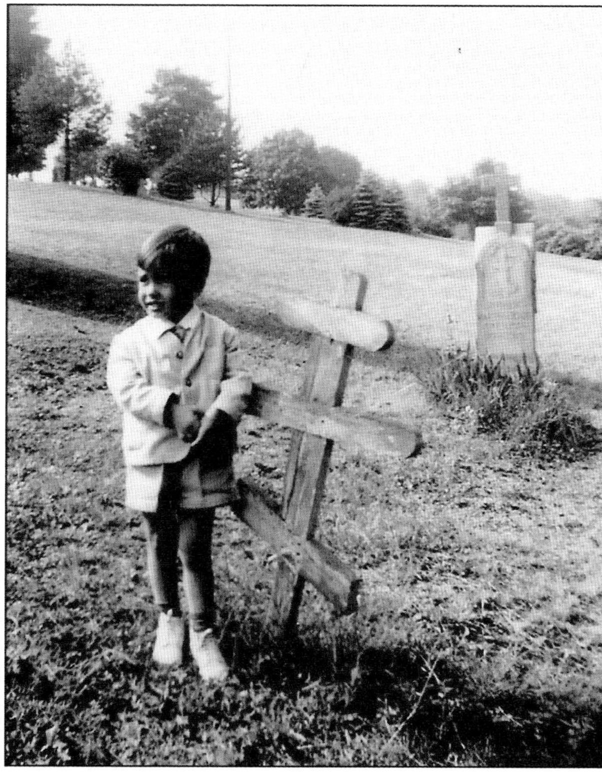

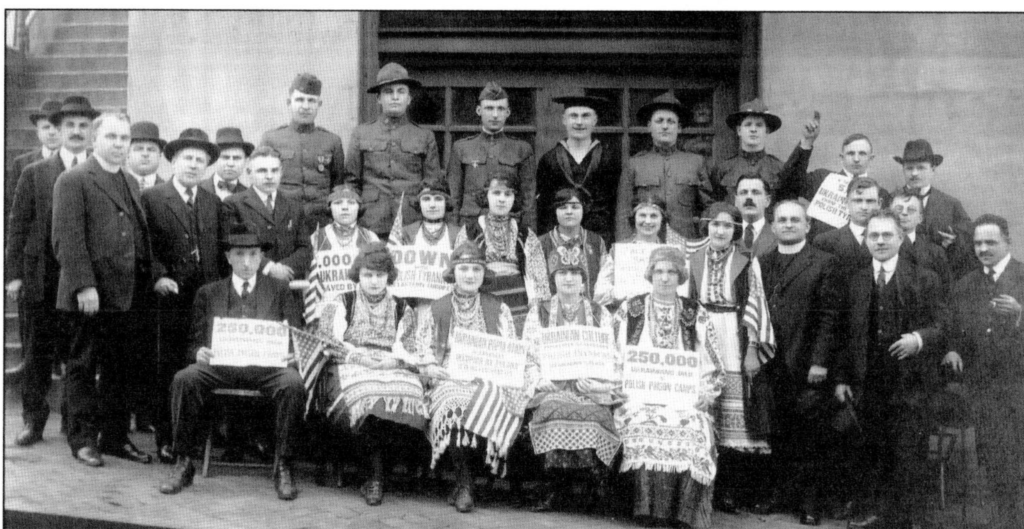

PROTESTING POLISH RULE. Treaties following World War I awarded the western Ukrainian territory of Galicia, or Halychyna in Ukrainian, to the newly reborn country of Poland. In this 1922 photograph, Ukrainians protest the policy of Polonization through which Ukrainian institutions were closed and the Ukrainian school system declined precipitously in lands where Ukrainians outnumbered Poles by two to one. Most of these western Ukrainian lands were returned to Ukraine following World War II, and Poland today is considered one of Ukraine's closest allies. (Courtesy of Joan Fedora.)

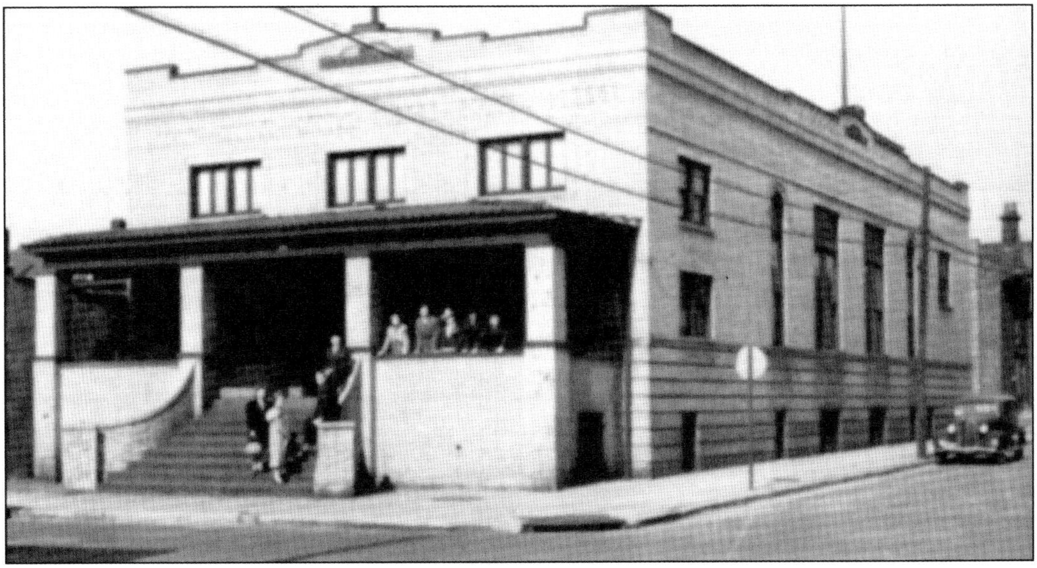

UKRAINIAN CITIZENS' CLUBS. Ukrainian citizens' clubs were formed beginning in the second and third decades of the 20th century in order to assist members in becoming U.S. citizens as well as to provide an arena for social interaction. The Ukrainian Citizens' Hall in Arnold (shown above), the Ukrainian Literary and Beneficial Association of Monessen, and the Ukrainian Citizens' Club of Jeannette all have closed. The Ukrainian American Citizens' Club of Carnegie, shown below and founded in 1927, is still active, as is the American Ukrainian Citizens' Club of Wilmerding, founded in 1945. In addition to sponsoring activities to maintain and perpetuate the Ukrainian culture, these clubs provide a safe gathering place for workers to meet their friends for a "shot and a beer" after a hard day's work. (Courtesy of Steve Pituch.)

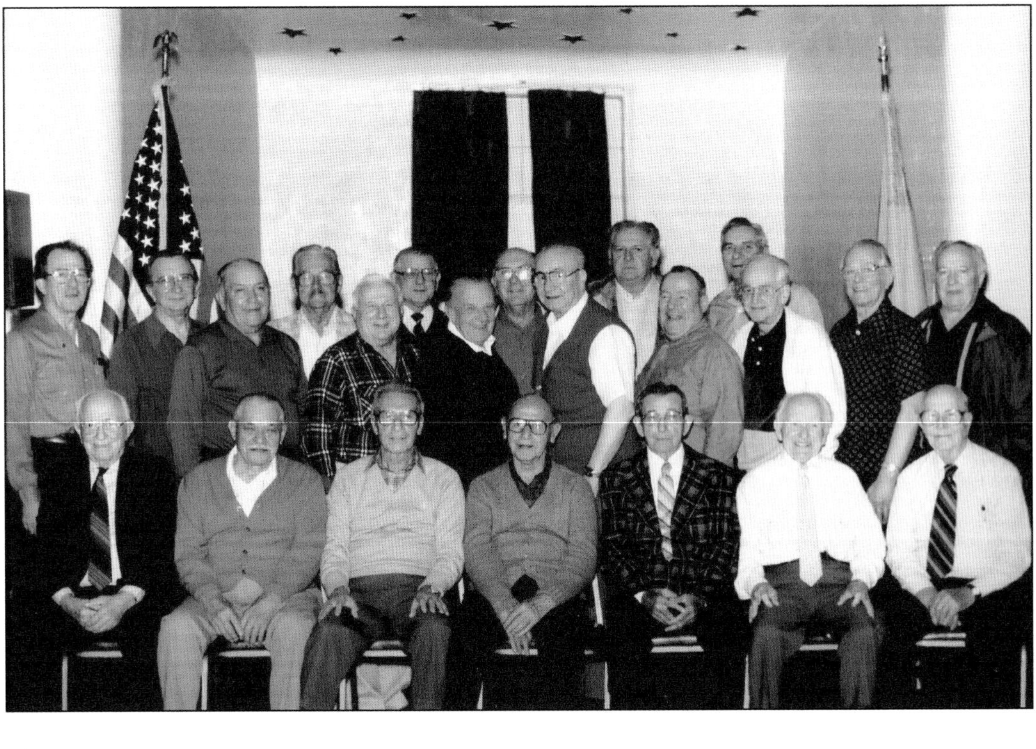

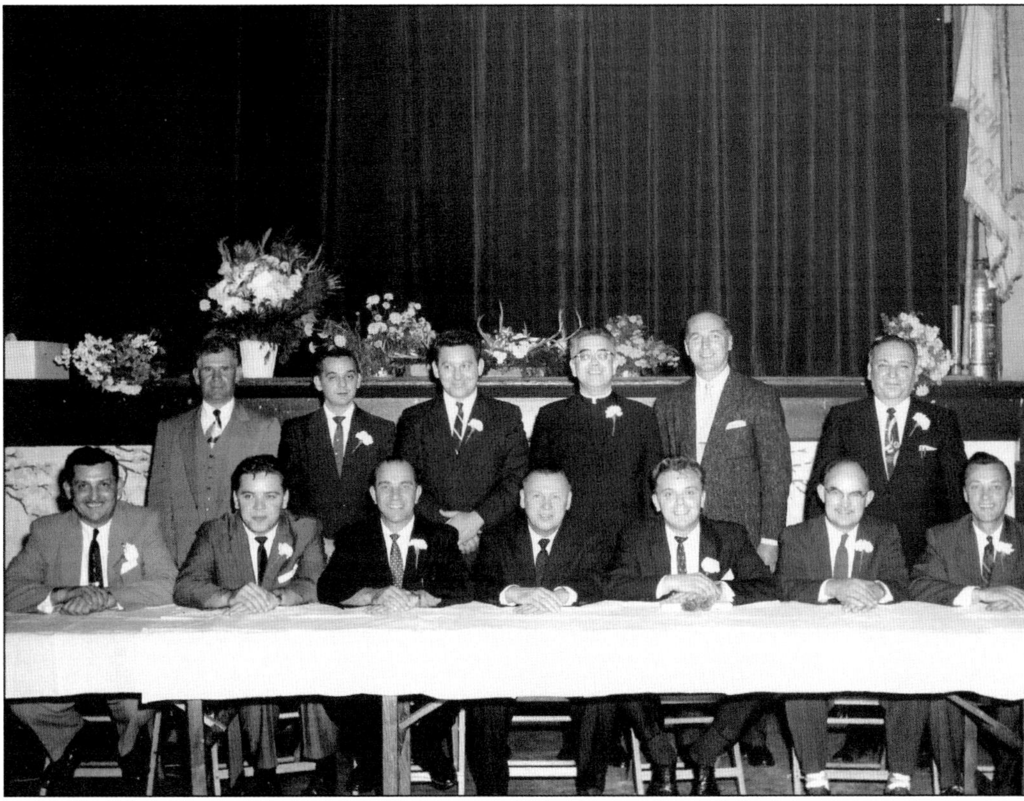

The Ukrainian National Home of McKees Rocks. Located close to St. Mary Ukrainian Orthodox Church, the Ukrainian Home of McKees Rocks was always a hub of Ukrainian activity, including New Year's dances and concerts, until its recent closure. (Courtesy of John Czuczman.)

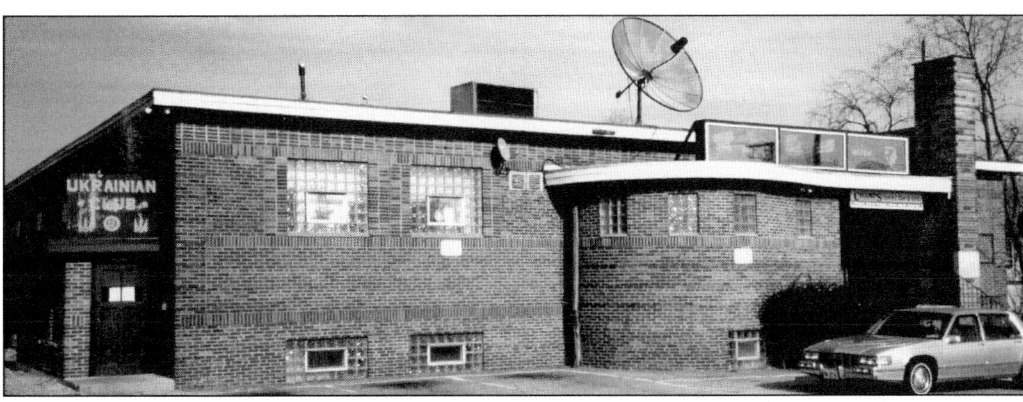

UNA Branch No. 120 Club, Aliquippa. Founded in 1917, the Aliquippa Ukrainian Club is still going strong. Over the years, it has hosted lessons in Ukrainian language, dancing, arts, and crafts, served as a ticket selling point for Ukrainian events, and provided scholarships for Ukrainian students. (Courtesy of Eli Matiash.)

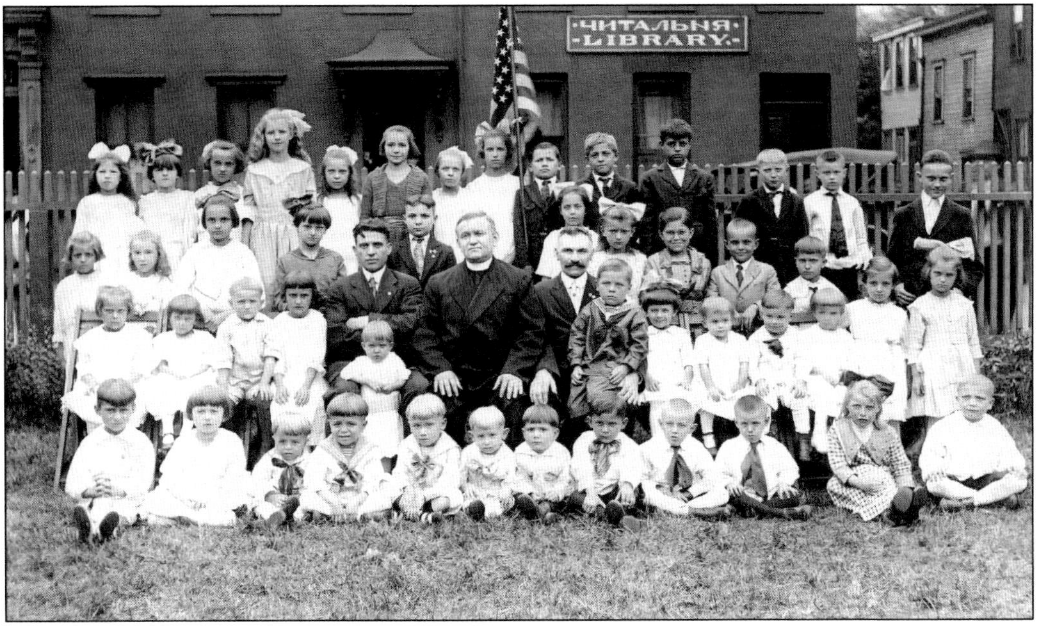

THE CHYTALNYA. Among the earliest examples of organized Ukrainian community life were reading rooms. These were organized by priests, UNA branches, and other organizations to develop cultural and intellectual knowledge among the Ukrainian people. This photograph is from such a reading room located in the Woods Run section of Pittsburgh in the second decade of the 20th century. (Courtesy of St. George Ukrainian Catholic Church.)

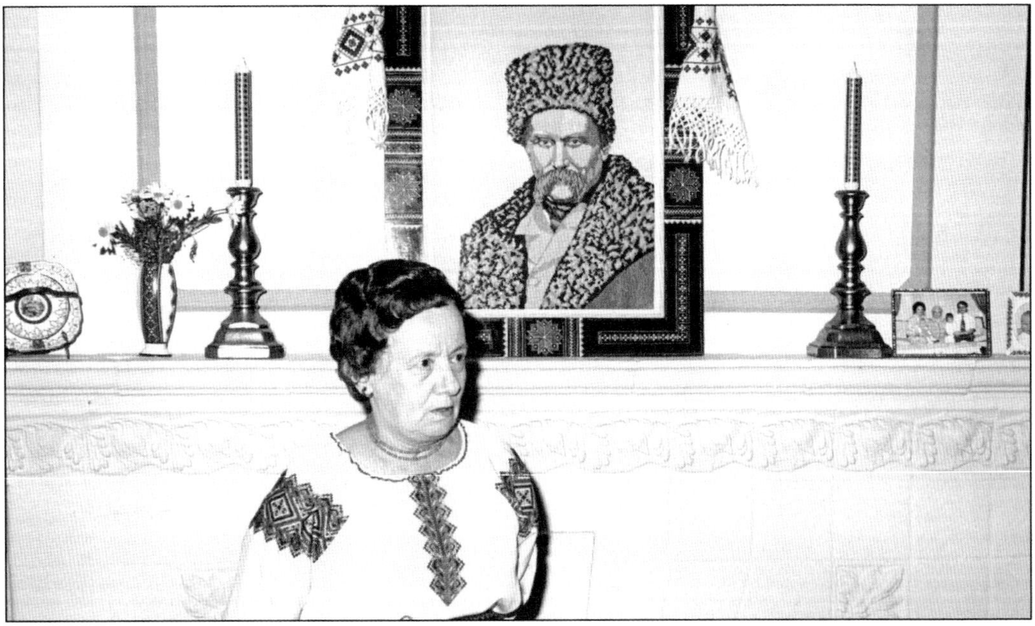

THE UKRAINIAN QUESTION. For many years, Ukrainians were frustrated by their fellow Americans' lack of understanding of their identity and struggled to educate them about their ancestral homeland through various means. In this photograph from Erie, a poetry reading is included in such an outreach program. (Courtesy of Ethnic Impressions Collection, Erie County Historical Society.)

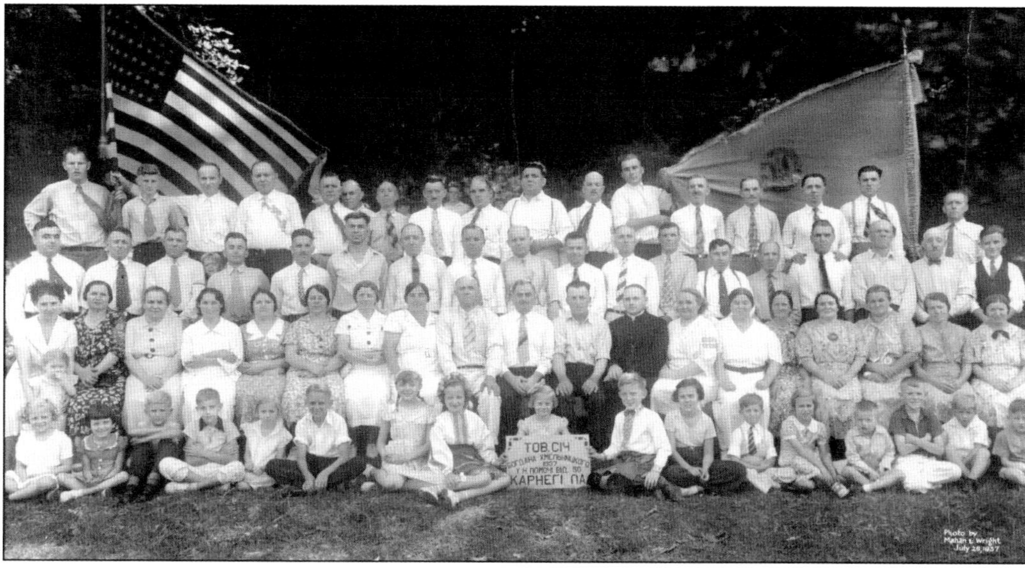

HONORING HEROES FROM THE PAST. Insurance fraternal branches such as this UNAA branch based in Carnegie, named their branches in honor of Ukrainian kozak heroes. In this 1937 photograph, children in the first row show that their branch is named after Ukrainian hetman Bohdan Khmelnytsky, who led the 1648–1654 uprising against the lords of the Polish-Lithuanian Commonwealth. (Courtesy of MASPPUOGCCC.)

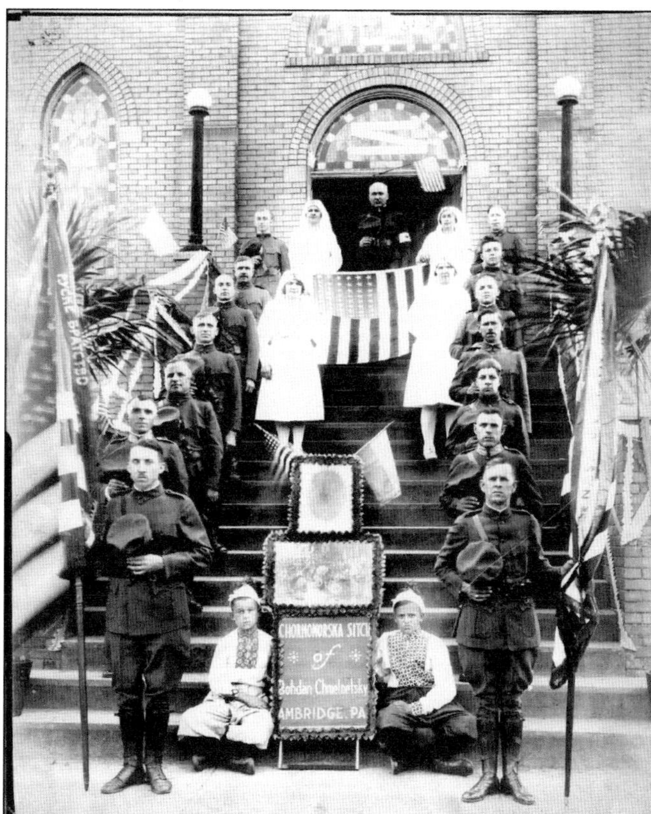

SICH. Founded as an athletic association, Sich catered to the younger generation of Ukrainian Americans and aimed to train them physically and spiritually. Over time, owing to frustration over the world community's lack of support for Ukrainian independence following World War I, the Sich organization developed military overtones. Members of the Ambridge Sich branch stand on the steps of St. Vladimir Ukrainian Orthodox Church around 1935. During a peaceful demonstration on October 29, 1933, members were attacked by alleged communists during their protest of the mistreatment of Ukrainians in the USSR. (Courtesy of St. Vladimir Ukrainian Orthodox Church.)

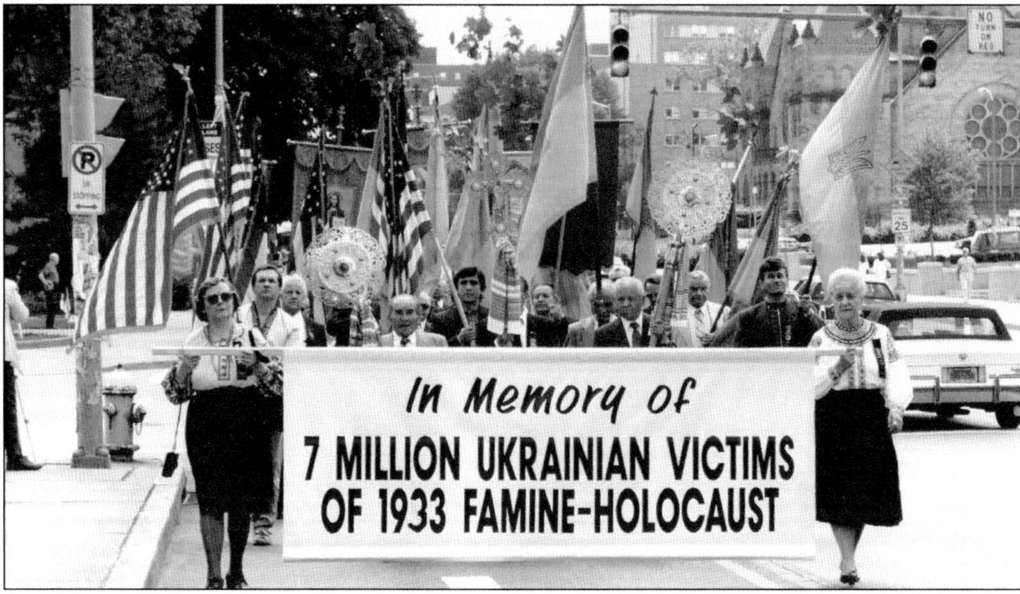

THE MAN-MADE FAMINE OF 1932–1933. The collectivization program of Soviet leader Josef Stalin led to the deaths of between 7 and 10 million Ukrainians during an 18-month period, as reports Robert Conquest, British-born author of the book *Harvest of Sorrow*. Western Pennsylvania Ukrainians commemorated the 60th anniversary of this tragedy with a march down Oakland's Fifth Avenue on their way to a *moleben*, or "requiem service," in Heinz Chapel. (Courtesy of Luba Hlutkowsky.)

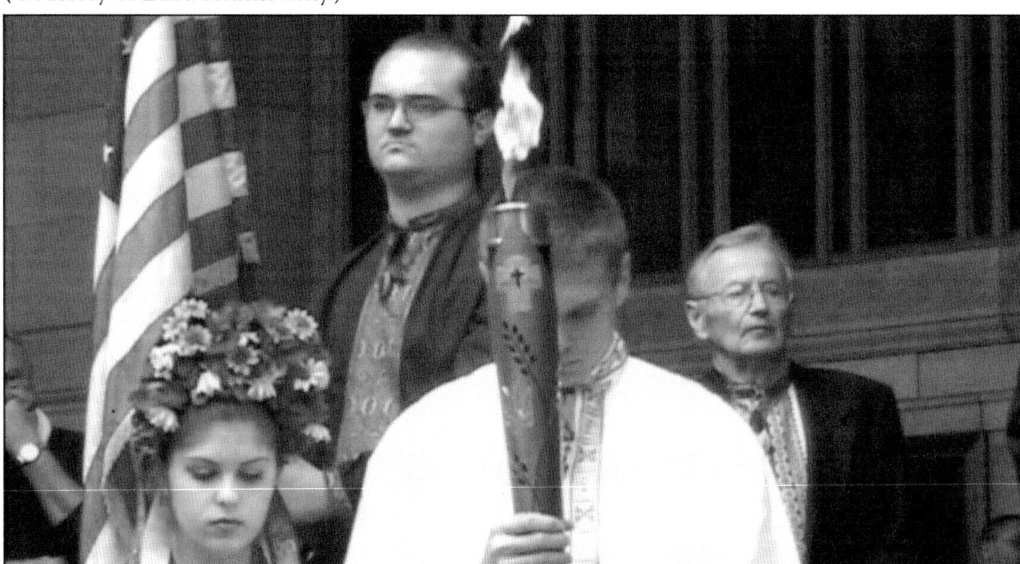

ETERNAL FLAME. Seventy-five years after the man-made famine, western Pennsylvania Ukrainians gathered on the steps of the Pittsburgh City-County Building to pass along an eternal flame, which traveled the world drawing attention to this tragedy. Pictured on the right is famine survivor Gregory Repa, who lived near Ukraine's capital of Kyiv and was the only member of his immediate family to survive the famine and was expelled from school for a time for not signing a document renouncing belief in God. (Courtesy of Yaroslaw Hodowanec.)

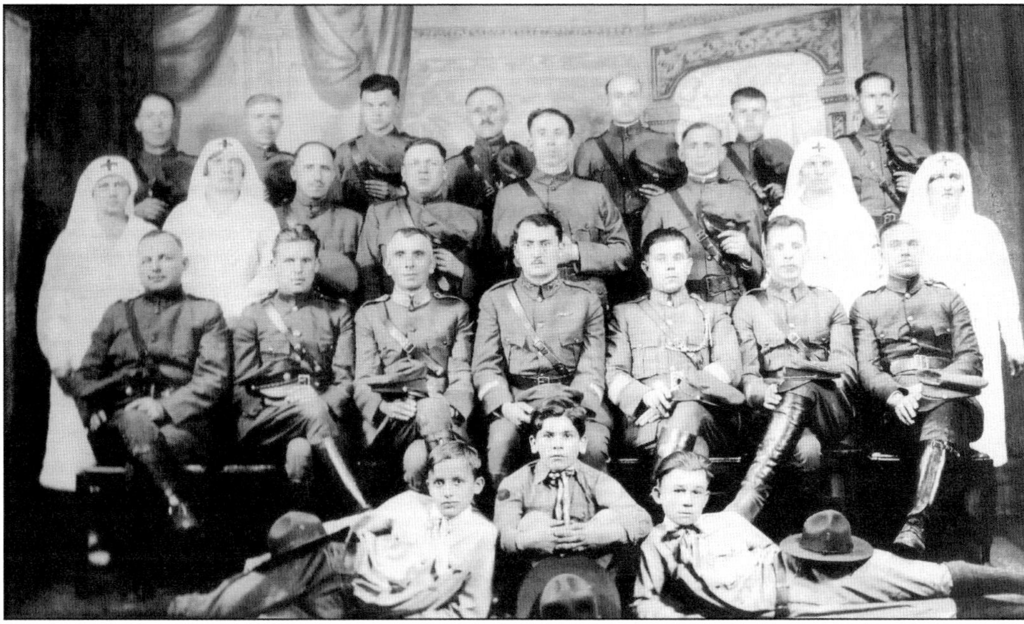

UKRAINIAN GOLD CROSS. Founded in 1931 as the Ukrainian Red Cross, this was a national organization of Ukrainian American women, who supported the nationalist cause. The organization had to change the *Red* in its name to *Gold* due to pressure from an American Red Cross ruling that only nation-states could use the name "Red Cross." Pictured are members of the Ambridge branch around 1935. (Courtesy of William Korey.)

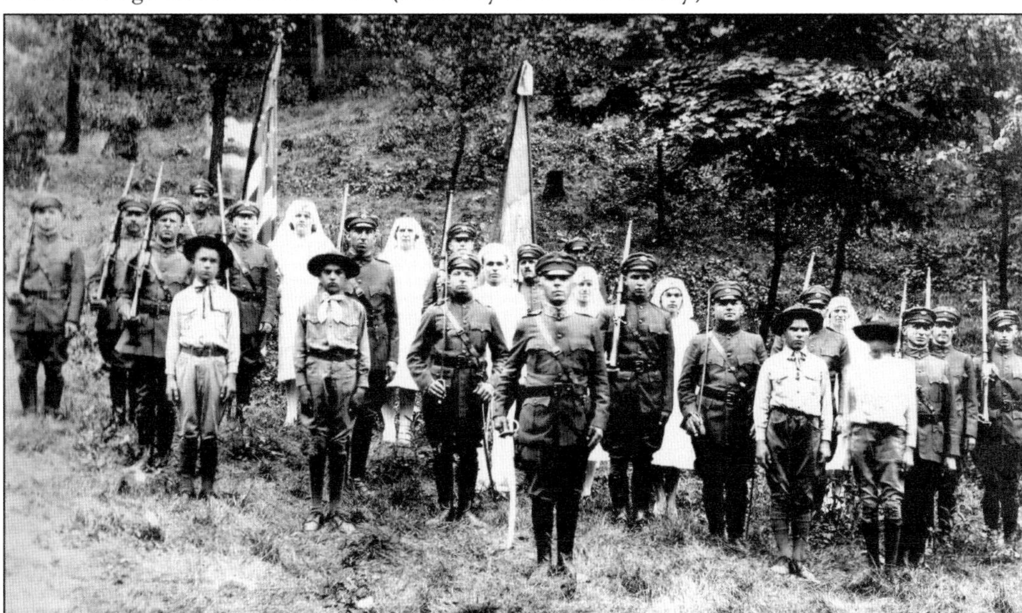

SICH MANEUVERS. During the "Red Decade," when communism was growing in strength and western powers did not believe reports of Soviet atrocities, members of some Sich branches began to perform military drills in preparation for a potential fight to liberate Ukraine. Here the Ambridge branch performs drills in the Gillingham Hollow area near Baden. (Courtesy of St. Vladimir Ukrainian Orthodox Church, Ambridge.)

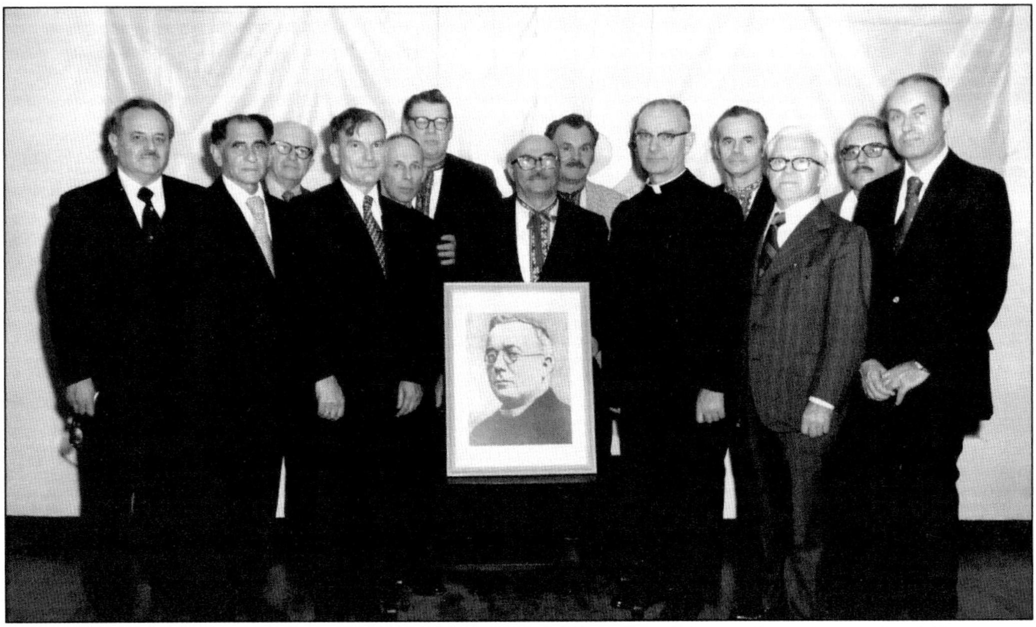

CARPATHO-UKRAINE. The Munich Pact of 1938 gave Ukrainians hope that a Carpatho-Ukrainian state would be realized. On March 15, 1939, the republic of Carpatho-Ukraine was declared but was crushed by Hungarian troops after only one day. This 1974 photograph shows western Pennsylvania Ukrainians gathering to commemorate the birth of Fr. Avhustyn Voloshyn, who was the president of this short-lived nation. (Courtesy of USWPFCU.)

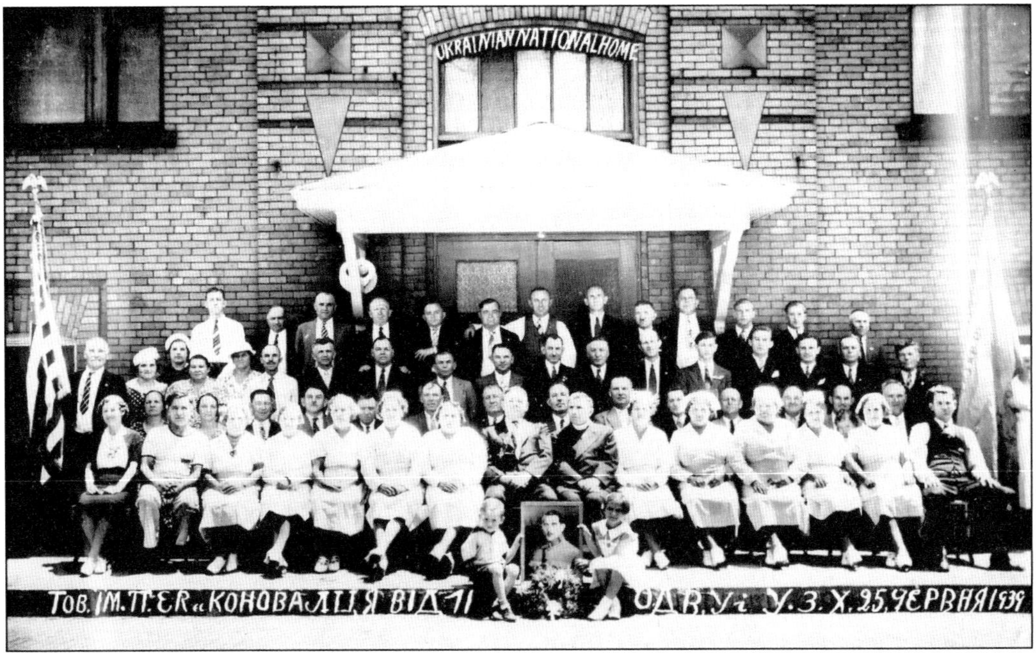

THE ORGANIZATION FOR THE REBIRTH OF UKRAINE. A political group formed in 1929, the Organization for the Rebirth of Ukraine (ODWU) was dedicated to the establishment of an independent Ukrainian state. Active throughout the United States, this 1939 photograph is of the McKees Rocks branch. (Courtesy of St. Mary Ukrainian Orthodox Church.)

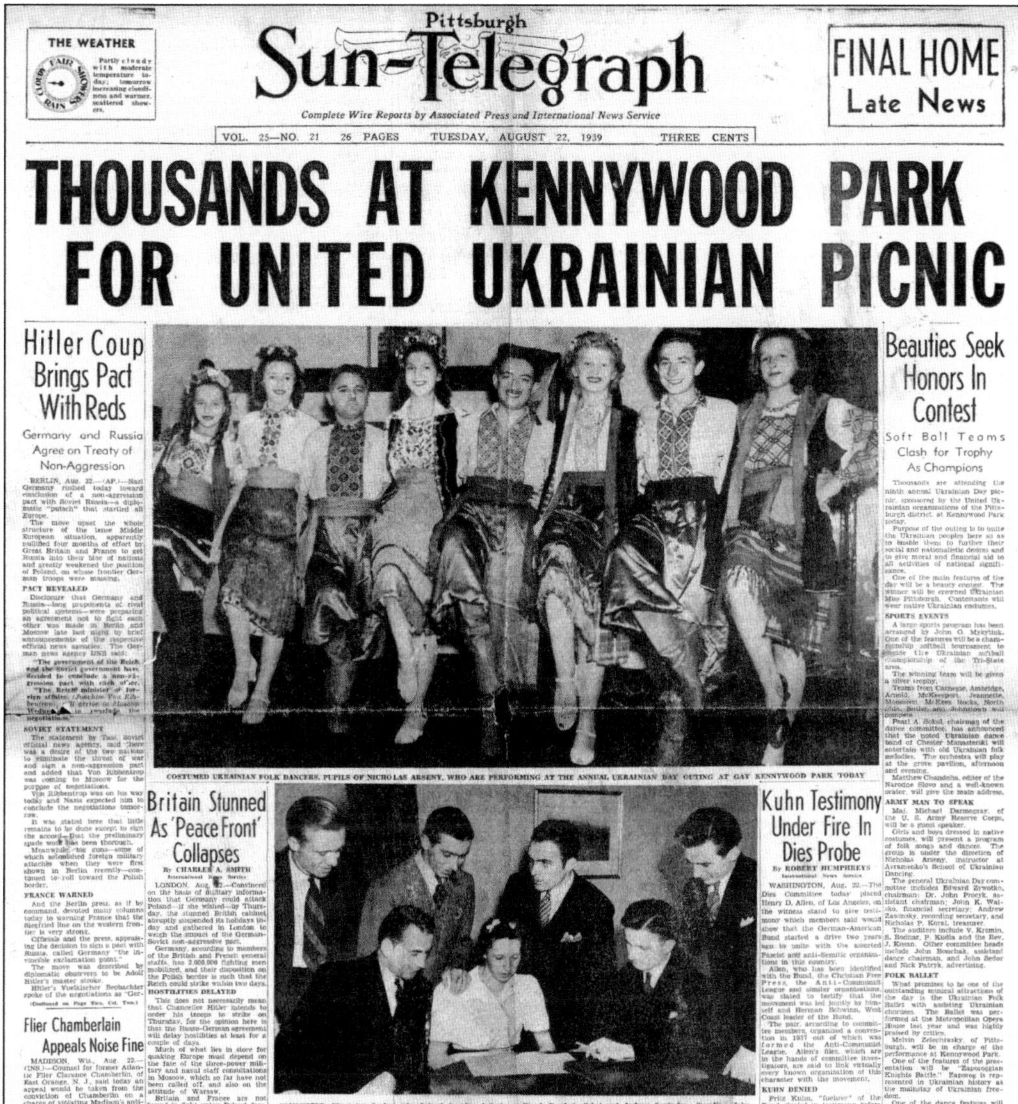

Pittsburgh Sun-Telegraph

THE WEATHER

FINAL HOME
Late News

Complete Wire Reports by Associated Press and International News Service

VOL. 25—NO. 21 26 PAGES TUESDAY, AUGUST 22, 1939 THREE CENTS

THOUSANDS AT KENNYWOOD PARK FOR UNITED UKRAINIAN PICNIC

Hitler Coup Brings Pact With Reds

Germany and Russia Agree on Treaty of Non-Aggression

Beauties Seek Honors In Contest

Soft Ball Teams Clash for Trophy As Champions

COSTUMED UKRAINIAN FOLK DANCERS, PUPILS OF NICHOLAS ARSENY, WHO ARE PERFORMING AT THE ANNUAL UKRAINIAN DAY OUTING AT GAY KENNYWOOD PARK TODAY

Britain Stunned As 'Peace Front' Collapses

Kuhn Testimony Under Fire In Dies Probe

Flier Chamberlain Appeals Noise Fine

More Reserves Called by Poland

Spanish Army Fliers Called, Portugal Hears

THE WINDS OF WAR. Western Pennsylvania Ukrainians gathered at Kennywood Amusement Park in West Mifflin for the ninth annual Ukrainian Day celebration at the park. The festival featured a Ukrainian Miss Pittsburgh pageant and a sports program including a championship softball tournament in which teams from Ambridge, Arnold, Butler, Carnegie, Jeannette, Johnstown, McKeesport, Monessen, and North Side Pittsburgh competed. The musical renderings of the "Ukrainian Caruso," singer Mykhaylo Holynsky, were heard as he made Pittsburgh his next stop after performing for the king and queen of England in Toronto, Canada, and his performance at the 1939–1940 New York World's Fair. The date of the newspaper is August 22, 1939—just 10 days before the Nazi invasion of Poland. On the reverse, an editorial claims that "Hitler is apparently a bloodless General, who wins wars without battles . . . There is now no likelihood of bloodshed in actual warfare . . . Russia has signed a friendly compact with Germany . . . we will have peace." (Courtesy of Cynthia Haluszczak.)

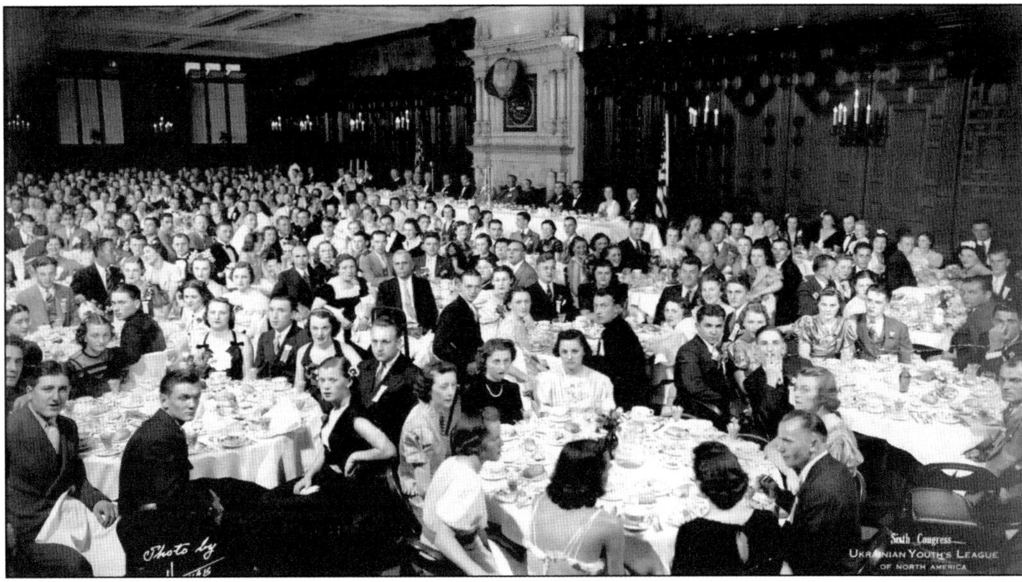

THE UKRAINIAN YOUTH LEAGUE OF NORTH AMERICA. Founded in 1933 and with branches throughout the United States, the Ukrainian Youth League of North America's sixth congress was held in Pittsburgh in 1938. Youth activities such as sports and cultural venues were the main thrust of this organization, which hoped to attract and retain the younger generation of American-born Ukrainians. (Courtesy of MASPPUOGCCC.)

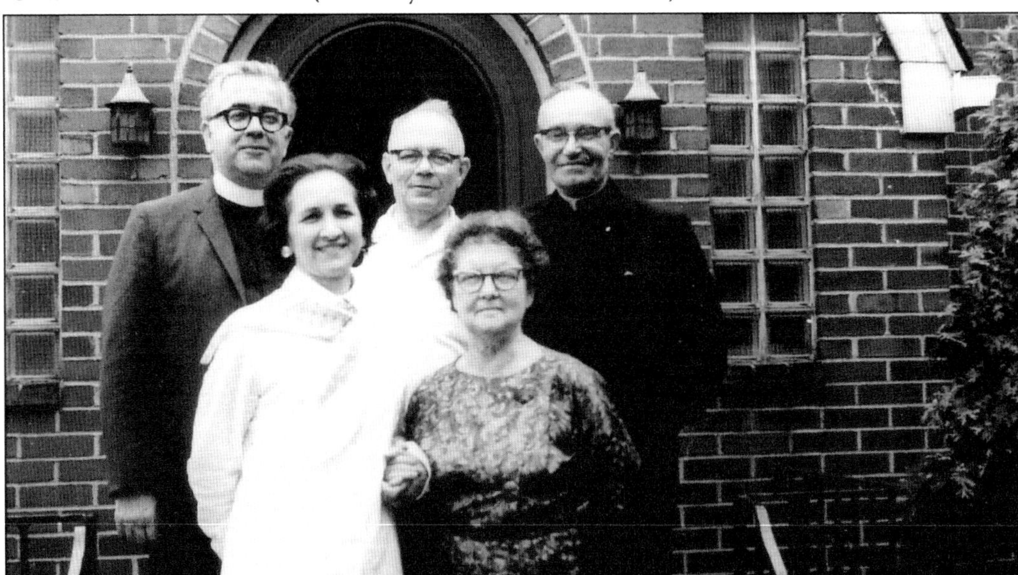

SERVICE OF A DIFFERENT KIND. Fr. Andrew Leschyshyn and Hieromonk Sviatoslav Magalias (back row right and center), photographed in 1969 at Holy Virgin Ukrainian Orthodox Church in Arnold, served in the Army of the Ukrainian National Republic, which was made up of various armed volunteer units. Becoming priests later in life, they continued to serve as warriors in a different sense. While the Ukrainian Autocephalous Orthodox Church flourished in the 1920s, it was brutally liquidated later when the Soviet government executed bishops and priests by the hundreds. (Courtesy of LAVRSHH.)

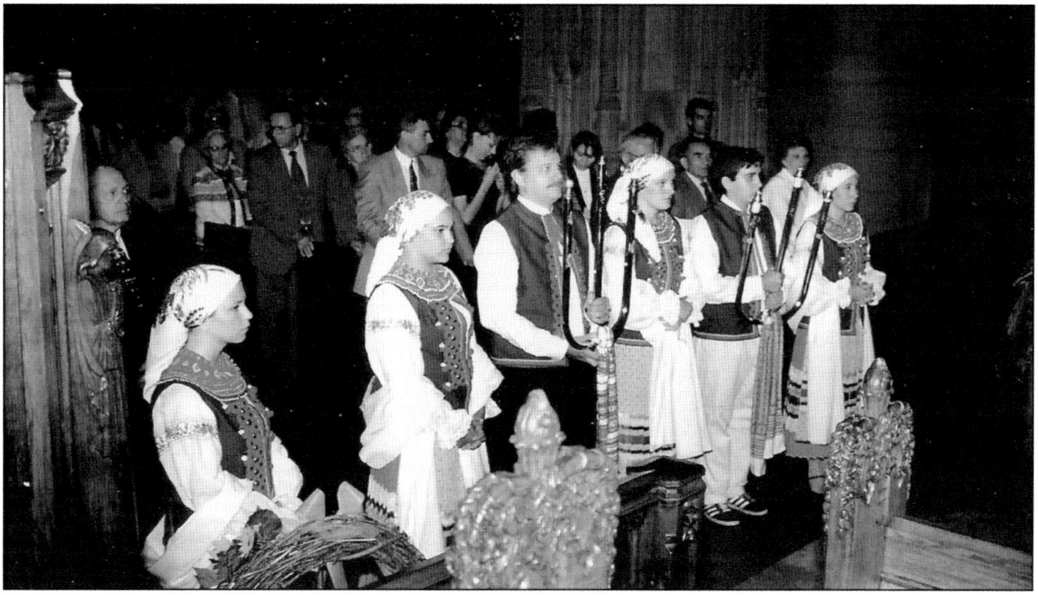

AKCIJA WISLA. Following World War II, the Polish government instituted a policy to disperse ethnic Ukrainians from their ancestral homeland in the Khol'mshchyna and Lemkivshchyna regions, which were awarded to Poland. In this 1997 photograph, western Pennsylvania Ukrainians gather in Pittsburgh's Heinz Chapel for a healing service to commemorate this expatriation named Akcija Wisla (Action Vistula), which split families from each other and their farmlands. (Courtesy of Michael Jula.)

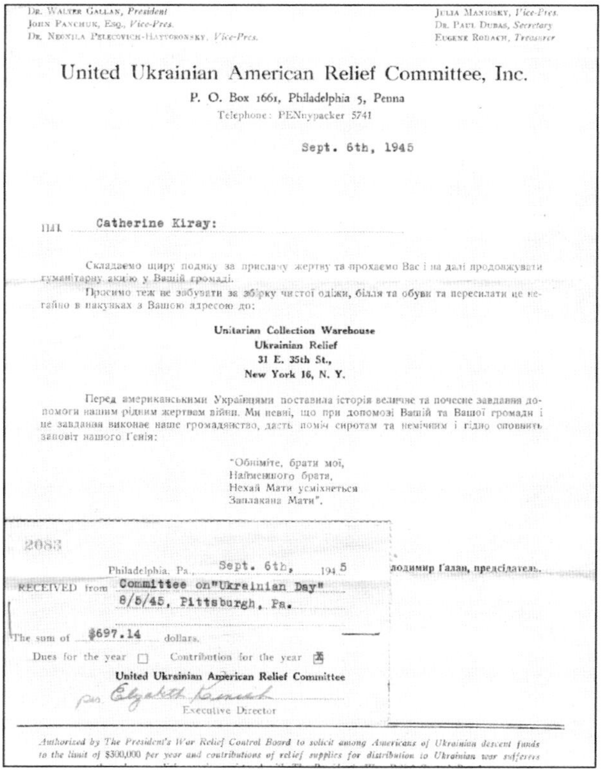

DR. WALTER GALLAN, *President*
JOHN PANCHUK, ESQ., *Vice-Pres.*
DR. NEONILA PELECOVICH-HAYTOKONSKY, *Vice-Pres.*

JULIA MANIOSKY, *Vice-Pres.*
DR. PAUL DUBAS, *Secretary*
EUGENE RODACH, *Treasurer*

United Ukrainian American Relief Committee, Inc.
P. O. Box 1661, Philadelphia 5, Penna
Telephone: PENnypacker 5741

Sept. 6th, 1945

Пані Catherine Kiray:

Складаємо щиру подяку за присланy жертву та просимо Вас і на далі продовжувати гуманітарну акцію у Вашій громаді.

Просимо теж не забувати за збірку чистої одіжи, білля та обуви та пересилати це негайно в пакунках з Вашою адресою до:

Unitarian Collection Warehouse
Ukrainian Relief
31 E. 35th St.,
New York 16, N. Y.

Перед американськими Українцями поставила історія величне та почесне завдання допомоги нашим рідним жертвам війни. Ми певні, що при допомозі Вашій та Вашої громади і це завдання виконає наше громадянство, дасть поміч сиротам та немічним і гідно сповнить заповіт нашого Генія:

"Обніміте, брати мої,
Найменшого брата,
Нехай Мати усміхнеться
Заплакана Мати".

...лодимир Галан, предсідатель.

2083

Philadelphia, Pa., Sept. 6th, 1945
RECEIVED from Committee on "Ukrainian Day" 8/5/45, Pittsburgh, Pa.
The sum of $697.14 dollars.
Dues for the year ☐ Contribution for the year ☒
United Ukrainian American Relief Committee
per Elizabeth [illegible]
Executive Director

Authorized by The President's War Relief Control Board to solicit among Americans of Ukrainian descent funds to the limit of $300,000 per year and contributions of relief supplies for distribution to Ukrainian war sufferers

ASSISTANCE. Western Pennsylvania Ukrainians have generously contributed financial assistance to their brethren in Ukraine during various times of needs such as floods, war, and other disasters. This letter shows that the amount of $697.14 was collected on Ukrainian Day in Pittsburgh and sent to the United Ukrainian American Relief Committee to send humanitarian aid to Ukrainian refugees in Europe. (Courtesy of Katherine Kiray.)

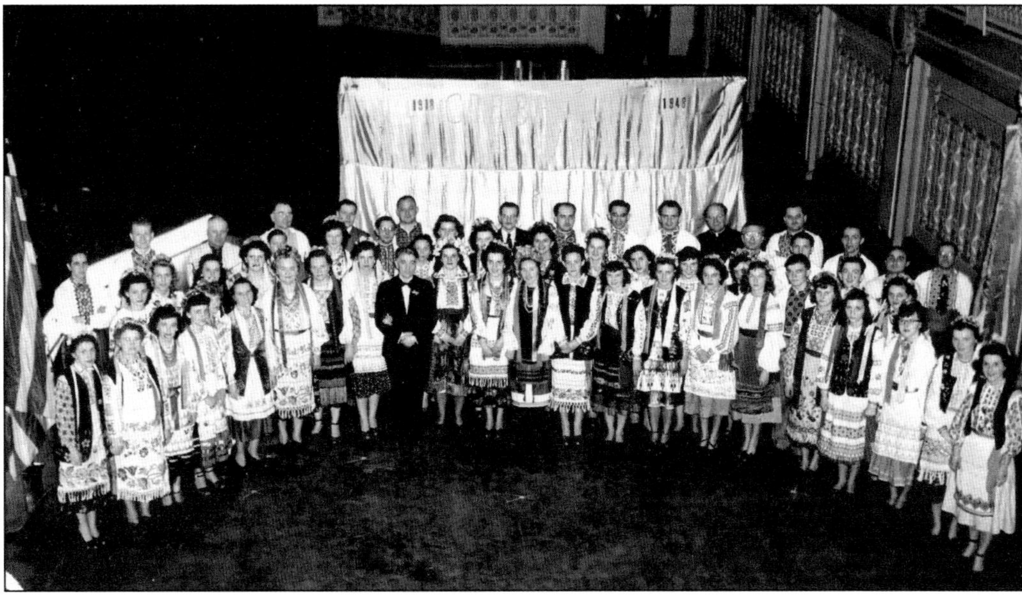

THIRD WAVE OF UKRAINIAN IMMIGRATION. In 1948, the U.S. Congress passed the Displaced Persons Act, which permitted Europeans displaced by World War II to enter the United States without regard to immigration quotas. Approximately 200 refugee families came to western Pennsylvania, some of whom immediately took part in this commemoration of the 30th anniversary of the 1918 Ukrainian independence at Soldiers and Sailors Memorial Hall. (Courtesy of Joanne Staroschak.)

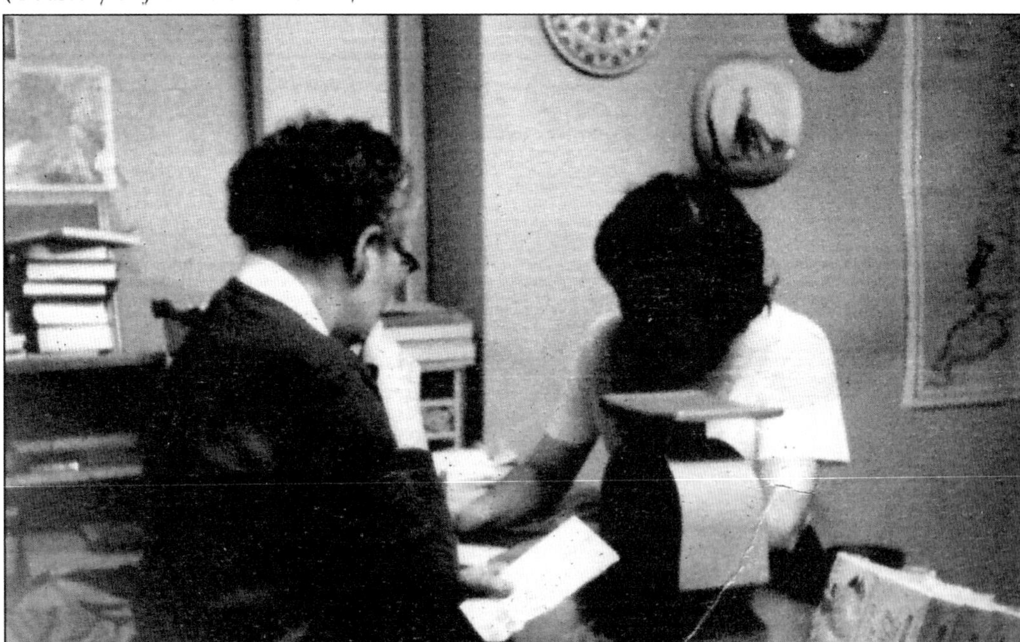

ASSISTANCE, 1960S. Many businesses sending parcels to Ukraine have existed over the years, which allowed western Pennsylvania Ukrainians to send clothing and foodstuffs to family members in need. This 1960s-era photograph was taken at Howerla Parcels, a South Side Pittsburgh institution still in operation. (Courtesy of Dana Krupnyk.)

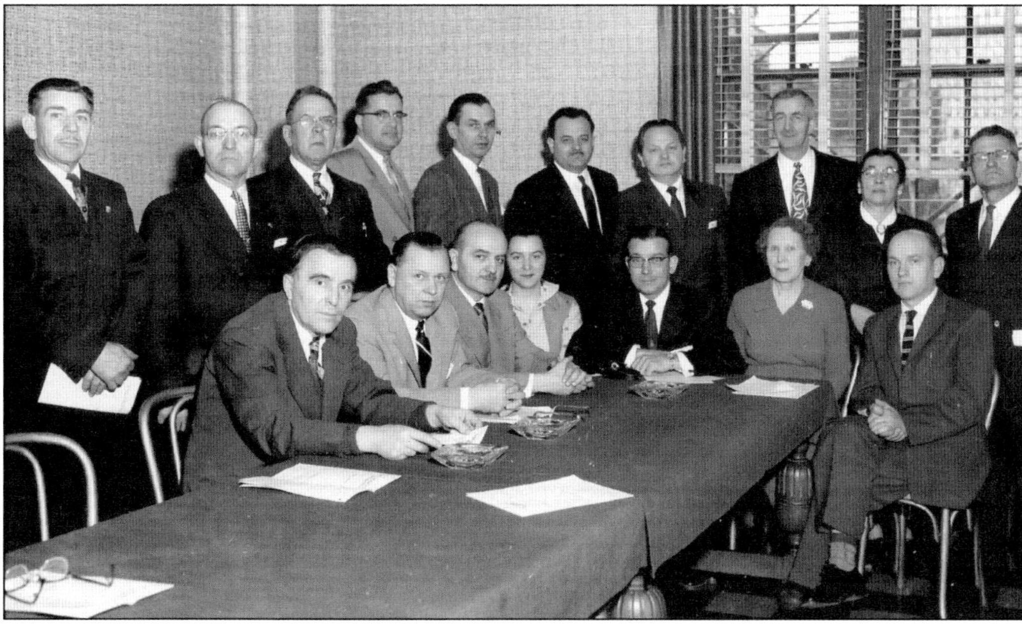

THE UNITED UKRAINIAN ORGANIZATIONS OF WESTERN PENNSYLVANIA. Founded in 1957, United Ukrainian Organizations of Western Pennsylvania (UUOWP) was formed to coordinate and reinforce activities in the broad territory of Ukrainian settlement in the area. Although short lived, the organization sponsored many commemorations of Ukrainian events, as well as Ukrainian Day at West View Park. (Courtesy of Michael Komichak.)

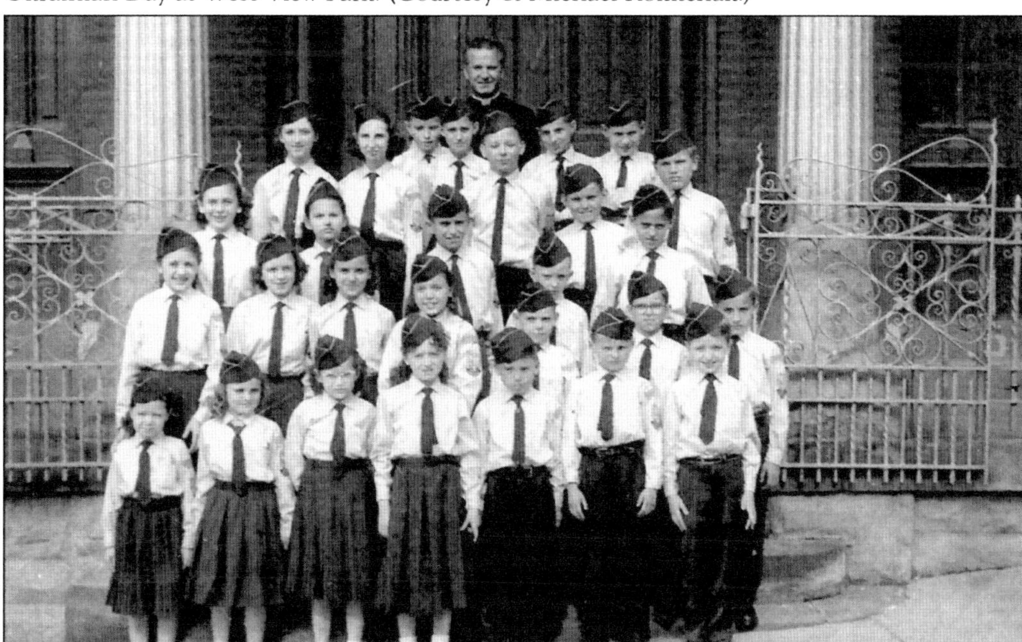

SUM. This Ukrainian youth group, whose acronym SUM stands for Ukrainian Youth Association, focuses on patriotism, sports, culture, and encampments. A branch located in Pittsburgh was active among third wave Ukrainian immigrants when this 1959 photograph was taken. (Courtesy of Yaroslaw Hodowanec.)

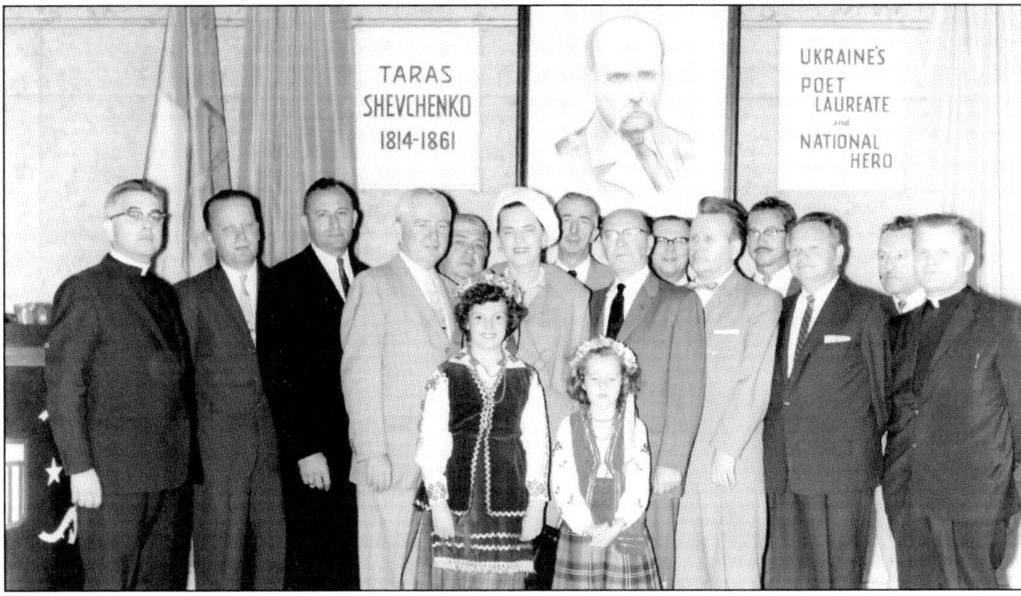

REMEMBERING SHEVCHENKO. Gathering to commemorate the life of Ukrainian poet-laureate Taras Hryhorovych Shevchenko has been an annual affair in Ukrainian communities throughout western Pennsylvania. Arguably the best known of Ukraine's historical figures, he led the reawakening of Ukrainian consciousness during the mid-19th century. Western Pennsylvania Ukrainians gather to commemorate the 100th anniversary of his death in 1961. (Courtesy of Roman Kyshakevych.)

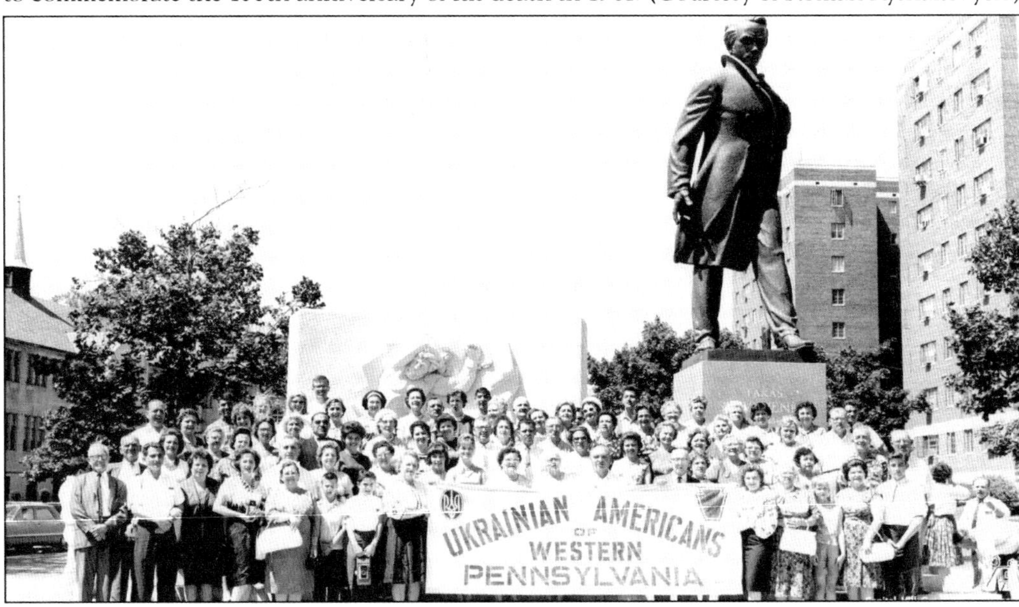

HONORING SHEVCHENKO. Pres. John Fitzgerald Kennedy explained the U.S. government's decision to erect a statue of Taras Shevchenko in Washington, D.C.: "We honor him for his rich contribution to the culture not only of Ukraine, which he loved so well and described so eloquently, but of the world. His work is a noble part of our historical heritage." Ukrainians from all over the United States formed committees to collect funds to pay for the building of the statue and gathered in Washington on July 24, 1964, for the statue's unveiling, which was overseen by former president Dwight D. Eisenhower. (Courtesy of St. Mary Ukrainian Orthodox Church, McKees Rocks.)

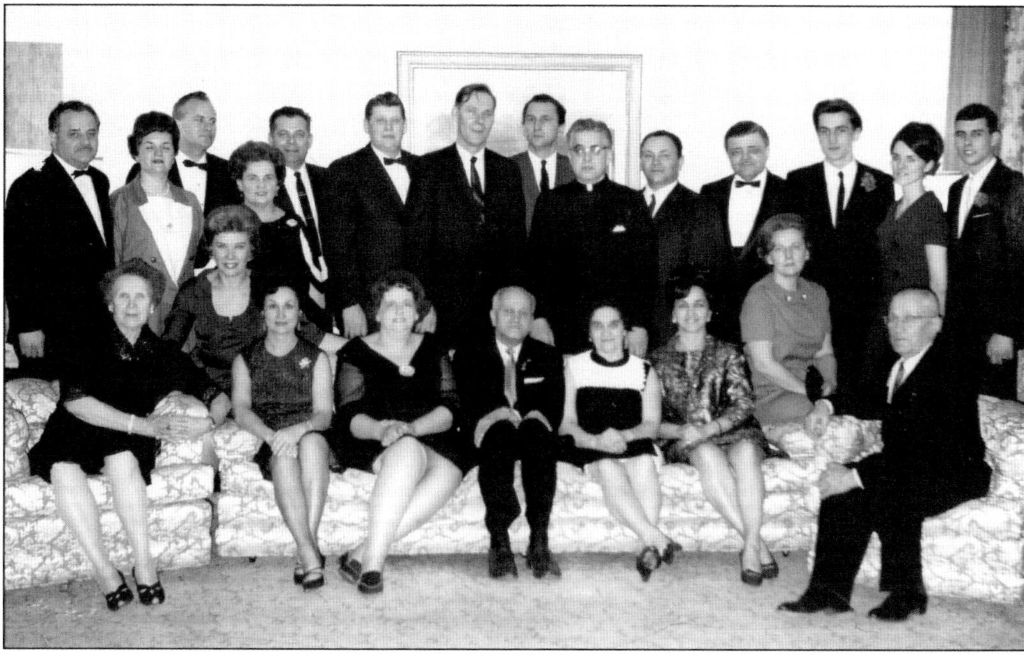

Government in Exile. The western Pennsylvania Ukrainian community greets president in exile of Ukraine Mykola Liwytzkyj in January 1968. Believing that the USSR was an occupying force in Ukraine, the government in exile advocated on behalf of the rights of all Ukrainians. (Courtesy of Roman Kyshakevych.)

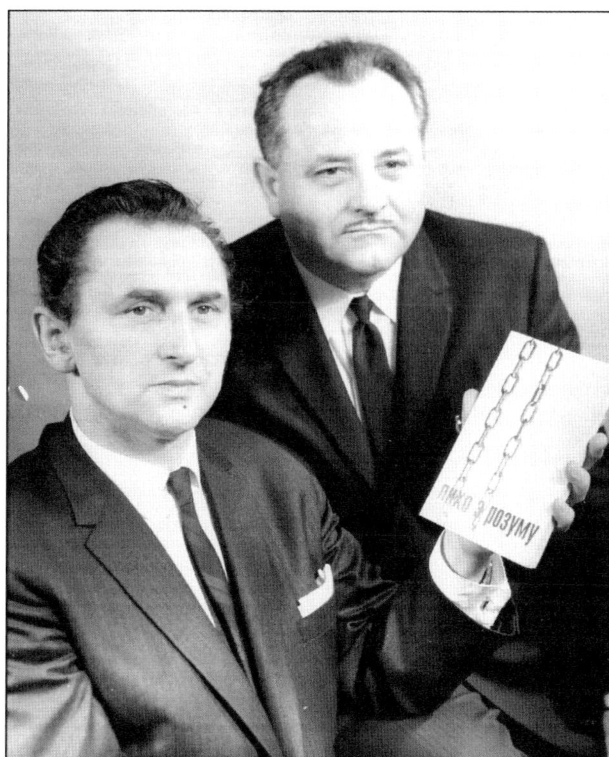

Dissidents. Citizens of the USSR who had the courage to protest the lack of personal freedoms and harsh repression by the Soviet government were known as dissidents. Local Ukrainian activists were photographed by the Pittsburgh Press for use in an article drawing attention to their plight. (Courtesy of Roman Kyshakevych.)

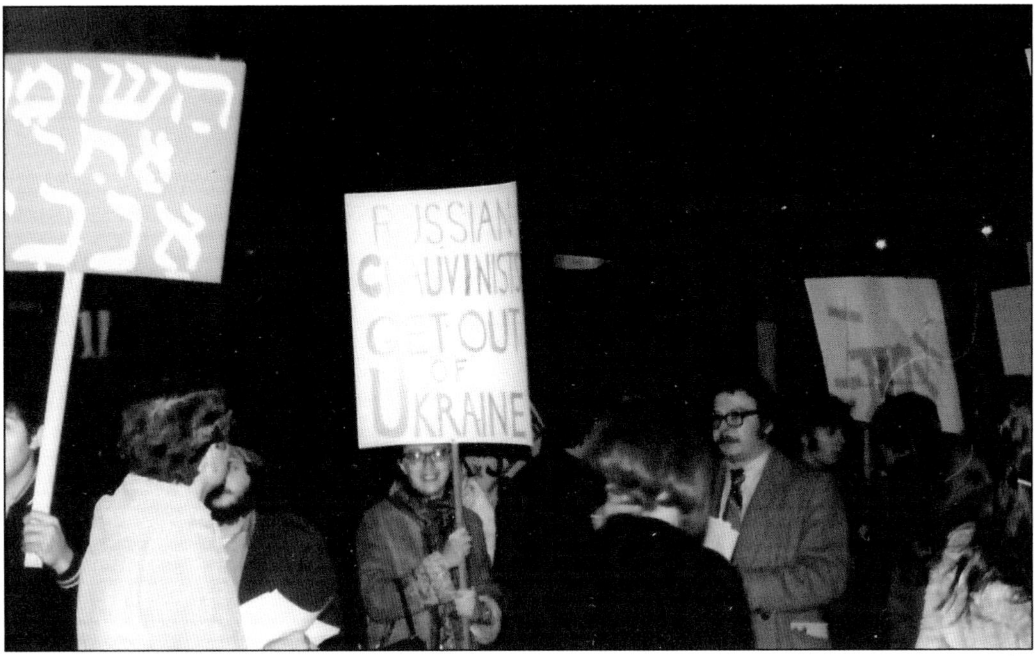

Protesting Soviet Oppression. Local Ukrainians joined Jews and Lithuanians to picket the March 30, 1971, performance of the Siberian Dancers and Singers of Omsk at Oakland's Syria Mosque. Protesters passed out literature to concertgoers outlining Soviet repressions. (Courtesy of Yaroslaw Hodowanec.)

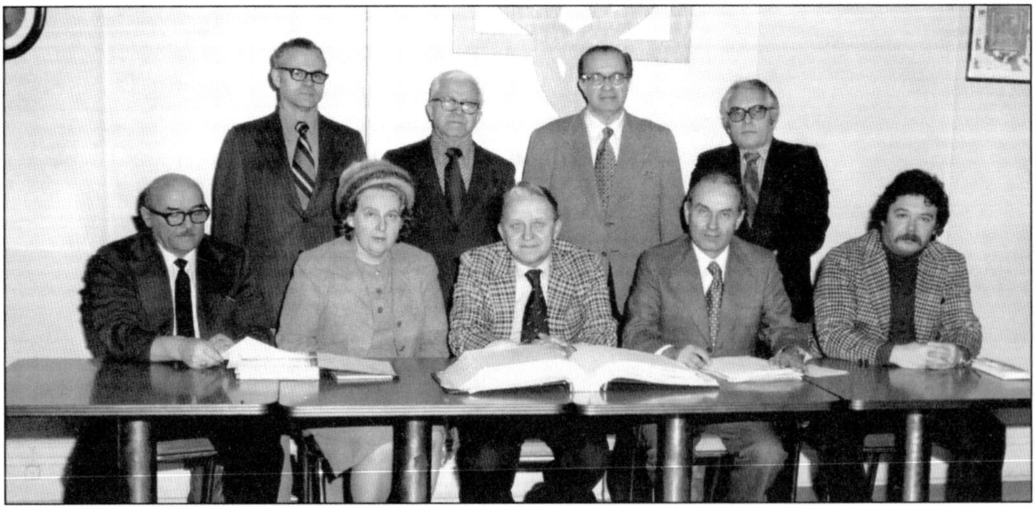

Samopomich. The board of directors and staff of the Ukrainian Selfreliance of Western Pennsylvania Federal Credit Union pose in 1976. Founded in 1974 to provide financial services to members of the Ukrainian community throughout western Pennsylvania, Samopomich (selfreliance in Ukrainian) has provided over $69,000 in donations to various Ukrainian causes since 1988 and over $17 million in loans to members. Pictured from left to right are (first row) Michael Baran, longtime manager Taisa Korchynsky, longtime treasurer Peter Naber, founder and president for 20 years Sydir Michael Tymiak, and current manager Yaroslaw Hodowanec; (second row) Andrew Germansky, Mykola Sywy, Chester Manasterski, and Pantelejmon Plaks. (Courtesy of USWPFCU.)

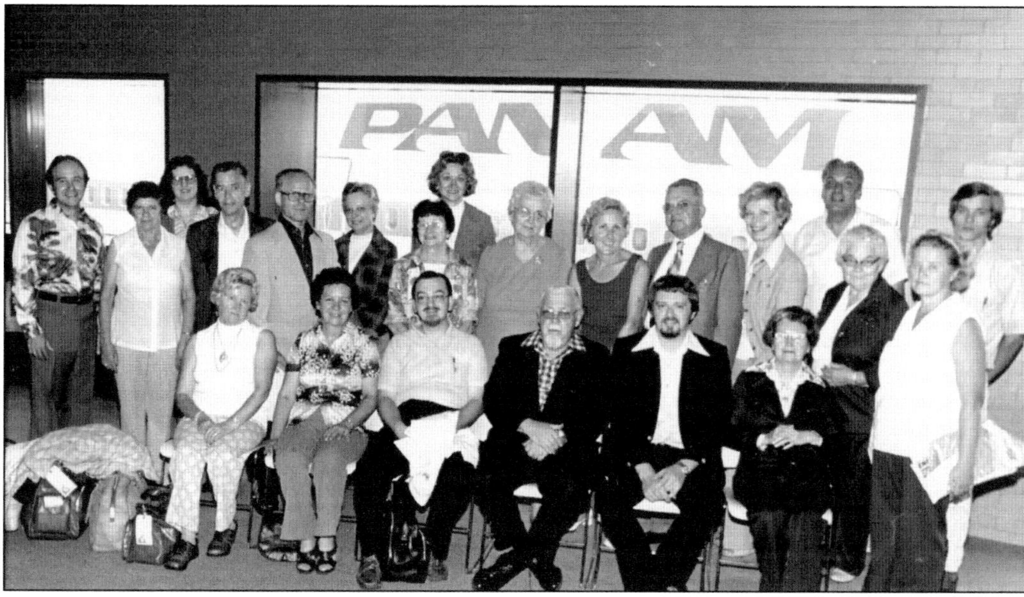

A THAW IN THE COLD WAR. Following summit meetings between U.S. and Soviet leaders in the 1970s, a liberalization of travel restrictions was instituted, and travel between the two countries by private citizens was allowed. In this 1978 photograph, Ukrainians from various parts of western Pennsylvania pose before their overseas adventure. Upon returning, they told of not being able to visit relatives in villages as well as other serious restrictions. (Courtesy of MASPPUOGCCC.)

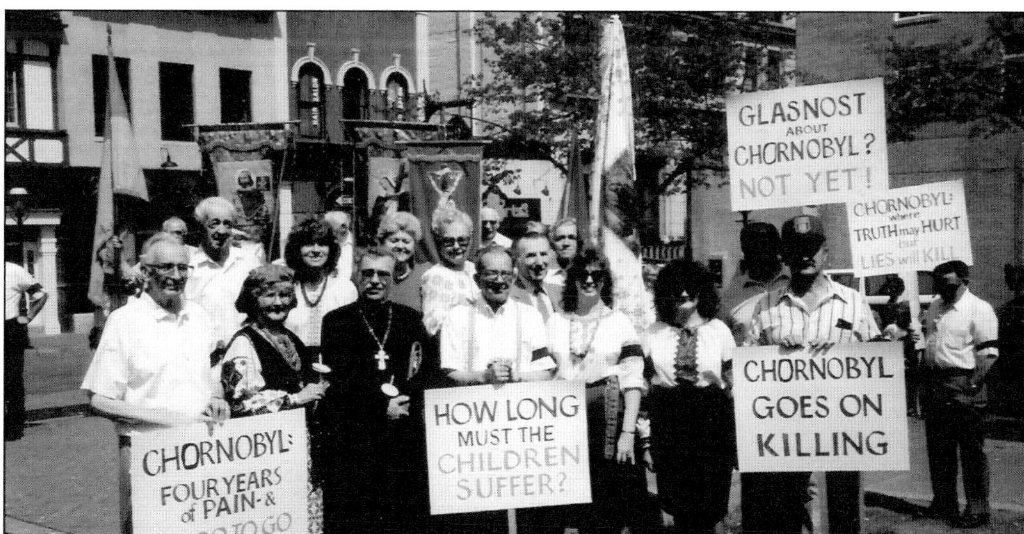

CHORNOBYL. On April 26, 1986, the nuclear reactor in Chornobyl, Ukraine, just north of capital city Kyiv, began to melt down. The press, which was controlled by the Soviet government, was not allowed to report on the disaster. The Soviet government allowed a May Day Parade in the streets of Kyiv to take place and did not admit to the tragedy until unusually high levels of radiation were detected over parts of northern Europe days later. Western Pennsylvania Ukrainians commemorate the fourth anniversary of this tragedy in Pittsburgh's Market Square in 1990. (Courtesy of Oksana Byczkalo.)

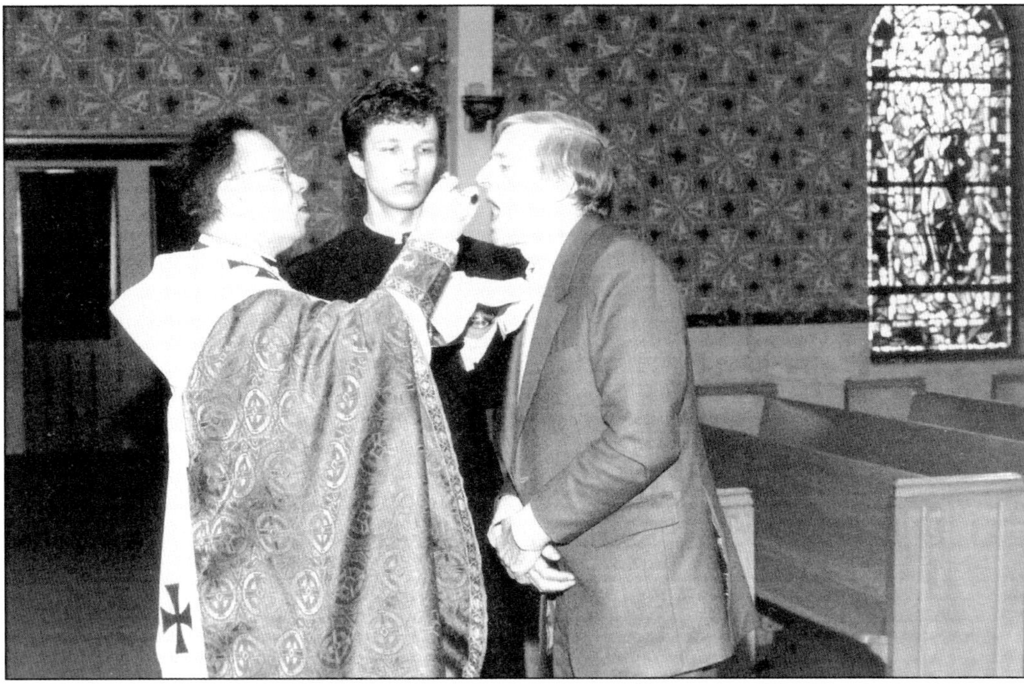

THE ISSUE OF RELIGIOUS FREEDOM. Conservative icon William F. Buckley Jr. takes communion at Holy Trinity Ukrainian Catholic Church in Carnegie during a 1987 visit to Pittsburgh to discuss religious freedom in the Soviet Union. (Courtesy of Michael Haritan.)

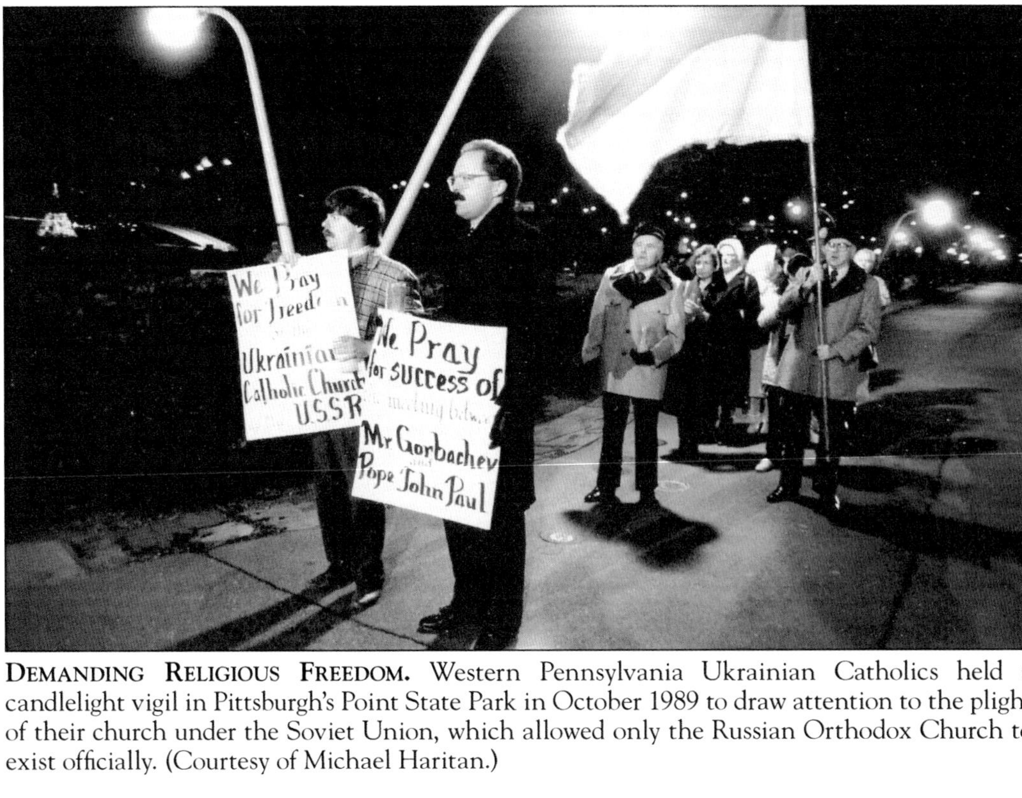

DEMANDING RELIGIOUS FREEDOM. Western Pennsylvania Ukrainian Catholics held a candlelight vigil in Pittsburgh's Point State Park in October 1989 to draw attention to the plight of their church under the Soviet Union, which allowed only the Russian Orthodox Church to exist officially. (Courtesy of Michael Haritan.)

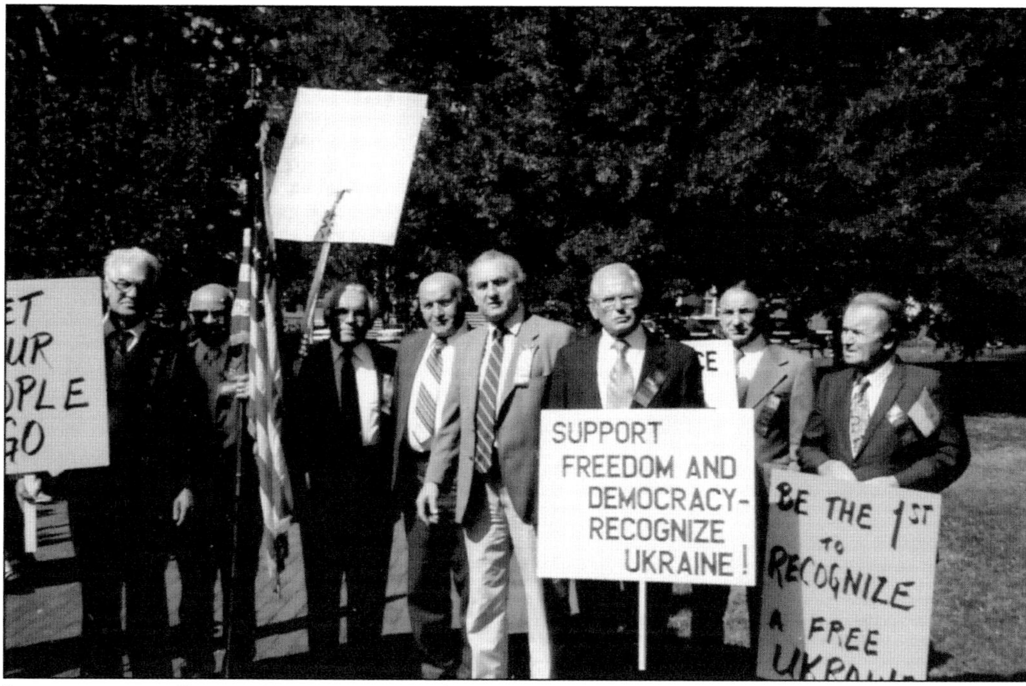

INDEPENDENCE RALLY. Western Pennsylvania Ukrainians travel to the nation's capital in 1991 to demand the United States' support of Ukraine's independence declaration during the final days of the Soviet Union. (Courtesy of Oksana Byczkalo.)

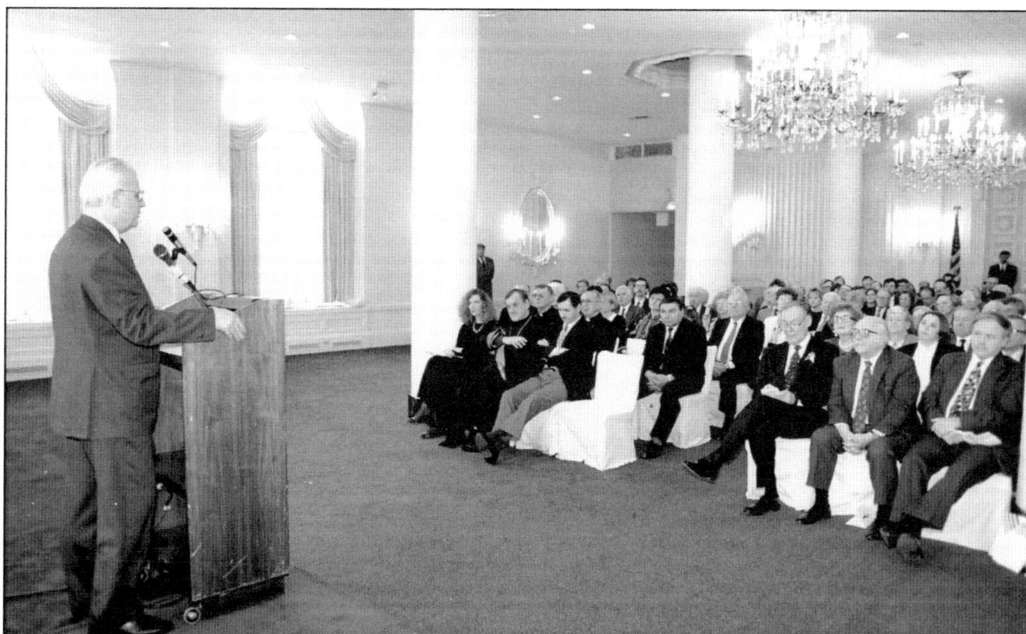

THE VISIT OF UKRAINIAN PRESIDENT LEONID KRAVCHUK. Leonid Kravchuk was the first democratically elected president of modern Ukraine and served as its president from 1991 until 1994. This photograph was taken during his stop in western Pennsylvania during a U.S. tour in January 1995. (Courtesy of Michael Haritan.)

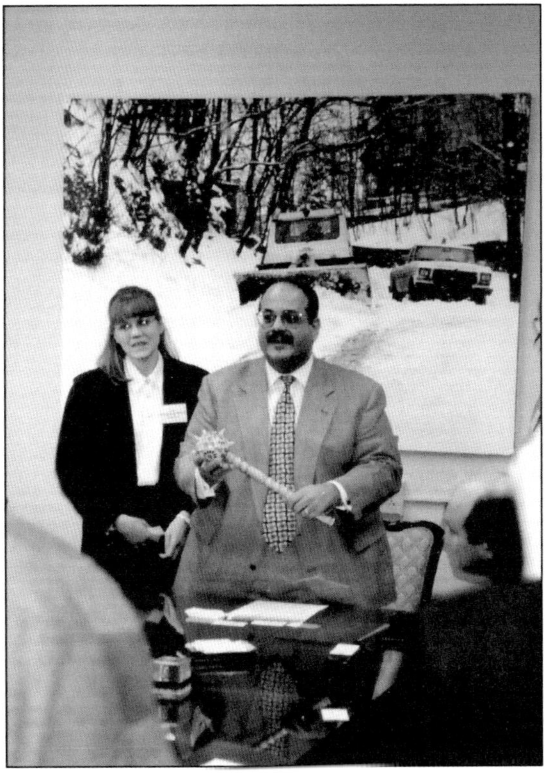

Symbolic Greeting from Citizens of Independent Ukraine. Pittsburgh deputy mayor Sal Sirabella receives a *bulava*—a staff of office from kozak times—given to him by a delegation of local government officials from Ukraine taking part in the Community Connections Program of the U.S. Department of State. These citizen diplomats visited the area in December 1996. (Courtesy of UCHI.)

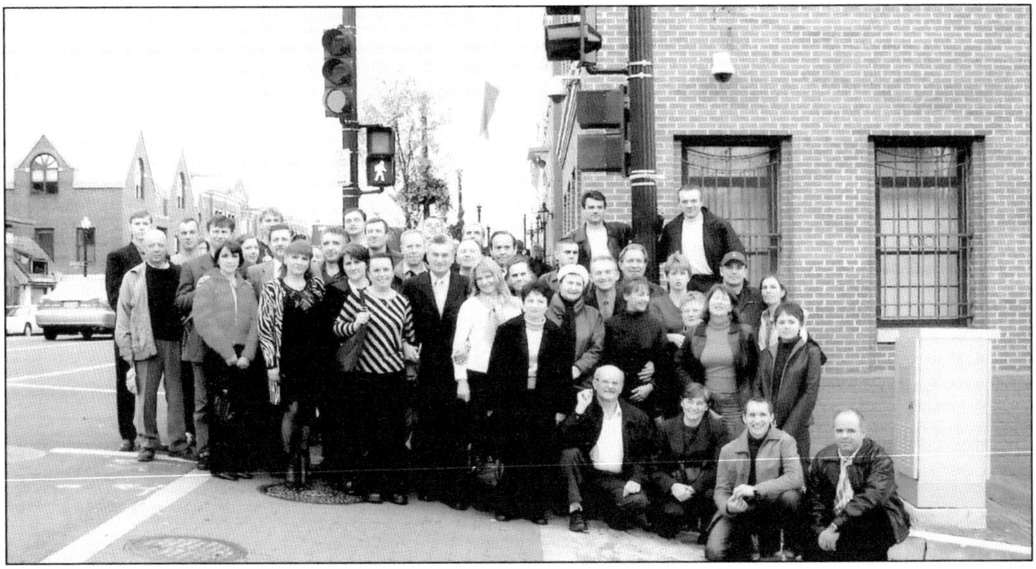

The Orange Revolution. Members of the fourth wave of Ukrainian immigration to the United States travel to the Ukrainian Embassy in Washington, D.C., to cast their votes for president of Ukraine in November 2004. Marred by voter fraud perpetrated by the then-current Ukrainian government, a people's protest arose, which forced new elections. Known as the Orange Revolution, this nonviolent protest movement saw millions of Ukrainian citizens take to the streets of Kyiv during the cold winter months and received worldwide attention. (Courtesy of Volodymyr Nakonechnyy.)

Two

CHURCH AND COMMUNITY

A CONNECTION FROM AGES TO AGES

Western Pennsylvania Ukrainian communities historically have had very strong ties to their churches, and in many communities, the church is the center of Ukrainian activity. Prior to the collapse of the USSR, many Americans did not understand what a Ukrainian was, and these Ukrainian churches served as repositories of knowledge about the Ukrainian people and as places to preserve their identity.

The Kyivan-Rus' state adopted Eastern Christianity in the year 988 from Constantinople, almost 70 years before the Christian Schism of 1054. Although most Ukrainians remained Orthodox, seven Ukrainian bishops attended the Council of Brest in 1596, where an Eastern Church administratively in union with Rome was created, later to be known as the Byzantine, Greek, or Ukrainian Catholic Church. This Ukrainian Catholic Church and its faithful were guaranteed retention of a married clergy, the Julian calendar, and various church theology and traditions. Unfortunately, their unique status was not familiar to Americans, and they experienced many prejudices and difficulties in maintaining these rights in their new homeland.

In Europe, the state, local gentry, and estate endowments provided financial support to churches. In the United States, these Ukrainian immigrants contributed generously from their modest incomes to build and maintain houses of worship in which to honor their Lord in the manner to which they were accustomed and desired. These differences conflicted with the established churches and provided for many disagreements—even among themselves. Property ownership, celibacy for priests, and various jurisdictional disputes were among the most serious issues, which led to internal divisions and conflicts. Some disagreements caused congregations to alternate between hiring Catholic and Orthodox priests, and some led to cases heard by the Pennsylvania Supreme Court. Certain parishes remain to this day uniquely independent under the law.

Historically, most western Pennsylvania Ukrainians have identified themselves as either Greek Catholics or Orthodox. Other Ukrainian Christian groups have had a significant presence as well, particularly in Pittsburgh. Of course, not all Ukrainian immigrants belonged to "Ukrainian" churches, and many have also brought aspects of their culture to socialist and organized worker organizations. Although some parishes have closed, there are 36 active Ukrainian churches in the area today.

Many Ukrainian churches follow the Julian calendar, which is why they celebrate Christmas on January 7 and occasionally celebrate Easter in May. Most Ukrainian priests are allowed to marry if they do so before they are ordained to the deaconate. Communion is given to children from the time they are baptized, and they receive the sacrament of first confession around age eight.

Many Ukrainian parish halls contain Ukrainian gift shops, and most parishes operate a kitchen, offering Ukrainian food for sale to parishioners and the general public. The Ukrainian language is still heard in many church services, and some parishes still sponsor Ukrainian folk dance groups and choirs. Ukrainians' ethnic and religious identities have always been so intertwined that when two of them meet for the first time, they usually ask each other, "What church do you go to?"

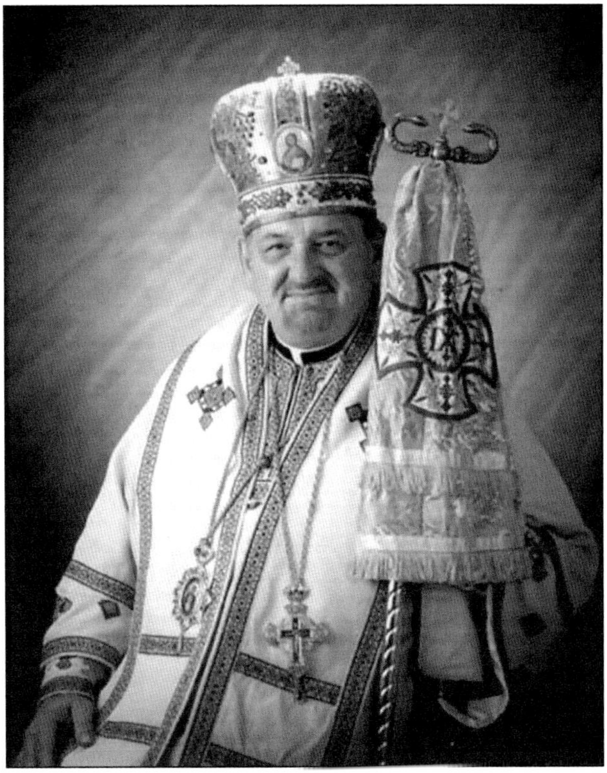

METROPOLITAN CONSTANTINE OF THE UKRAINIAN ORTHODOX CHURCH OF THE UNITED STATES OF AMERICA. A child of St. Vladimir Ukrainian Orthodox Church on the South Side of Pittsburgh, Theodore Buggan was ordained a priest in 1967 and bishop in 1972, being elevated to the position of metropolitan of Ukrainian Orthodox faithful in the United States, Europe, and Australia in 1992. He returned to Pittsburgh in 1994 and maintains his See from his childhood home on the city's South Side. (Courtesy of UOCUSA.)

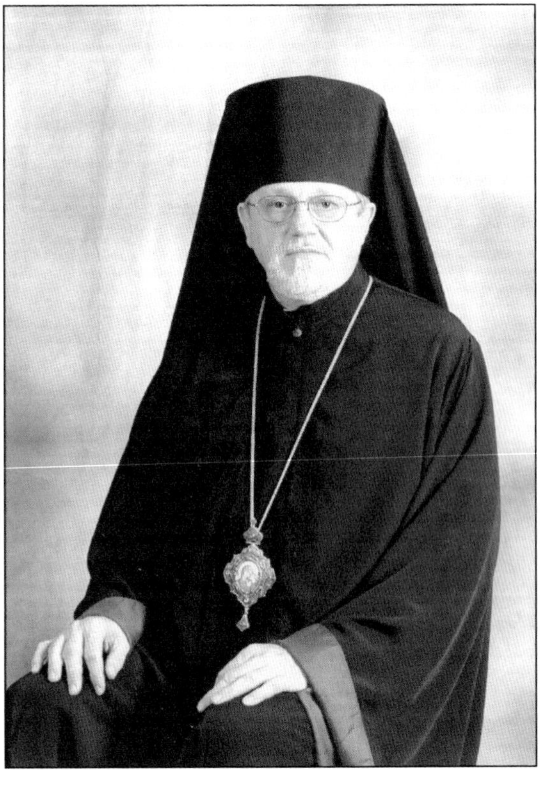

ARCHBISHOP ANTONY OF THE UKRAINIAN ORTHODOX CHURCH OF THE UNITED STATES OF AMERICA. John Scharba was born in Sharon and upon his ordination in 1972, was assigned pastoral duties at St. Vladimir Ukrainian Orthodox Church in Ambridge. Upon his elevation to Episcopal service in 1985, he was given the name Antony. Over the years, he has served as editor of the church's *Ukrainian Orthodox Word English Edition*, as rector of St. Sophia Seminary, and as president of the Consistory of the Church since 1995. (Courtesy of UOCUSA.)

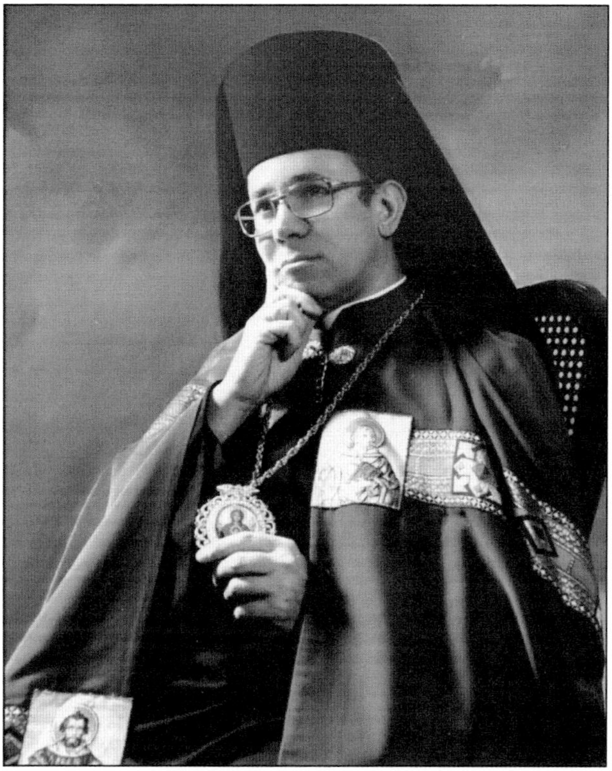

Bishop Robert Moskal of the Ukrainian Catholic Church. Born in Carnegie, Robert Michael Moskal was ordained to the holy priesthood in 1963 and served his first Divine Liturgy at his home parish. He has served at the Archbishop's Chancery in Philadelphia, edited the Archdiocesan weekly *The Way*, served as pastor in Warrington, Pennsylvania, and was elected for a four-year term as president of the Providence Association of Ukrainian Catholics of America. He was elevated to Episcopal service as first prelate of the newly formed Diocese of St. Josaphat in 1984. (Courtesy of the UCDSJP.)

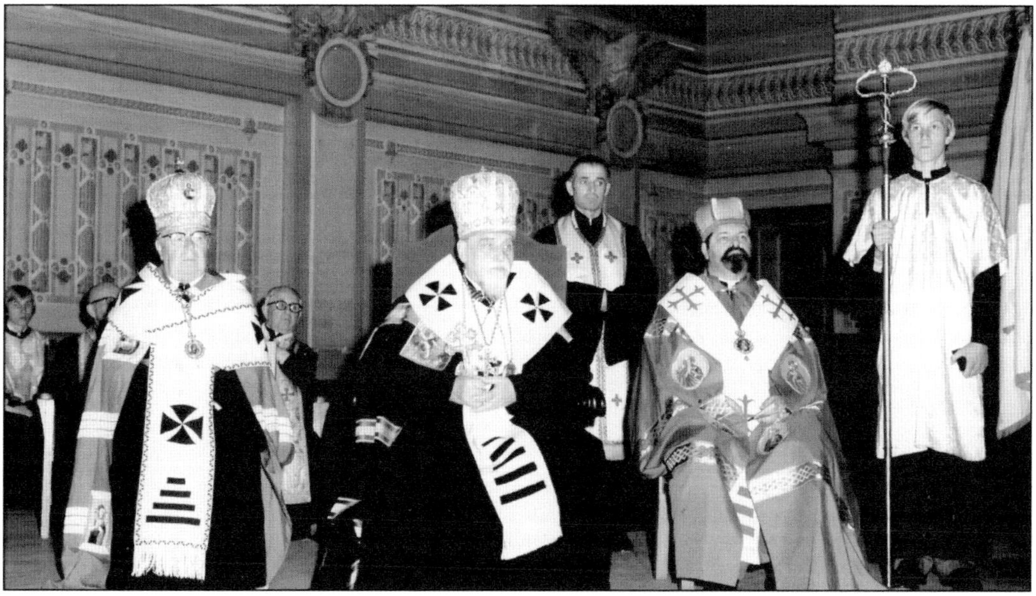

Visit of Cardinal Josef Slipyj. Elected metropolitan of L'viv in 1944, one year later Josef Slipyj (second from left) was arrested and condemned to eight years of prison and forced labor by the Soviet government. Consequent sentences kept him in prison until, with the assistance of Pope John XXIII, he was released in 1963. Ten years later, he visited Pittsburgh and, during a ceremony at Soldiers and Sailors Memorial Hall in Oakland, challenged those in attendance to build a stronger community, suggesting the founding of a financial institution. (Courtesy of Melody Sachko.)

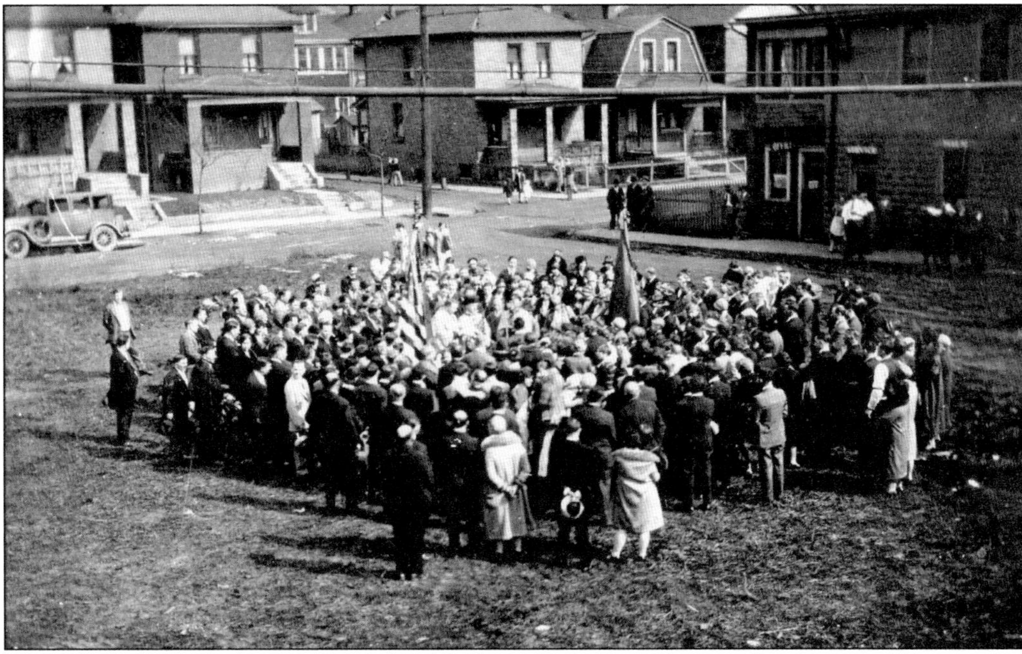

GROUNDBREAKING. Parishioners gather at the groundbreaking for the construction of St. Vladimir Ukrainian Orthodox Church in Ambridge in 1928. The Ukrainian Orthodox Church in Ukraine was reborn following World War I and many of its parishes in the United States opened in the 1920s. (Courtesy of St. Vladimir Ukrainian Orthodox Church.)

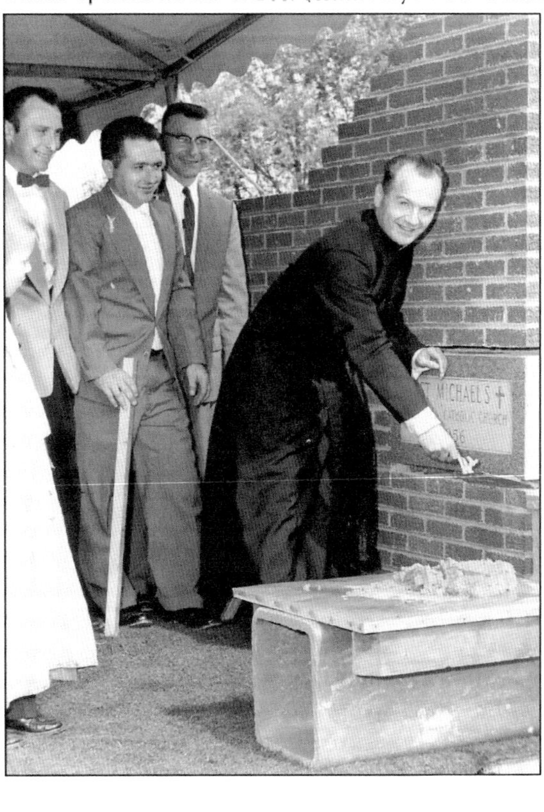

LAYING THE CORNERSTONE. Fr. Michael Bochnewich of St. Michael Ukrainian Catholic Church in West Leechburg lays finishing touches to the cornerstone of the church during its construction in 1956. The first Ukrainian immigrants to this Westmoreland County coal-mining town arrived in 1909, and by 1930, there were 15 Ukrainian families. The 2000 census data showed 5 percent of town residents were of Ukrainian ancestry. (Courtesy of Pat Morovich.)

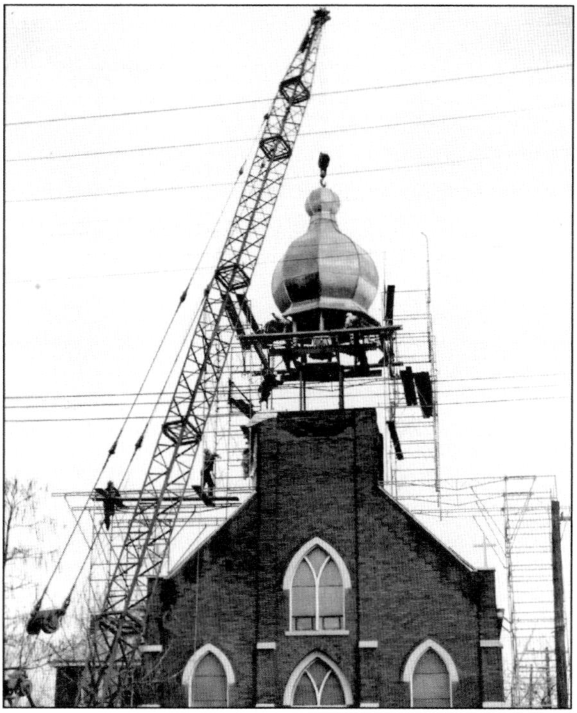

DOMES. Most Ukrainian churches are topped with onion- or pear-shaped domes reflecting the Ukrainian Baroque architectural style, which emerged in the 17th and 18th centuries. Eastern rite Christianity teaches that through his son Jesus Christ, God has come to live among us, and these domes symbolize the act of God the Father reaching out to his children and enveloping them in his love. The newly organized parish of St. John the Baptist Ukrainian Catholic Church in McKees Rocks bought an independent Polish congregation building as a place of worship in 1942 and soon replaced its spire with this dome. The local press contained articles detailing the new technology, which allowed the dome to be lifted into place, as previously this was considered too dangerous and domes were built in place. (Courtesy of St. John the Baptist Ukrainian Catholic Church.)

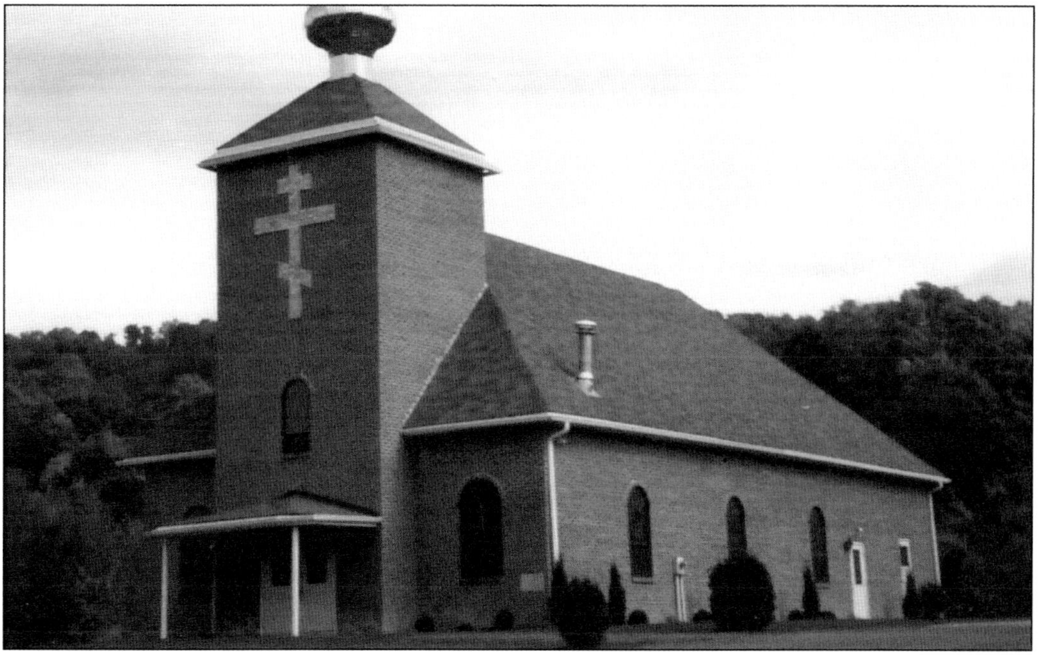

THREE-BARRED CROSS. Most Ukrainian churches use the Eastern or three-barred cross like the one placed among the bricks at St. John the Baptist Ukrainian Orthodox Church in Dixonville. The top bar represents the headboard, where Jesus's sentence was written and the diagonal bar represents the footrest, wrenched loose by Jesus writhing in intense agony. It is raised to the left side, toward the righteous criminal who said to Jesus, "Remember me when you come into your kingdom." (Courtesy of UOCUSA.)

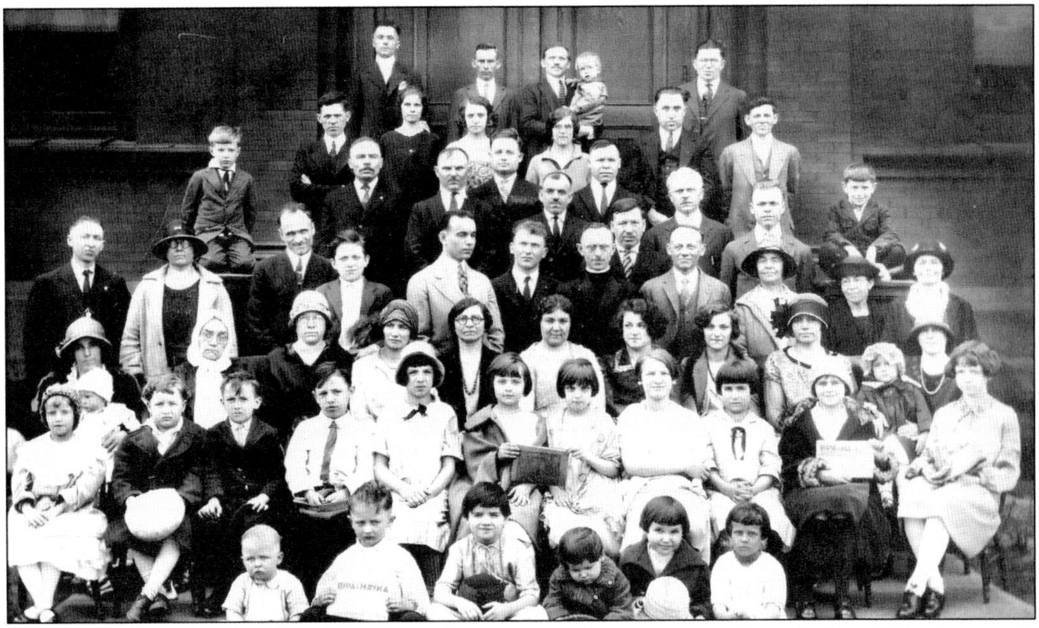

The First Ukrainian Presbyterian Church of Pittsburgh. Founded in 1913, the parish was located a short distance from St. John the Baptist Ukrainian Catholic Church on Carson Street on Pittsburgh's South Side. Parishioners pose in front of the church in 1926, some of whom are holding copies of the newspaper *Vira Nauka* or "faith and science" in English. (Courtesy of Margaret A. Klimko.)

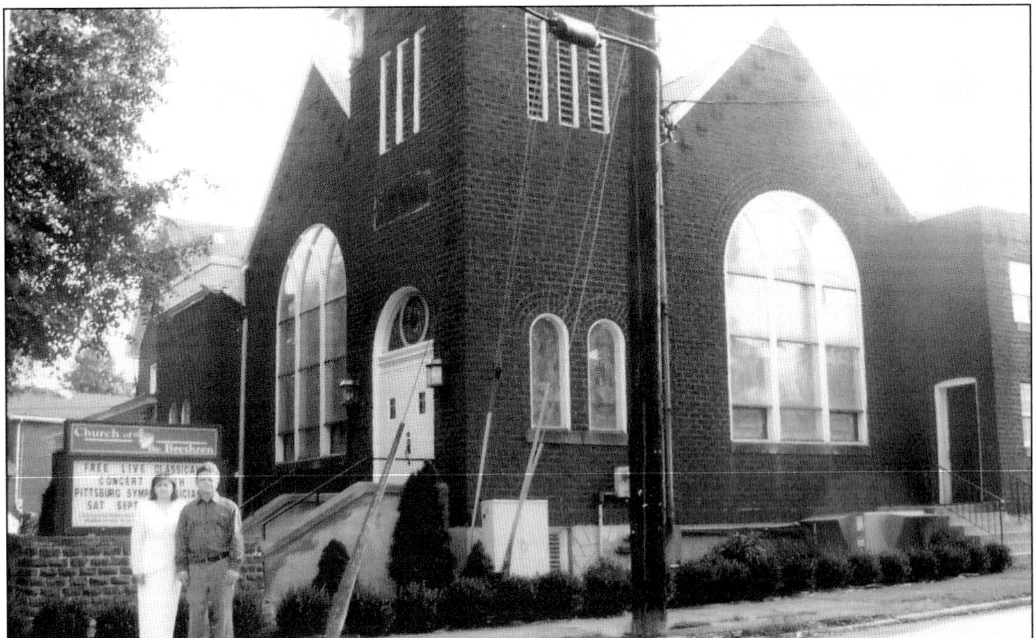

The Slavic Evangelical Baptist Church. Many church members arrived in the United States during the 1980s and early 1990s as refugees from religious persecution in the USSR. Church pastor Viktor Mikhnyuk and his wife stand in front of their parish located in Pittsburgh's Greenfield neighborhood. (Courtesy of Pastor Viktor Mikhnyuk.)

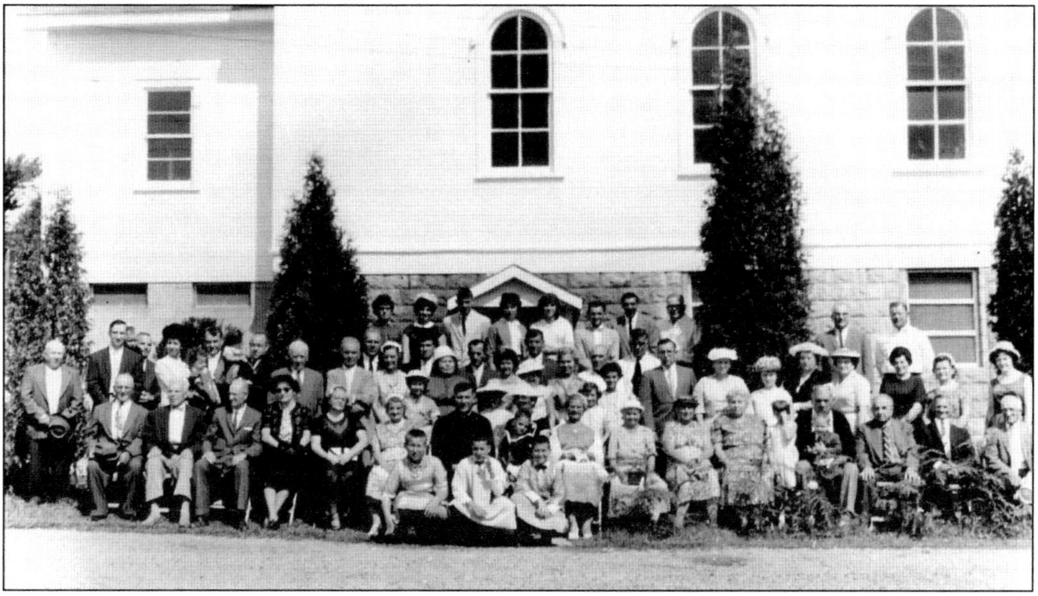

SLICKVILLE. Members of Holy Ghost Ukrainian Orthodox Church are pictured next to their church in Slickville, the last "coal patch" town to be built in Westmoreland County. Coal companies built these model towns to provide better living conditions for their employees and some say to deter unionization efforts. (Courtesy of Holy Ghost Ukrainian Orthodox Church.)

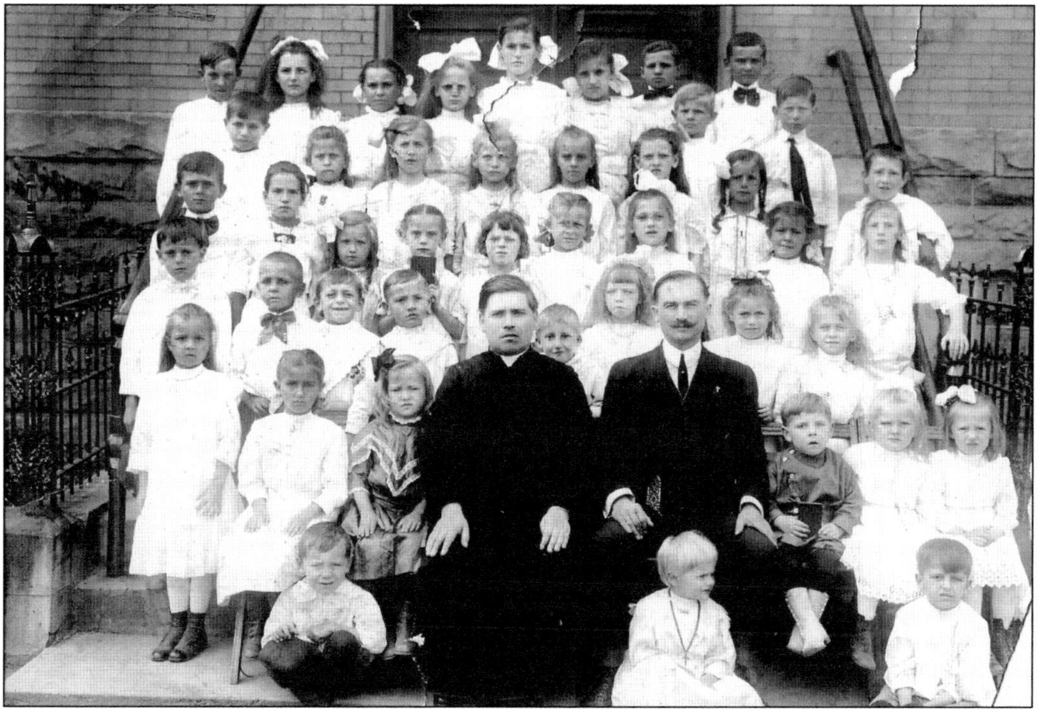

FORD CITY ROMANCE. Children at Patronage of the Blessed Virgin Mary Ukrainian Catholic Church pose with their spiritual leader and their teacher in this photograph taken in 1913. The little girl in the front row with her eyes on the boy to her left eventually married him and they lived together as man and wife for over 60 years. (Courtesy of Pat Morovich.)

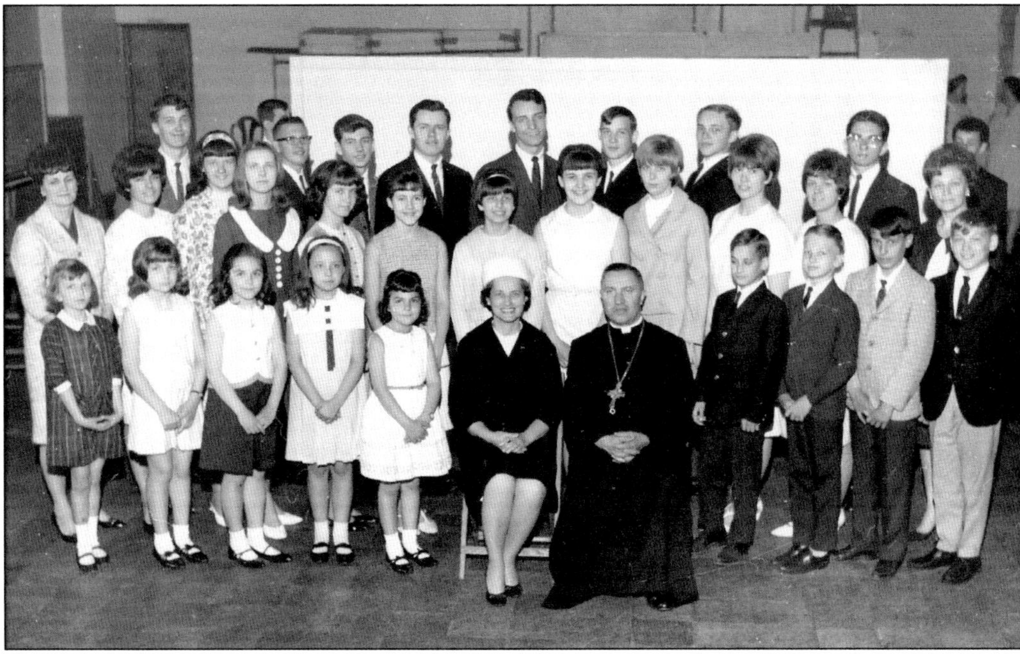

JUNIOR CHOIR, MONESSEN. Eastern-rite churches, by tradition, do not use musical instruments. Responses are either sung by the congregation or by church choirs. St. Nicholas Ukrainian Orthodox Church was founded in 1908 as SS. Peter and Paul Ukrainian Greek Catholic Church, and the city of Monessen was a prominent Mon Valley steel town during the industry's heyday. (Courtesy of Helen Guzensky.)

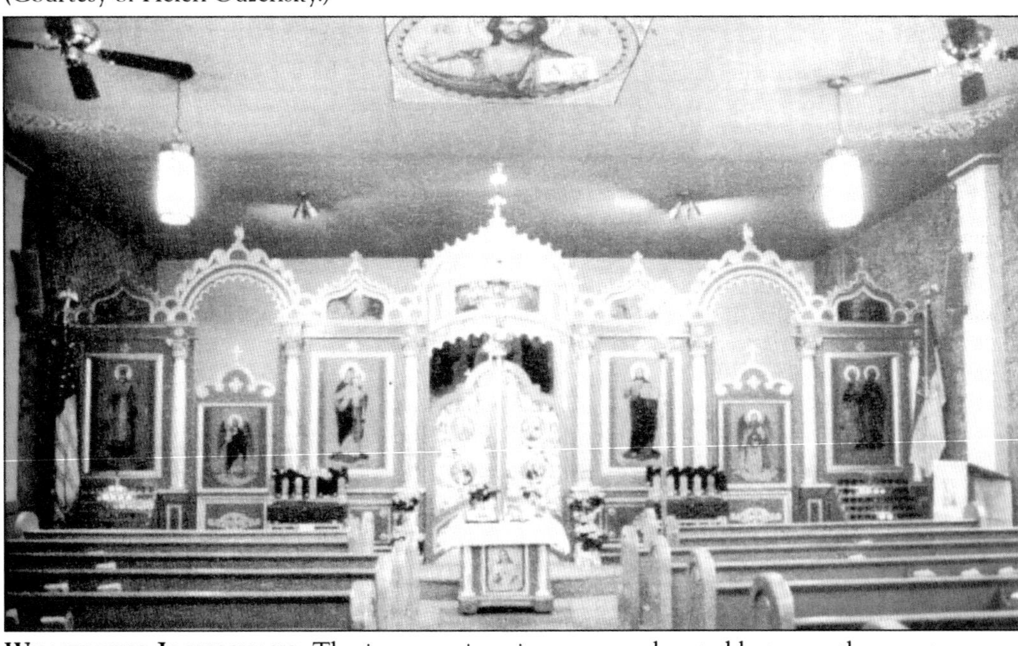

WILMERDING ICONOSTASIS. The iconostasis or icon screen, located between the sanctuary and nave, is another vital element in most Ukrainian churches. This screen is located at SS. Peter and Paul Ukrainian Catholic Church in Wilmerding—a location of one of the former Westinghouse Air Brake Company's factories. (Courtesy of UCDSJP.)

THE FIRST TO SERVE IN NANTY GLO. Fr. Ivan Paley was the first priest assigned to Holy Ascension Ukrainian Orthodox Church in the Cambria County town of Nanty Glo. *Nanty glo* is a Welsh term translating to "streams of coal," and though logging was its first industry, coal mining brought many settlers from Europe and fueled the growth of the town early in the 20th century. (Courtesy of Irene Nestor.)

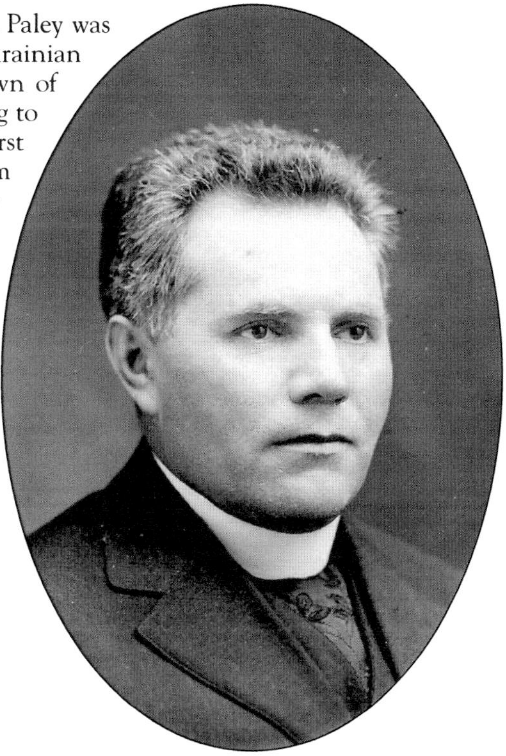

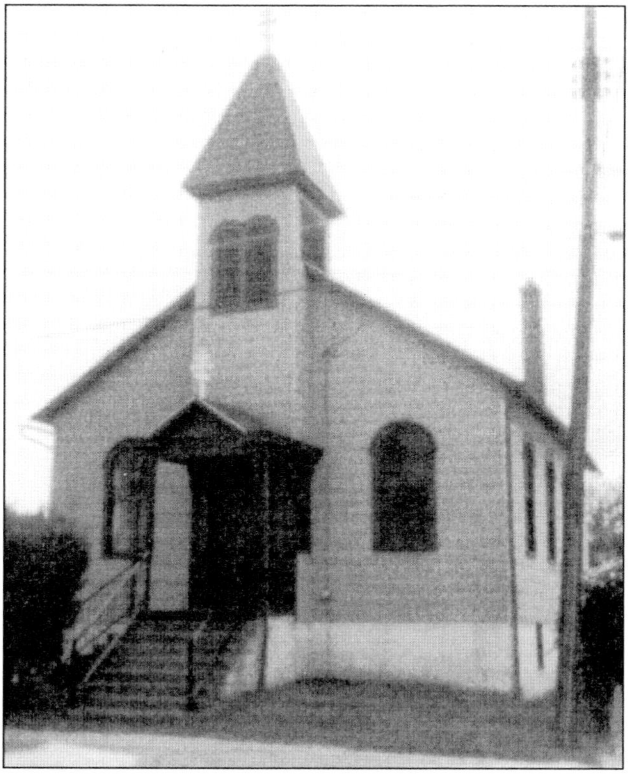

NEW ALEXANDRIA. Nativity of the Blessed Virgin Mary Ukrainian Catholic Church was founded in this Westmoreland County town in 1906. A wooden church was built the following year, and a parish hall soon after, which would serve as a social and cultural center for teaching Ukrainian language, customs, and church music. (Courtesy of UCDSJP.)

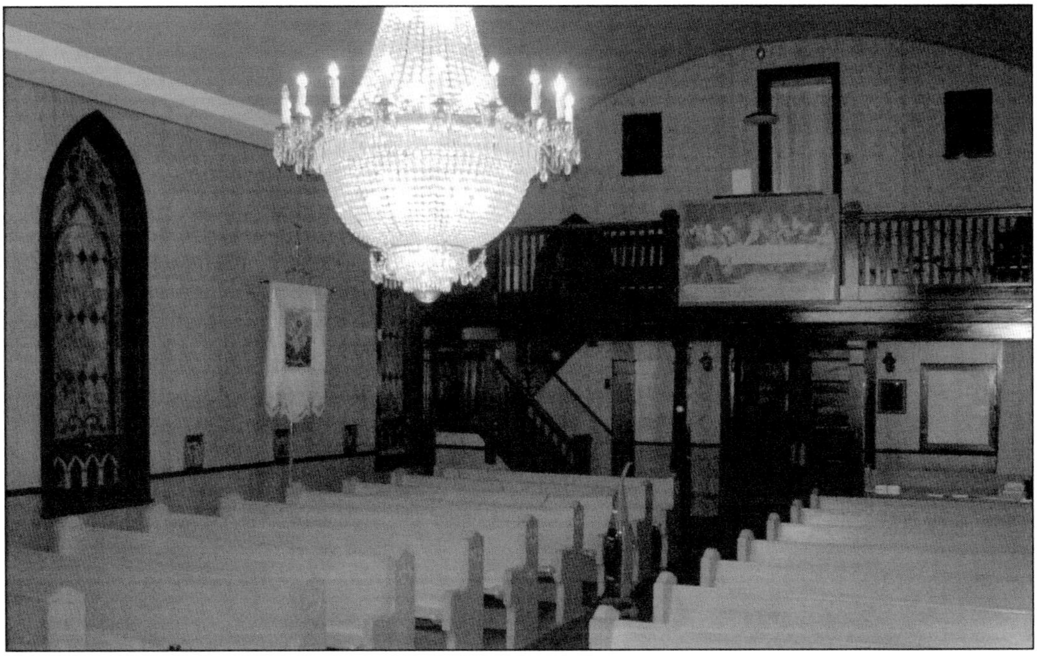

SMITHMILL. The chandelier is an important facet of Eastern-rite churches, representing the heavens and creation regenerated in Christ. Founded in 1917, ground was broken for St. Vladimir Ukrainian Orthodox Church in 1919, and construction was completed in 1921. This Clearfield County parish actively collects food, clothing, and other necessities for those in need in surrounding communities. (Courtesy of Fr. John Haluszczak.)

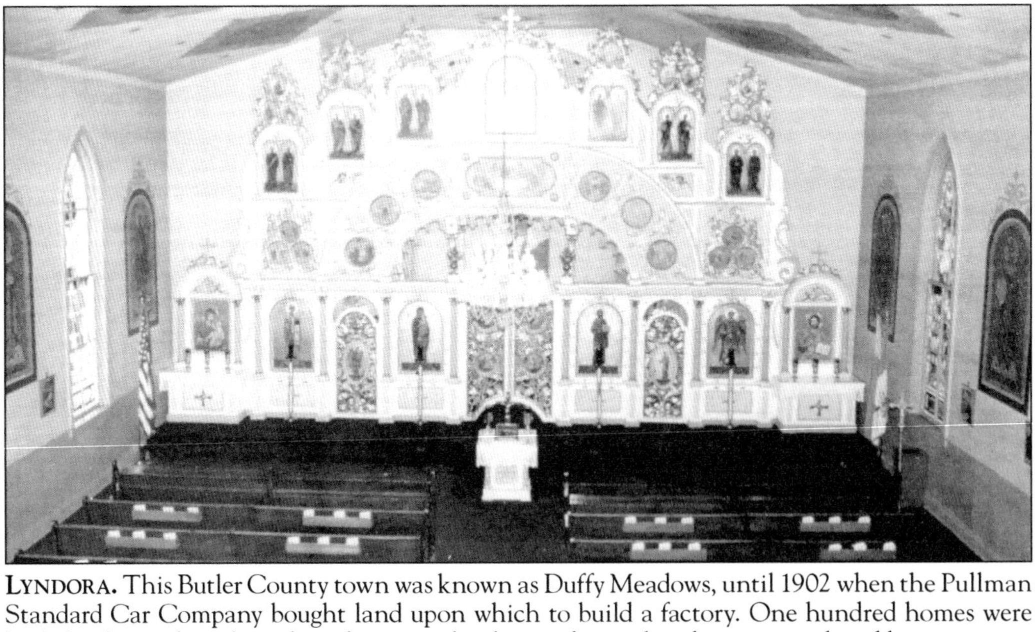

LYNDORA. This Butler County town was known as Duffy Meadows, until 1902 when the Pullman Standard Car Company bought land upon which to build a factory. One hundred homes were built for the workers, but when this proved to be too few, railroad cars were placed between rows of the new homes to serve as additional housing. The cars were painted red and this residential area became known as Red Row. Local Ukrainians founded St. Michael Ukrainian Catholic Church, pictured here in 1906. (Courtesy of UCDSJP.)

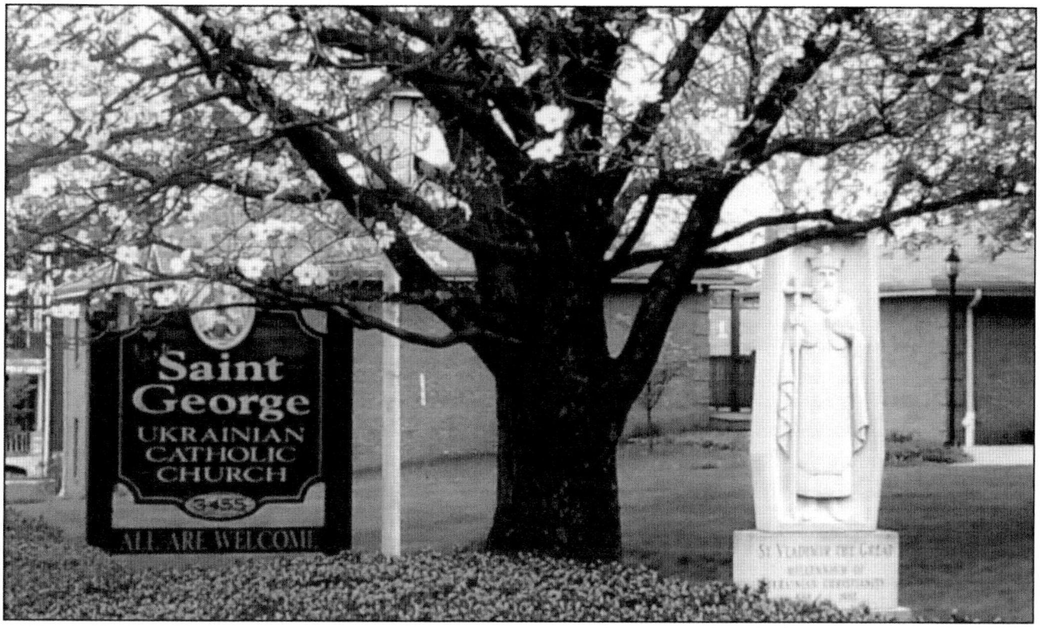

ST. VOLODYMYR. St. Volodymyr (Vladimir) was the Grand Prince of Kyivan-Rus', who in 988 converted to Christianity and proceeded to baptize his country in the Christian faith. The parishioners of St. George Ukrainian Catholic Church on Pittsburgh's North Side erected this statue in the saint's honor in 1988, during the millennium year of Christianity in Ukraine. (Courtesy of St. George Ukrainian Catholic Church.)

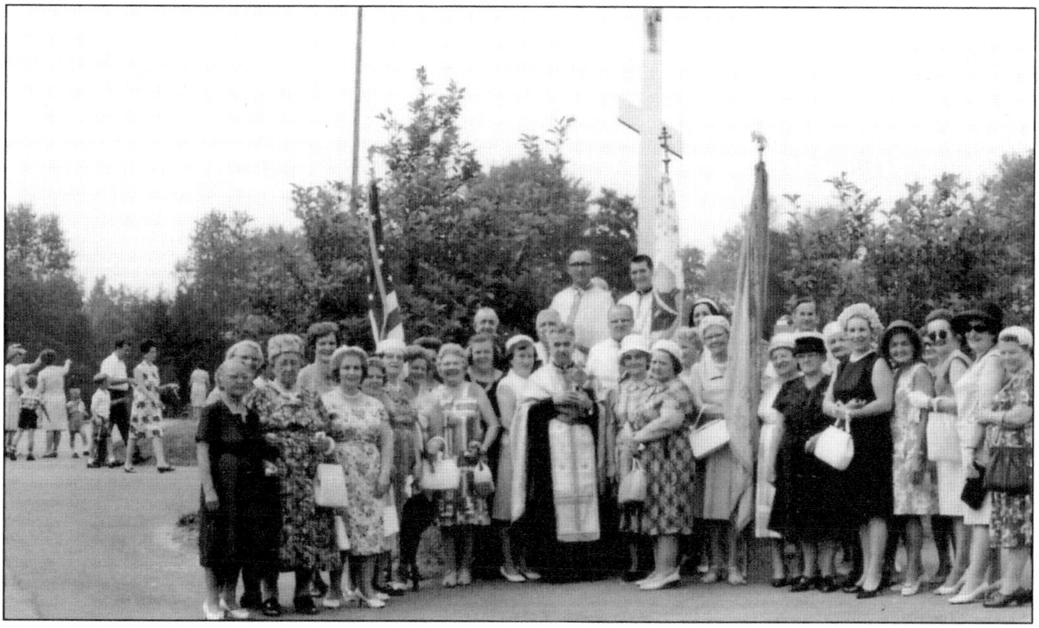

PARISH CEMETERY. Most Ukrainian churches in western Pennsylvania have their own cemetery, and the cemetery of St. Mary Ukrainian Orthodox Church in McKees Rocks is located in nearby Stowe. In the past, it was a common tradition to march in an organized procession from the church to the cemetery (sometimes quite a distance) on Memorial Day, St. Thomas Sunday (the week after Easter), or on Pentecost/Green Sunday. (Courtesy of LAVRSHH.)

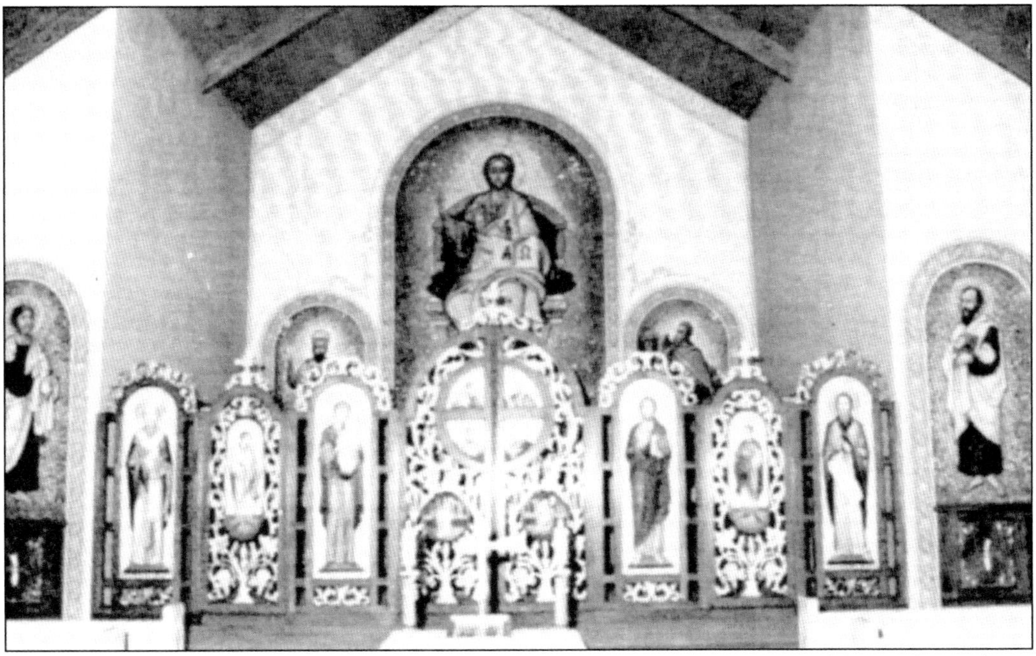

ALIQUIPPA. Many Ukrainians came to this Beaver County town, attracted by work in places like the Jones and Laughlin Steel Company and local railroads. The town was named for the Seneca Indian queen Aliquippa. This icon screen was installed in SS. Peter and Paul Ukrainian Catholic Church in the early 1980s. (Courtesy of UCDSJP.)

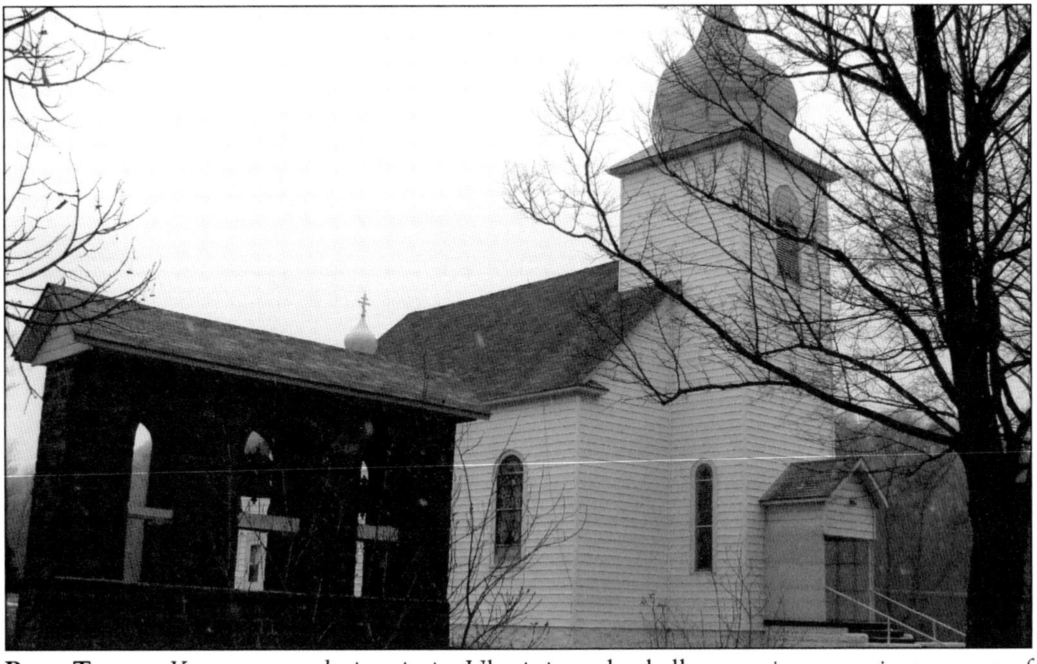

BELL TOWER. Known as a *dzvinytsia* in Ukrainian, the bell tower is an ancient aspect of Ukrainian church architecture, whose tolling declares joy, celebration, or mourning. Although somewhat rare in the United States, this bell tower stands next to SS. Peter and Paul Ukrainian Orthodox Church in Bakerton, Cambria County. (Courtesy of Fr. John Haluszczak.)

OLD-COUNTRY ARCHITECTURE. Immaculate Conception of the Blessed Virgin Mary Ukrainian Catholic Church in Barnesboro (recently renamed Northern Cambria) was founded by Ukrainian immigrants attracted to jobs in local mines in 1911. Parishioners decided in 1966 to build a new wooden church in the Ukrainian Hutzul style popular in the Carpathian Mountains. (Courtesy of Michael Haritan.)

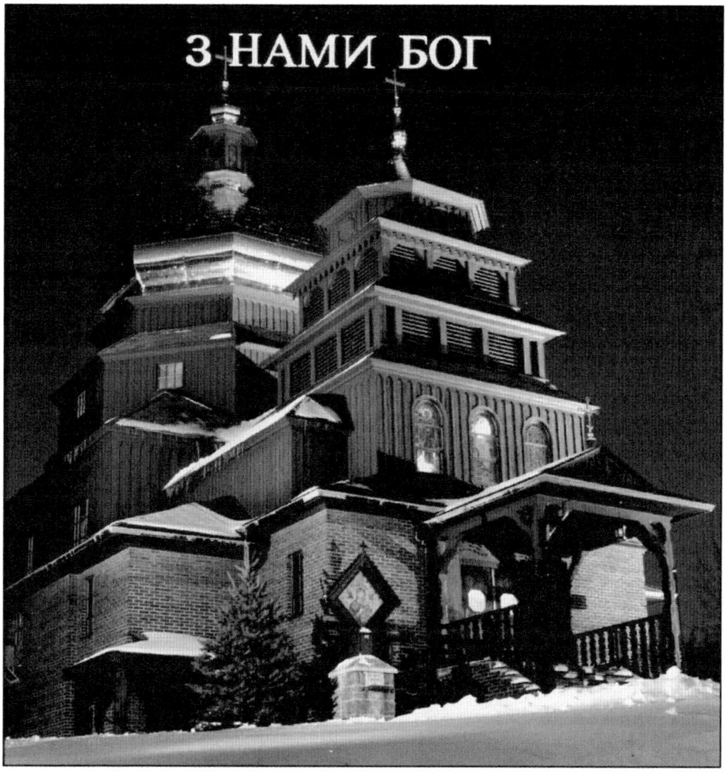

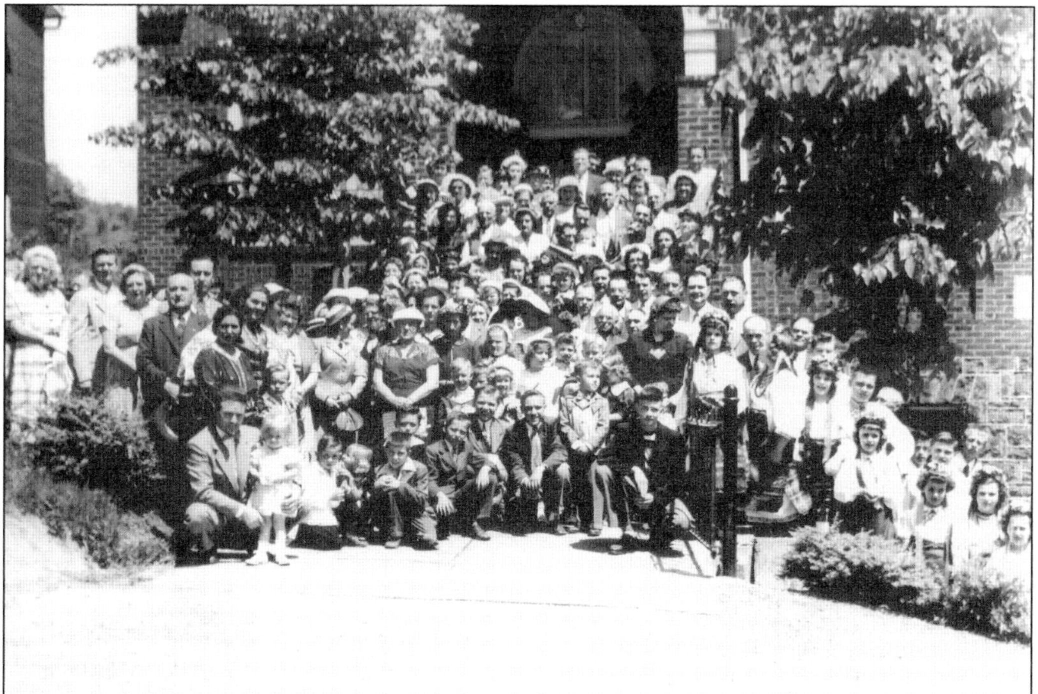

LYNDORA. Parishioners of SS. Peter and Paul Ukrainian Orthodox Church in this Butler County town pose with their spiritual father in this early-1950s photograph. (Courtesy of Barb Pupi.)

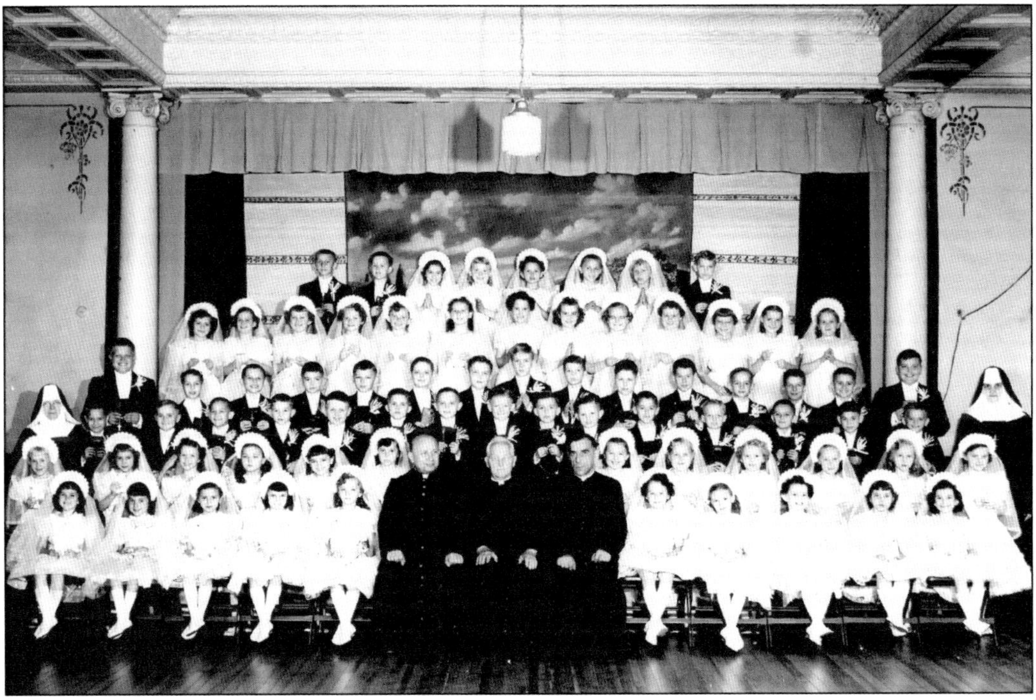

BECOMING RESPONSIBLE IN THE EYES OF THE CHURCH. The sacraments of holy confession and Holy Communion mark the maturation of a child as he or she comes to understand what sin is. In the Eastern Rite, the innocence of children is understood, and they receive the host from the time of baptism. The photograph above is of children from St. John the Baptist Ukrainian Catholic Church on Pittsburgh's South Side in 1954, and the second is from Holy Virgin Ukrainian Orthodox Church in Arnold around 1918. (Above, courtesy of Debra Meyer-Kincak; below, courtesy of Steve Pituch.)

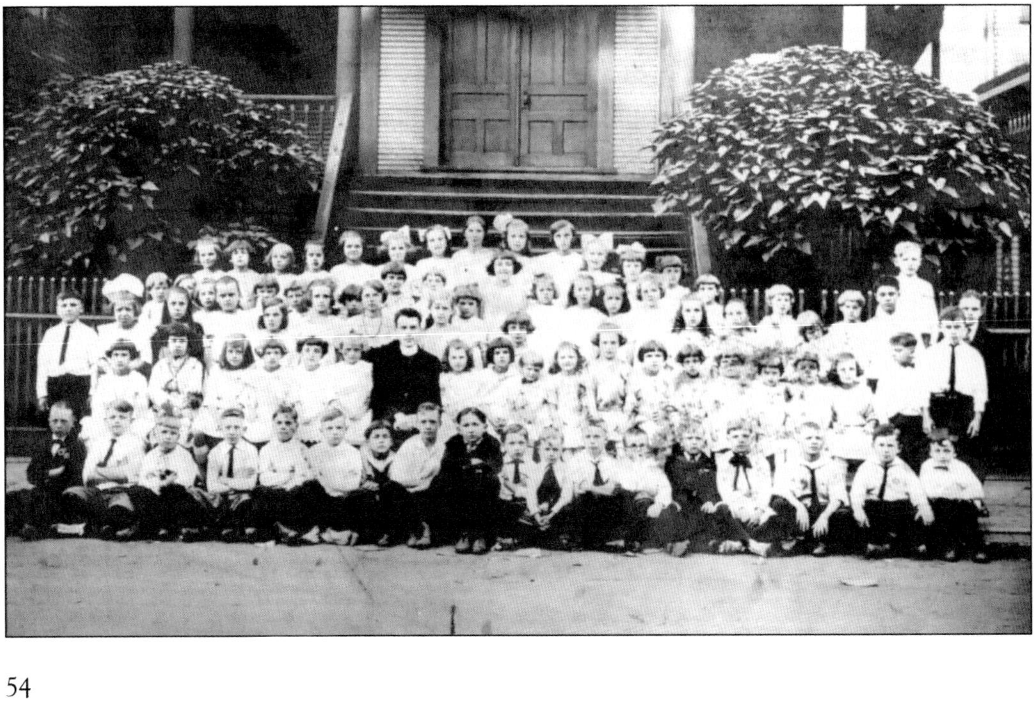

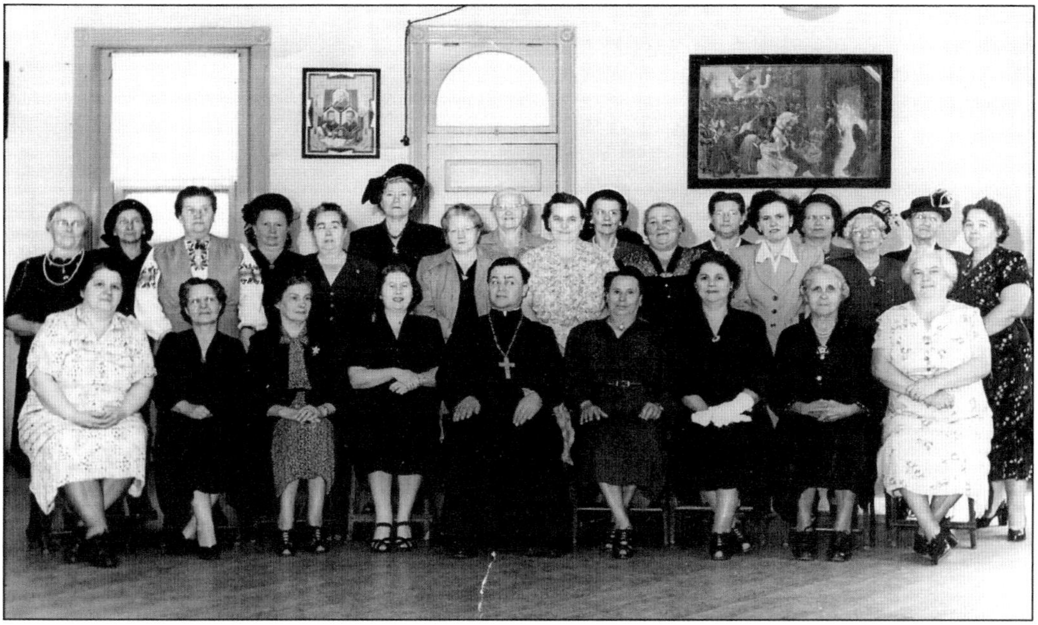

SISTERHOODS. Sisterhoods have always been popular in Ukrainian churches, providing important functions including decorating the church, preparing church-sponsored meals, and promoting culture and education. The members of the sisterhood of St. Vladimir Ukrainian Orthodox Church in Pittsburgh's South Side pose with their spiritual father around 1948. (Courtesy of Katherine Kiray.)

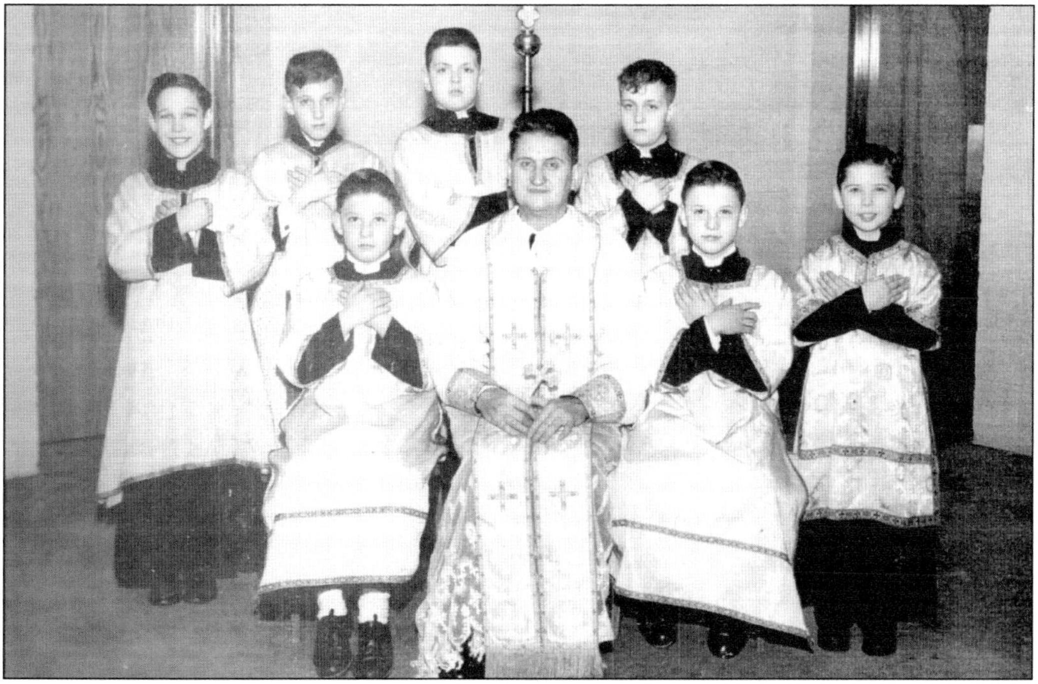

ALTAR BOYS. Young men from St. John the Baptist Ukrainian Catholic Church in McKeesport pose with their spiritual father in this late-1950s photograph. Altar boys assist the priest with the service in addition to the *tserkovnyk*, who is a church man or elder. (Courtesy of UCDSJP.)

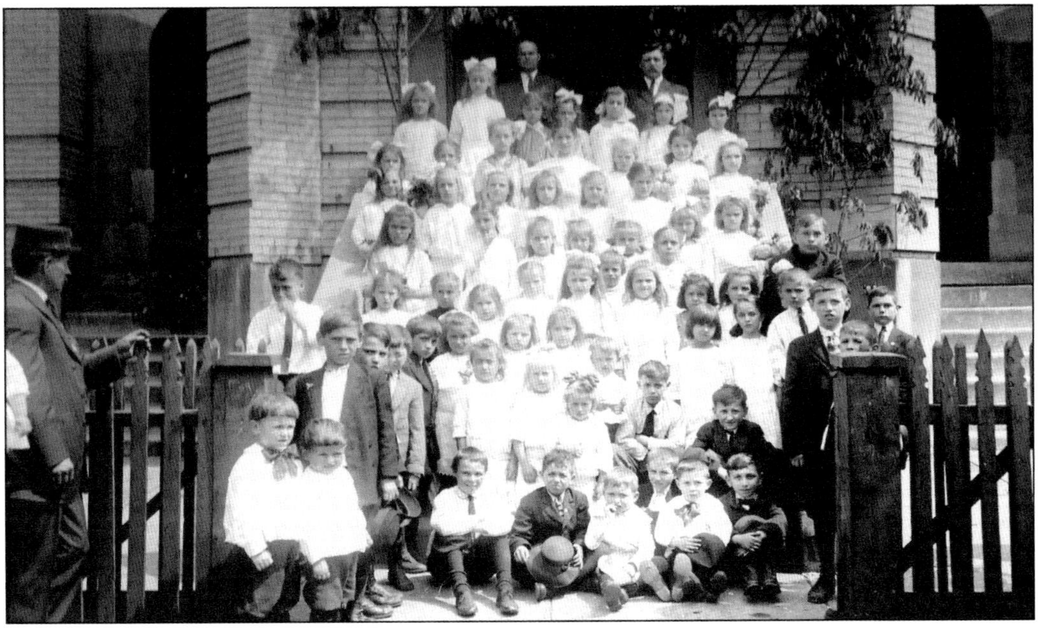

PENTECOST. Children from SS. Peter and Paul Ukrainian Orthodox Greek Catholic Church in Carnegie pose in front of the church on the feast of Pentecost around 1918. Boughs of trees holding green leaves are used to decorate the inside and outside of the church on Green Sunday, representing the color of life and the Holy Spirit. Often this holy day marks the end of either the church school year and/or the day when children receive their first confession. (Courtesy of MASPPUOGCCC.)

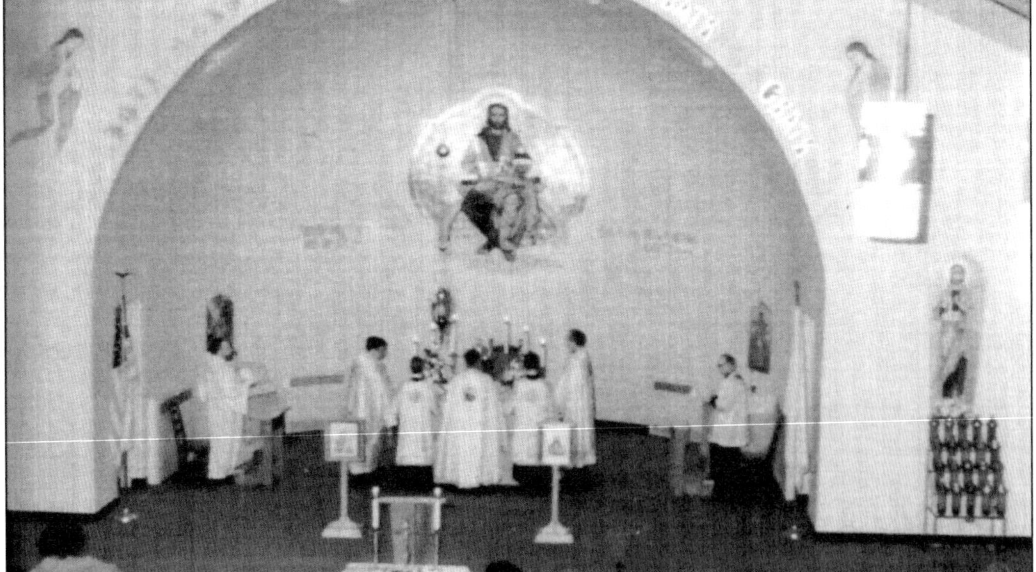

LATROBE. Ukrainian immigrants settled in this Westmoreland County industrial center in the early decades of the 20th century. This photograph of the interior of Assumption of the Blessed Virgin Mary Ukrainian Catholic Church, shows the words "Holy, Holy, Holy," in old church Slavonic, painted on the wall adjoining the sanctuary. (Courtesy of UCDSJP.)

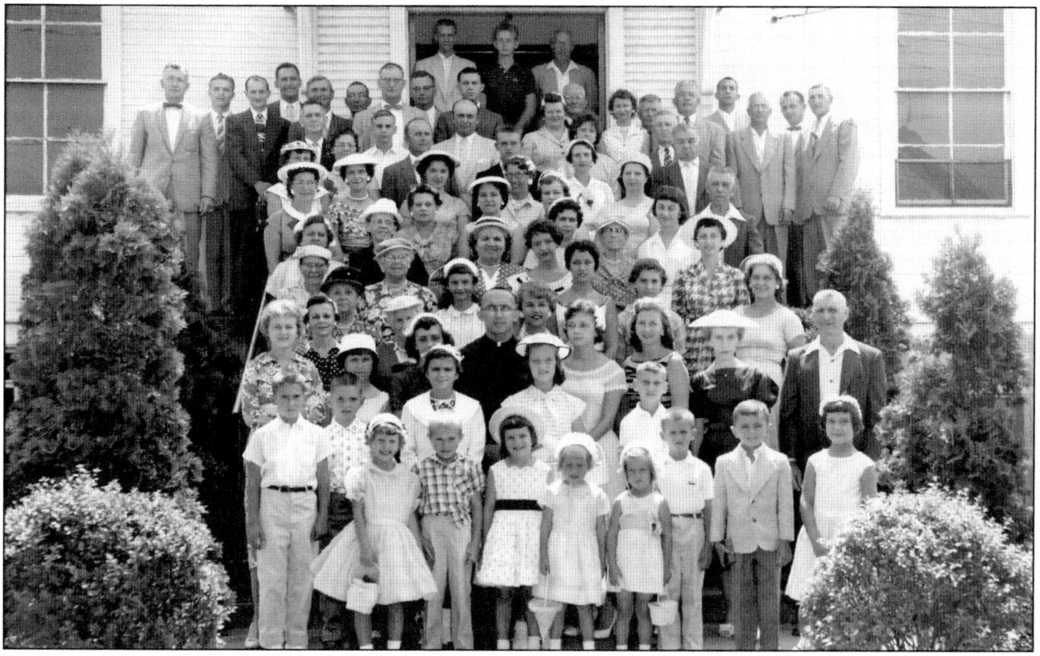

JEANNETTE. Known as the "Glass City" in recognition of the many glass plants found in the area, this Westmoreland County town attracted many Ukrainian immigrants. In this 1959 photograph, parishioners of St. Michael Ukrainian Orthodox Church pose with their spiritual leader, Fr. Martin Telenson. (Courtesy of Anna Mae Selembo.)

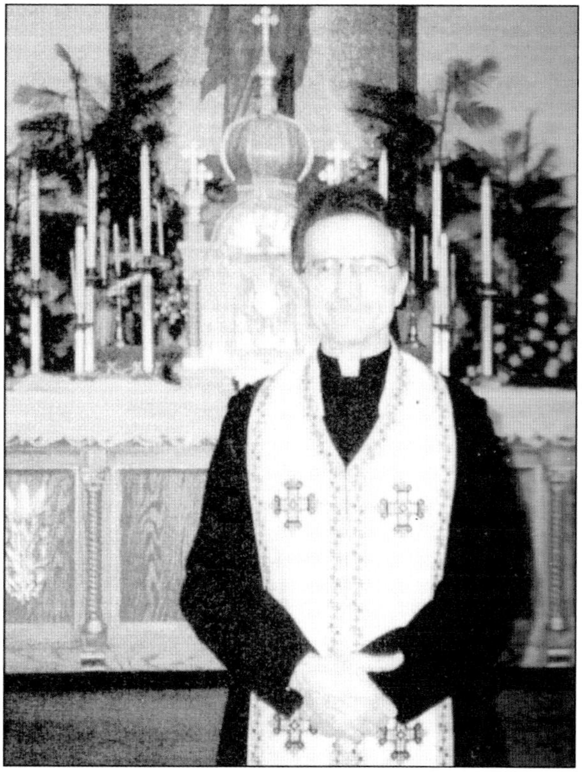

ST. JOHN THE BAPTIST UKRAINIAN CATHOLIC CHURCH. Nestled in the mountains of Cambria County, the city of Johnstown was a major center for the production of barbed wire in the late 1800s. Immigrants from Ukraine and other lands were attracted by jobs at Bethlehem Steel Company and other steel manufacturing and fabricating plants. Rev. John Dorozynsky stands before the altar of the church with a tabernacle in the shape of a church of the Ukrainian Baroque style. (Courtesy of UCDSJP.)

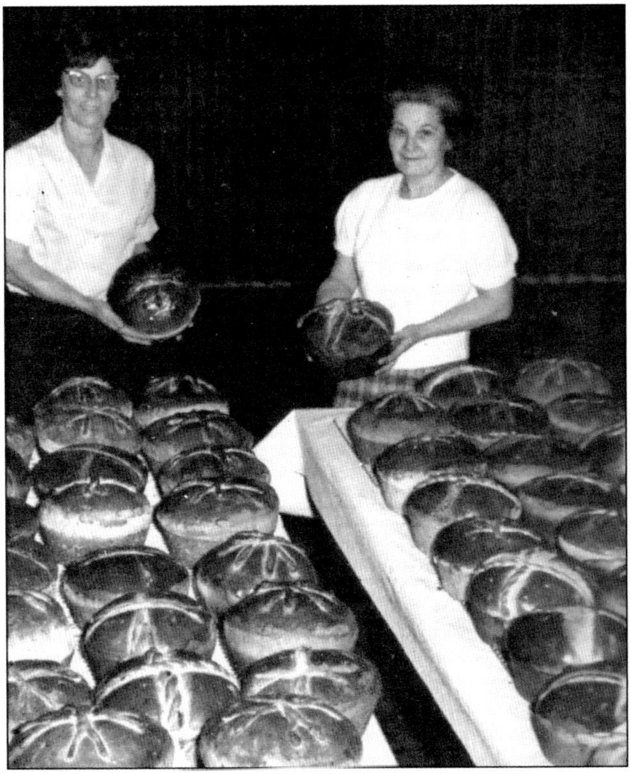

THE BREADBASKET OF CARNEGIE. Ukraine has been known for centuries as the "breadbasket of Europe" due to the location of one-third of the world's black soil or *chornozem* on Ukrainian lands. Here the ladies of Holy Trinity Ukrainian Catholic Church in Carnegie prepare traditional Ukrainian Easter *paska* for sale to church members and the public. (Courtesy of Holy Trinity Ukrainian Catholic Church.)

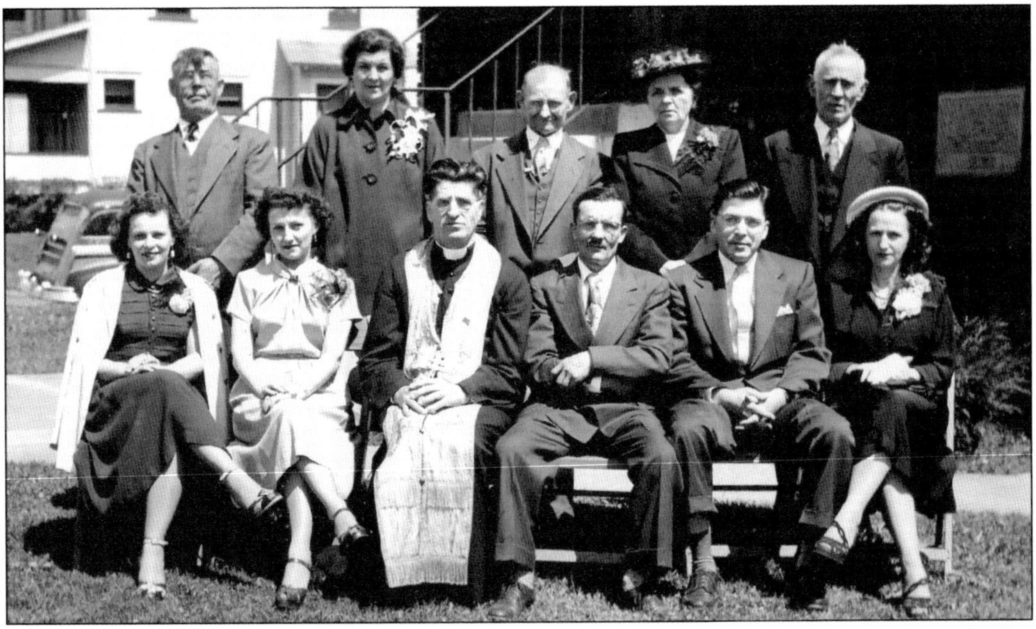

NEW CASTLE ANNIVERSARY. The 25th anniversary committee of Holy Trinity Ukrainian Orthodox Church poses with spiritual leader Rev. Stephen Musiychuk. In 1900, this Lawrence County town was one of the fastest growing cities in the United States. Jobs in its tinplate mill, which was the largest in the United States at the time, as well as steel and paper mills and car construction plants, attracted many Ukrainian immigrants. (Courtesy of Fr. Dea. Dennis Lapushansky.)

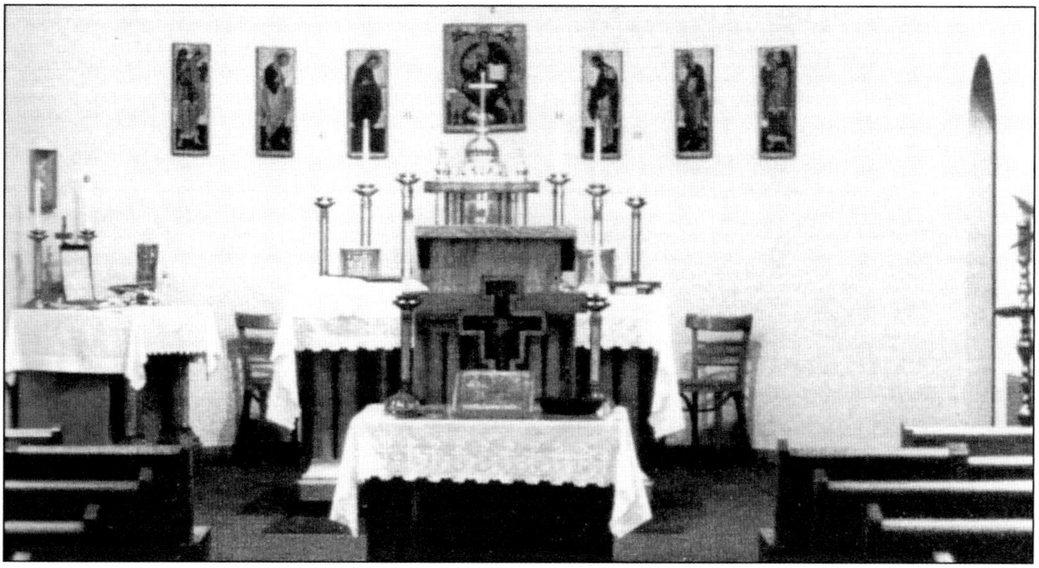

CANDELABRA. A seven-branched candelabra is found in most Eastern-rite churches behind the altar, signifying the seven gifts of the Holy Spirit from Revelations. This photograph from Immaculate Conception of the Blessed Virgin Mary Ukrainian Catholic Church in Altoona shows the candelabra with the tabernacle in the center. (Courtesy of UCDSJP.)

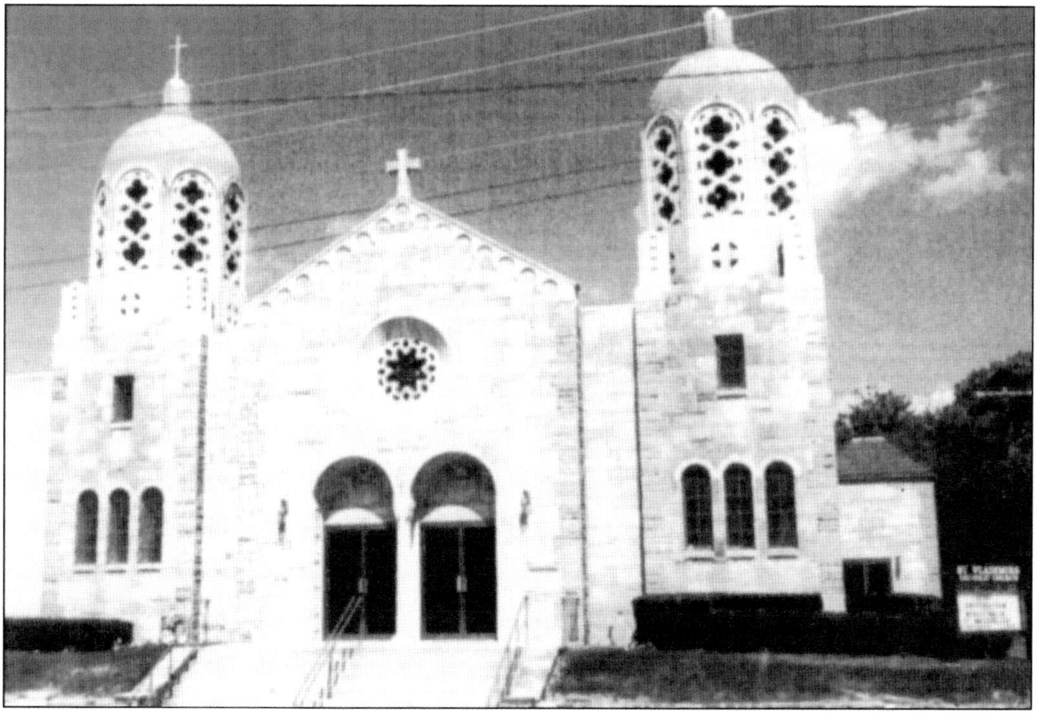

ARNOLD AND NEW KENSINGTON. Founded in 1911, St. Vladimir Ukrainian Catholic Church operated a parochial day school from 1936 through 1979. Arnold was a part of New Kensington until 1896, and both of these Westmoreland County boroughs drew Ukrainian immigrants through to the presence of companies like the Pittsburgh Reduction Company (later named Alcoa) and Chambers Glass Company. (Courtesy of UCDSJP.)

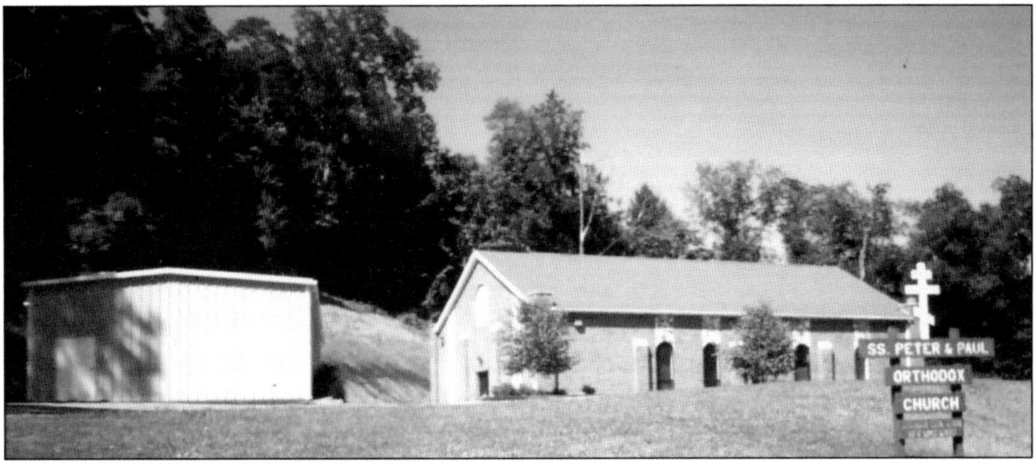

JOHNSTOWN. SS. Peter and Paul Ukrainian Orthodox Church is located in this Cambria County town, made famous by the great flood of May 31, 1899, as well as others in 1936 and 1977. Already a major manufacturing center, steel manufacturing and fabricating expanded rapidly in the area in the late 1800s, attracting many Ukrainian immigrants. (Courtesy of UOCUSA.)

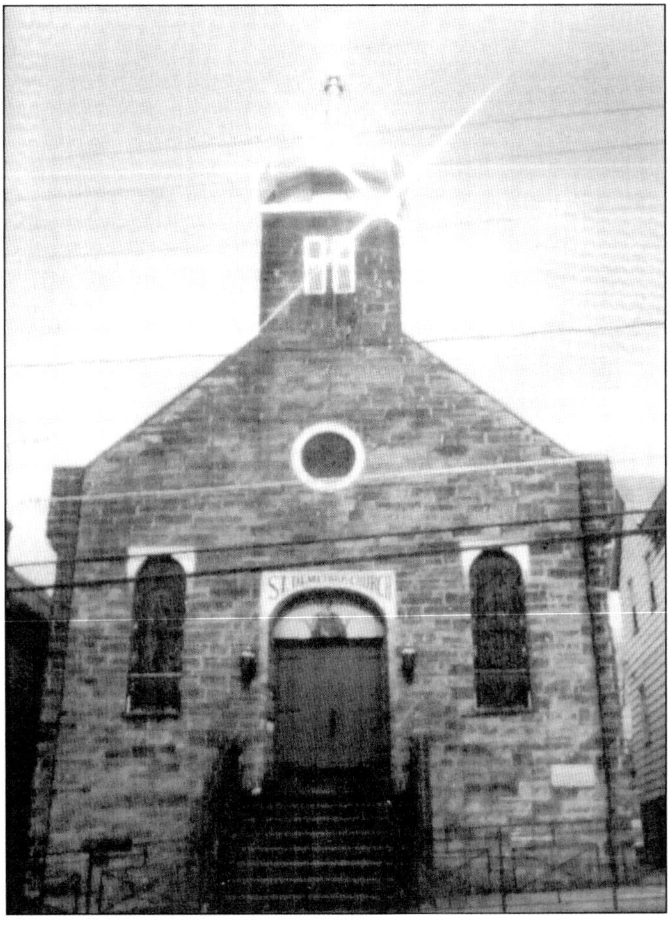

ST. DEMETRIUS UKRAINIAN CATHOLIC CHURCH. Founded in 1910 in Jeannette, Ukrainians were attracted to jobs in the town's many glass factories and other industries. Estimates indicate that at one time Jeannette factories produced between 70 and 85 percent of the world's glass, and familiar company names include Fort Pitt Glass and Westmoreland Glass. (Courtesy of UCDSJP.)

UKRAINIAN DAY IN AMBRIDGE. SS. Peter and Paul Ukrainian Catholic Church organized this annual event in conjunction with affiliate organizations: the Providence Association, UNA, George Washington Ukrainian Citizens' Club, church choir, Sisterhood of the Apostleship of Prayer, Ukrainian Junior Women's Club, Ukrainian Dancing School Association, and UWA. (Courtesy of Christine Sochocky.)

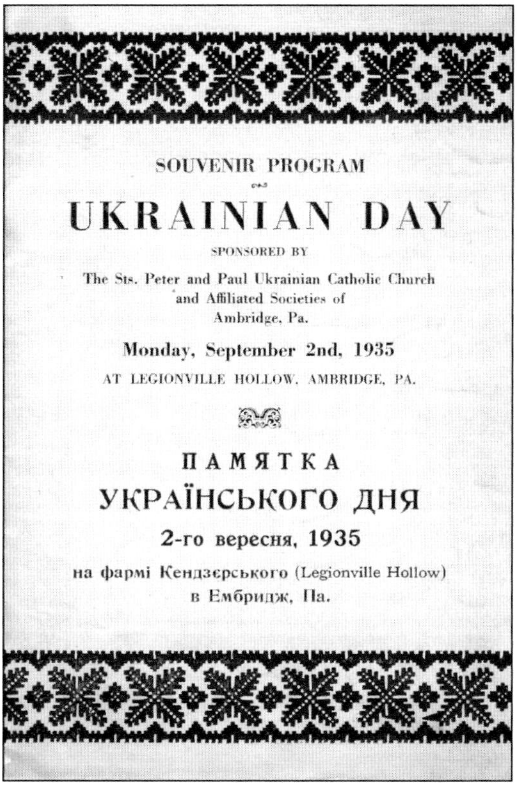

SOUVENIR PROGRAM

UKRAINIAN DAY

SPONSORED BY

The Sts. Peter and Paul Ukrainian Catholic Church
and Affiliated Societies of
Ambridge, Pa.

Monday, September 2nd, 1935

AT LEGIONVILLE HOLLOW, AMBRIDGE, PA.

ПАМЯТКА

УКРАЇНСЬКОГО ДНЯ

2-го вересня, 1935

на фармі Кендзерського (Legionville Hollow)
в Eмбридж, Па.

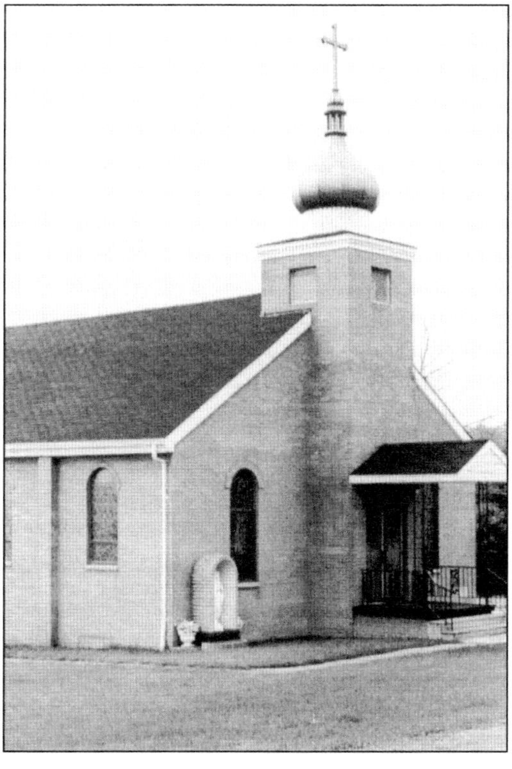

PROTECTION OF THE BLESSED VIRGIN MARY UKRAINIAN CATHOLIC CHURCH IN REVLOC. Originally housed in a former Latin-rite church building, the Monroe Coal Company donated a new church and property to the parish next to company-built housing in 1926. (Courtesy of UCDSJP.)

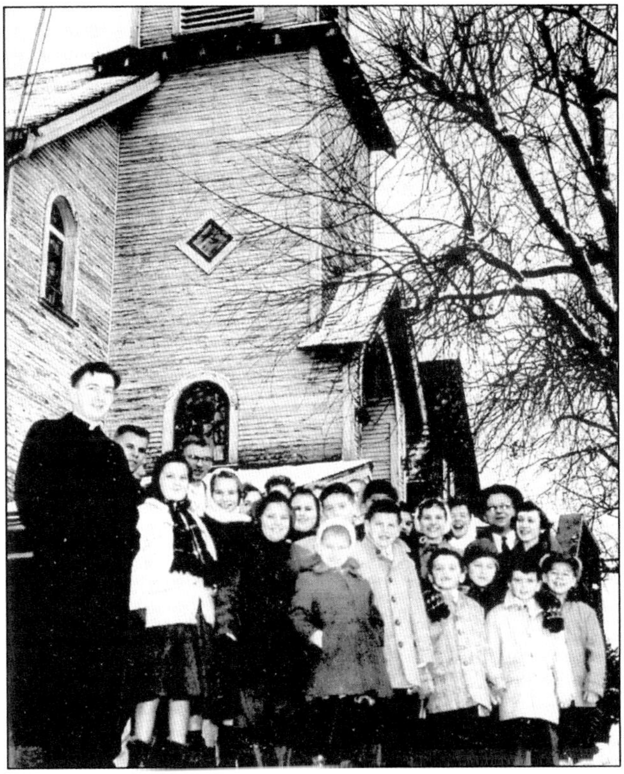

SHARON. The city of Sharon, located in Mercer County, attracted Ukrainian immigrants with jobs in coal mines, rolling mills, furnaces, and boiler and machines shops, among others. This early-1950s photograph shows the church school children of St. John the Baptist Ukrainian Orthodox Church with Fr. William Diakiw, who was born in Sharon. (Courtesy of Fr. Dea. Dennis Lapushansky.)

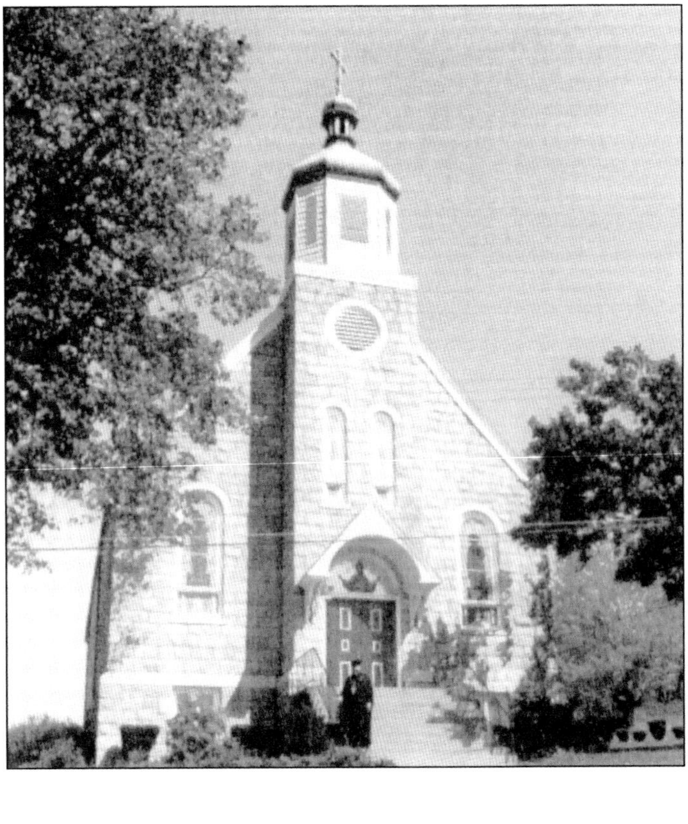

RAMEY, CLEARFIELD COUNTY. Founded in 1893, Annunciation of the Virgin Mary Ukrainian Catholic Church is the ninth-oldest Ukrainian Catholic Church in the United States. Efforts to organize this parish were begun by Rev. Ivan Wolansky, the first Ukrainian priest to come to the United States and who was instrumental in organizing religious and community life in the first days of Ukrainian immigration to America. (Courtesy of UCDSJP.)

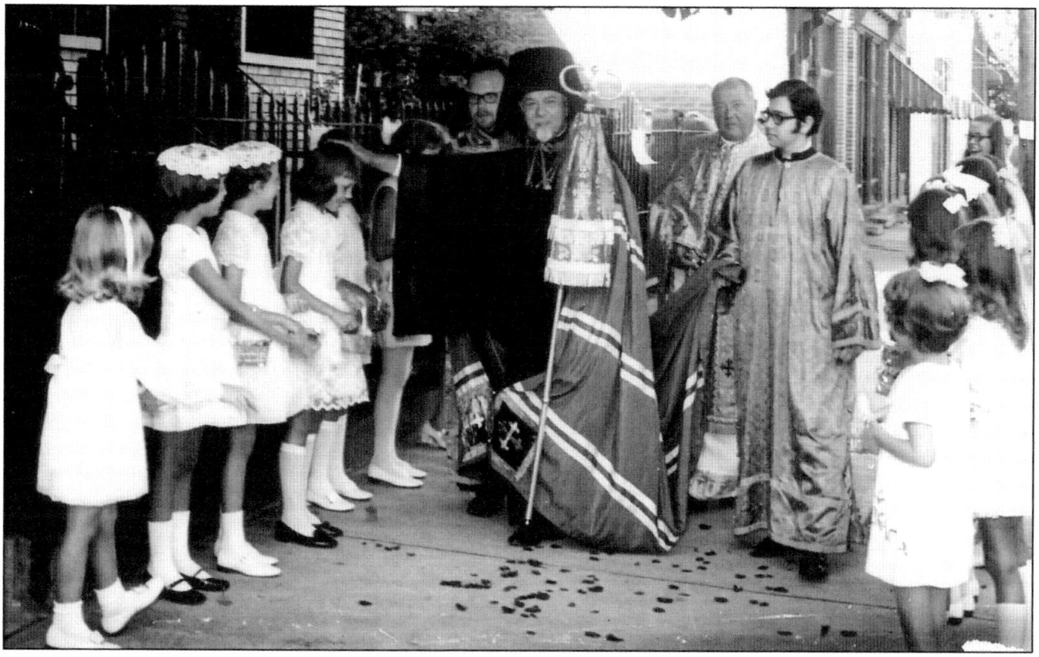

PATRIARCH MSTYSLAV. Children of St. Mary Ukrainian Orthodox Church in McKees Rocks prepare the way for then-Bishop Mstyslav during his visit to the parish in 1970. Bishop Mstyslav served as a Ukrainian representative from Volhynia to the Polish Sejm from 1930 to 1939 and spent time in both Polish and Nazi prisons. He was ordained a priest in 1942, became metropolitan of the Ukrainian Orthodox Church of the United States of America after the death of Metropolitan John Theodorovich in 1971, and was enthroned as Patriarch Mstyslav I in 1990 at St. Sophia Cathedral in Kyiv. (Courtesy of LAVRSHH.)

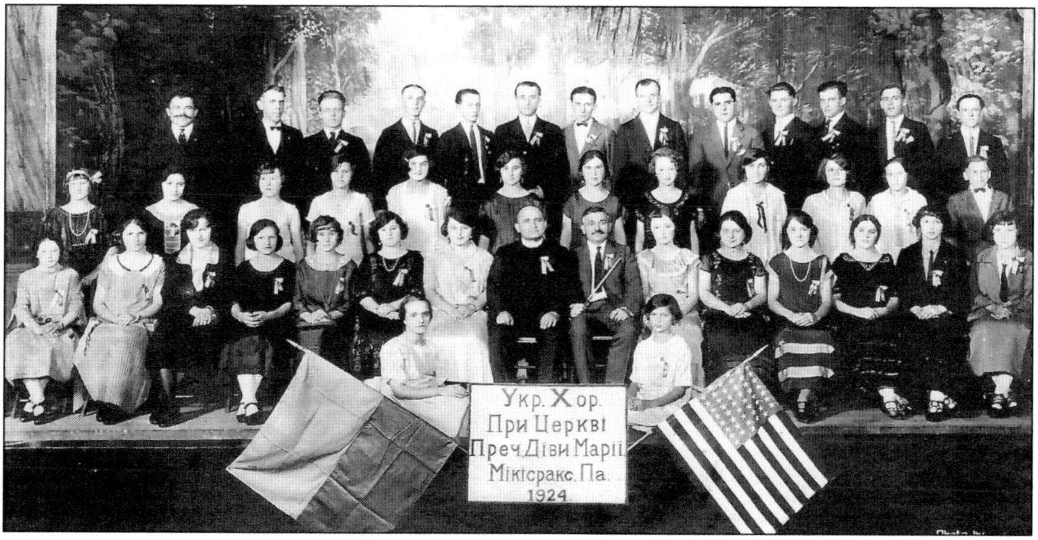

ST. MARY'S CHOIR. Members of the choir of St. Mary's Greek Catholic Church (later known as St. Mary's Ukrainian Orthodox Church) in McKees Rocks pose with a sign written in the Ukrainian language in this 1924 photograph. Ukrainian is an East Slavic language related to but no more similar to Russian than Portuguese is to Spanish. (Courtesy of St. John the Baptist Ukrainian Catholic Church.)

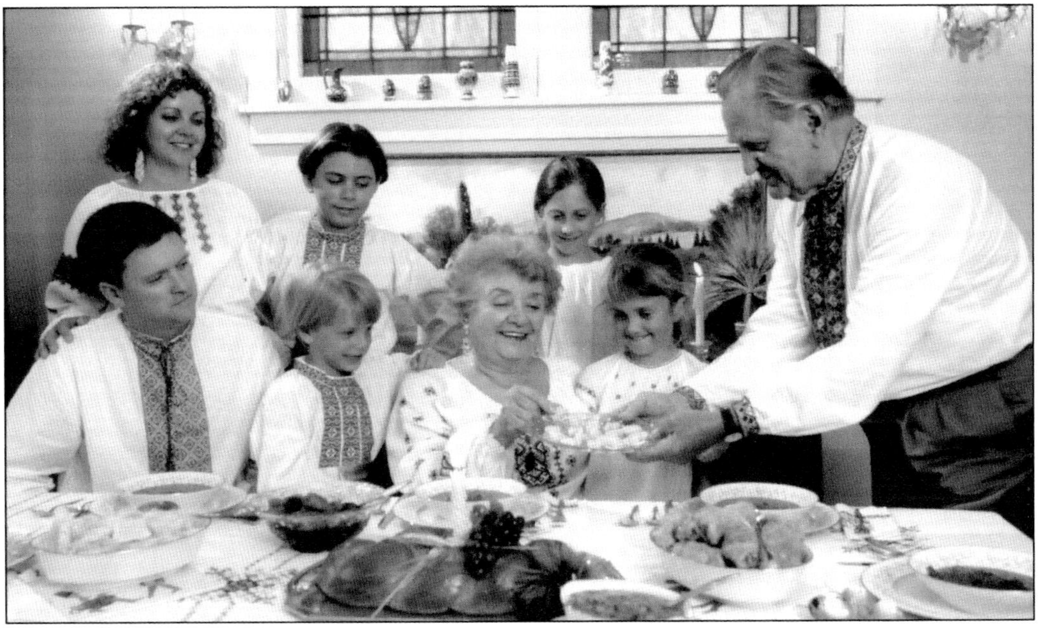

SVYATA VECHERYA—CHRISTMAS EVE SUPPER. Celebrated on January 6 before church service, the "holy supper" is a meal containing 12 meatless dishes in remembrance of the 12 apostles. Dishes include *kutya*, *holubtsi*, fish, *varenyky*, dried fruit, vegetables, and mushrooms, among others. This 1994 photograph was taken for use in a Christmas seal project of the Diocesan Resource Committee of St. Josaphat's Diocese in Parma. (Courtesy of Michael Haritan.)

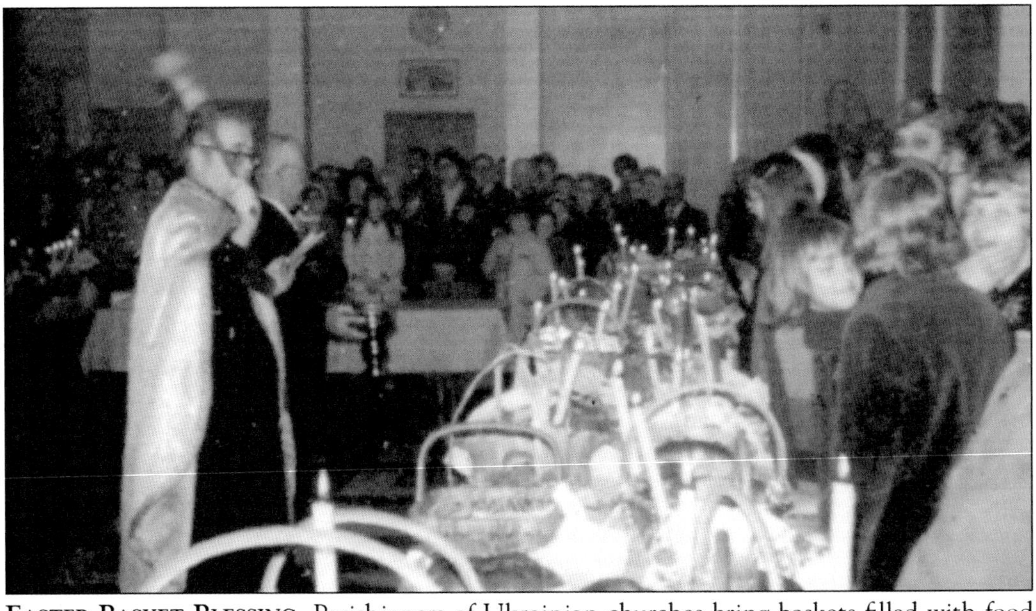

EASTER BASKET BLESSING. Parishioners of Ukrainian churches bring baskets filled with food to break the fast to their parish halls after the resurrection service. They have abstained from meat and dairy products during the 40-day Lenten period and the seven-day Passion Week fast (Eastern-rite Lent starts on a Monday). In this 1970 photograph, Fr. Stephen Hallick-Holutiak blesses parishioners' baskets with holy water, sanctifying them to celebrate Pascha in the home. (Courtesy of LAVRSHH.)

Wedding Rituals. During the wedding ceremony, the bride and groom wear crowns signifying their union, God crowning them with glory and honor establishing them as king and queen of their new household. Their hands are tied, and they walk around the altar three times signifying the dance of Isaiah—the beginning of their new life with the Gospel being its center. This 1970s photograph was taken at SS. Peter and Paul Ukrainian Orthodox Greek Catholic Church in Carnegie. (Courtesy of Marlane Pawlosky.)

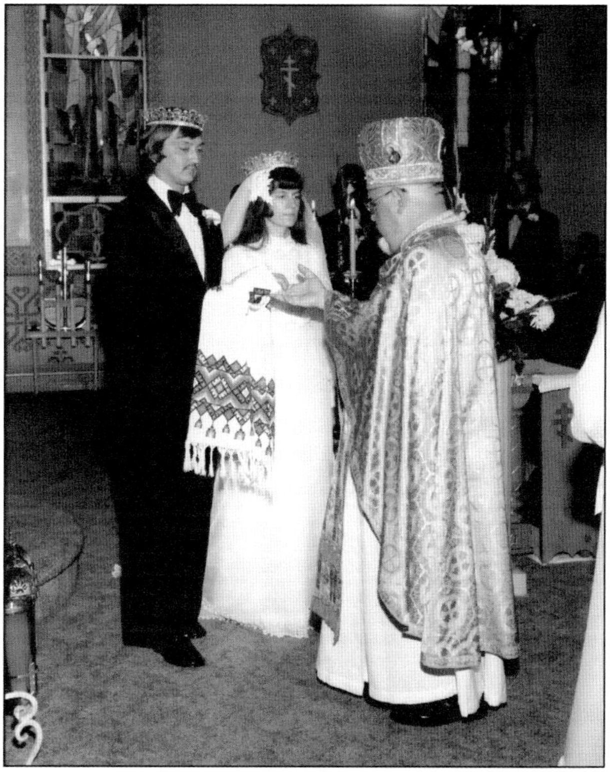

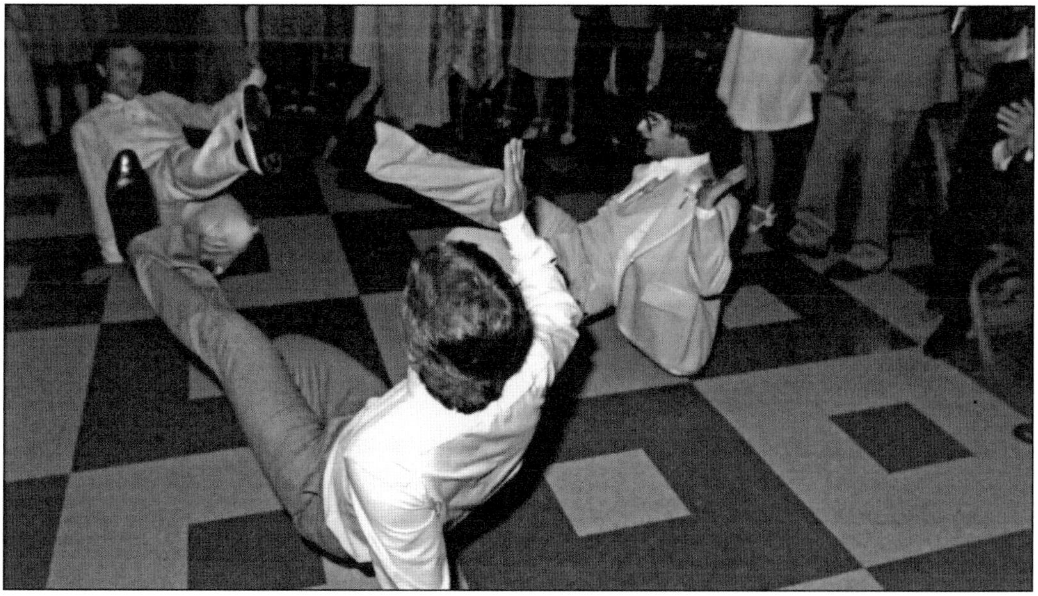

The Kolomiyka. A Ukrainian wedding reception is not complete without the dancing of the *kolomiyka*—an opportunity for guests to show off their dancing prowess. In this 1982 reception photograph from Ambridge, male guests show off their athletic ability by doing *presyadky*. It will be the women's turn next, and a friendly dancing competition ensues to lively Ukrainian dance music sometimes lasting as long as a half hour. (Courtesy of William Haluszczak and Carol Holobinko.)

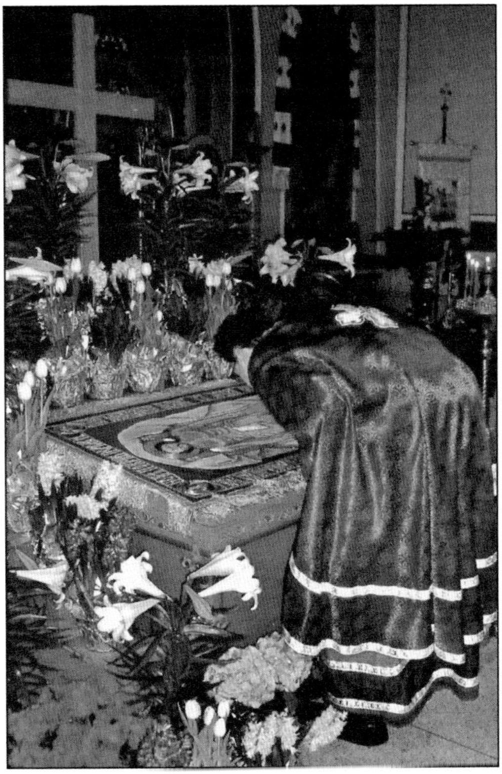

THE *PLASHCHANYTSYA*. The holy shroud is laid out immediately following services on Passion Friday and remains in the church until the Resurrection Matins. This photograph from St. George Ukrainian Catholic Church on Pittsburgh's North Side shows the proper veneration of the holy shroud. (Courtesy of St. George Ukrainian Catholic Church.)

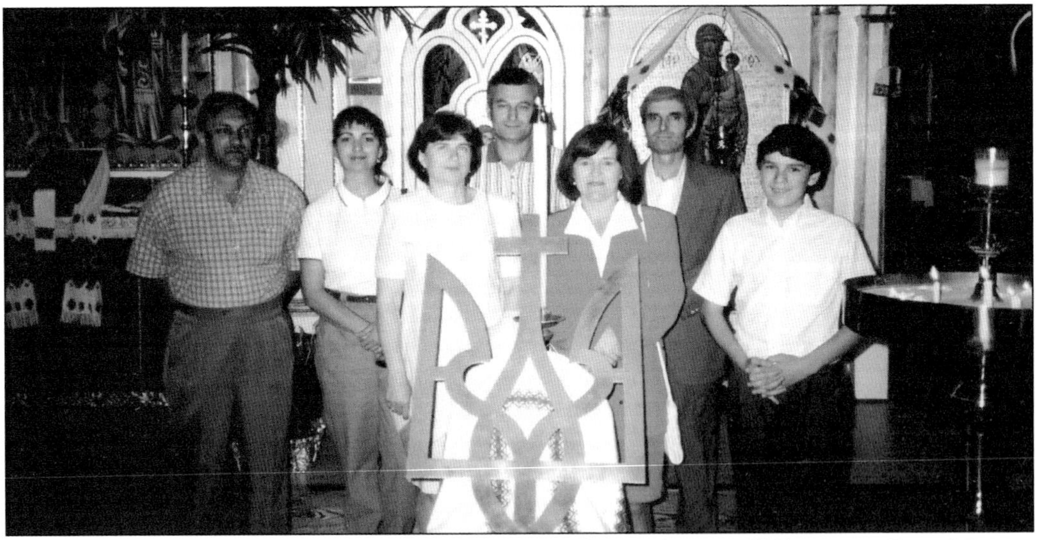

THE *TRYZUB*. The *tryzub*, or "trident," originated as the royal crest of Ukrainian Grand Prince Volodymyr in the 10th century. Adopted without the cross as the national symbol of the UNR in 1918, it became a symbol of Ukrainian identity and independence throughout the turmoil of the 20th century. It was adopted as the national seal of Ukraine in 1991 upon the declaration of Ukrainian independence after the dissolution of the USSR. Here Volodymyr's tryzub with a cross was refurbished by artist Zinoviy Bohonok (second from right) and was reattached to the Ukrainian Hall of SS. Peter and Paul Ukrainian Orthodox Greek Catholic Church in Carnegie. (Courtesy of MASPPUOGCCC.)

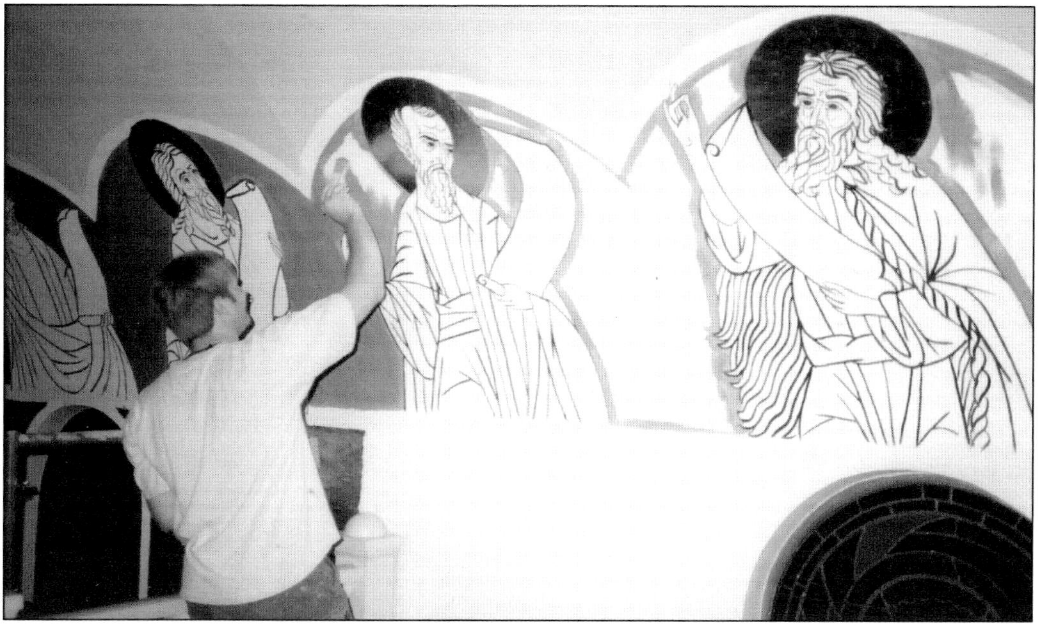

ICON PAINTING. Icons are a defining feature of Eastern-rite churches and date from the earliest days of Christianity. They are windows to the spiritual world and demonstrate how the church uses all five human senses to teach the faithful about God. Local iconographer Michael Kapeluck applies one of the many layers of paint that went into creating these icons at SS. Peter and Paul's in Carnegie. (Courtesy of MASPPUOGCCC.)

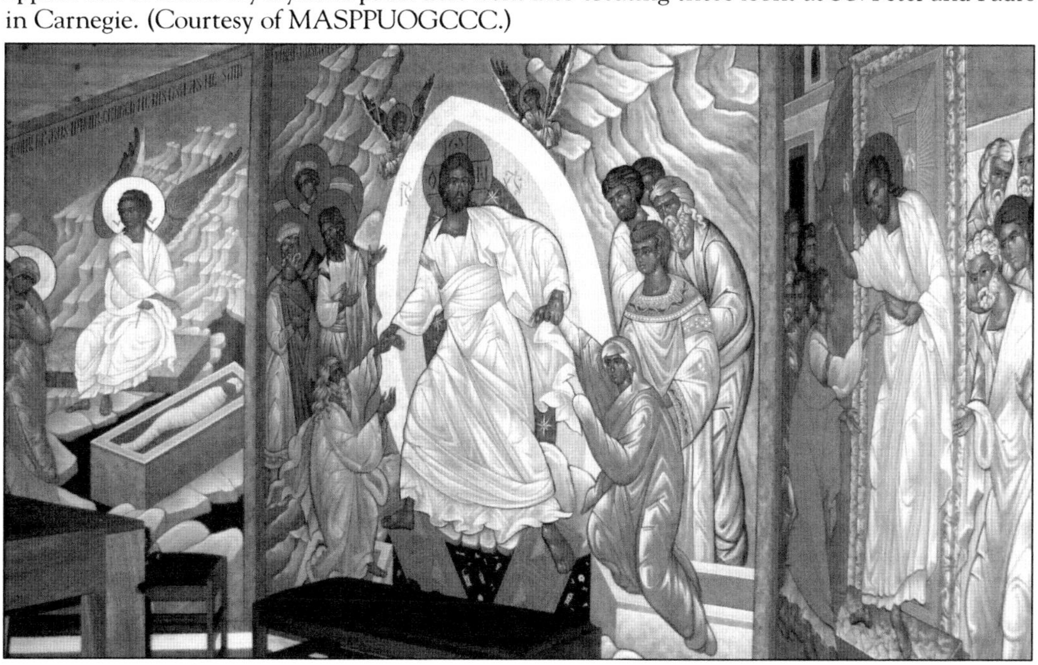

ICON SCREEN. The St. Thomas Chapel of All Saints Ukrainian Orthodox Church Camp in Emlenton is a wooden building reminiscent of church architecture in the Ukrainian Carpathian Mountains. Over 70 icons were commissioned and installed inside the chapel for veneration of the faithful. This icon screen details mankind's fall from paradise and return in Christ's resurrection and ascension. (Courtesy of Stephen Sheptak.)

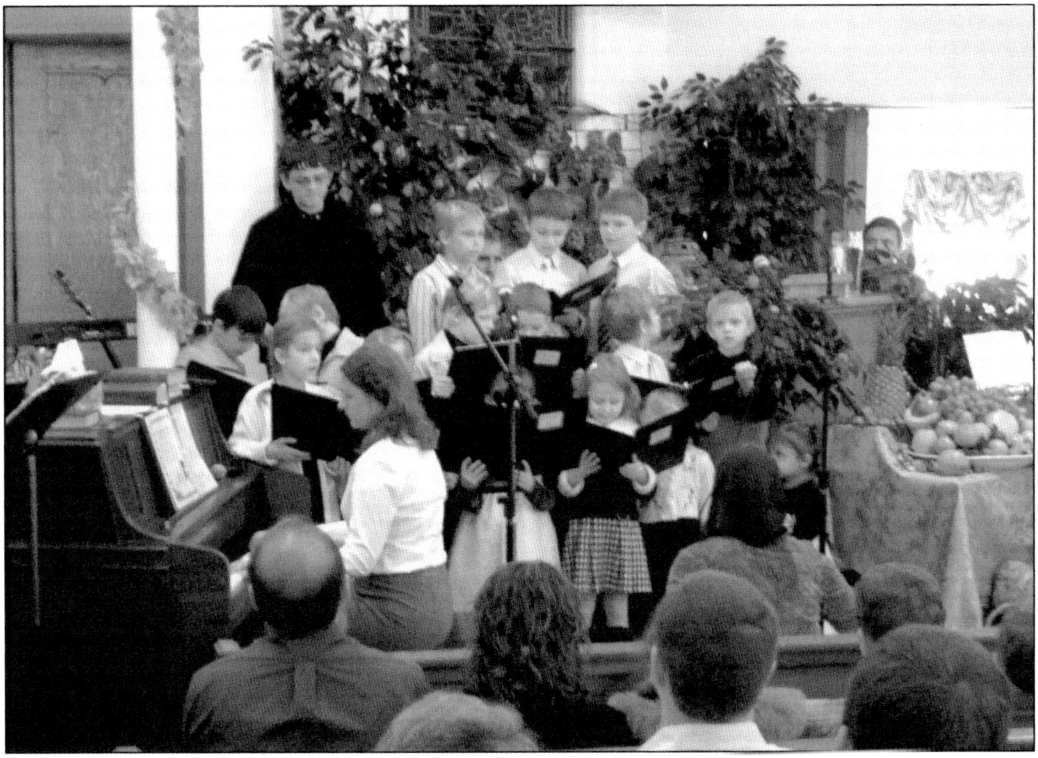

ZHNYVA. Children from the Slavic Evangelical Baptist Church participate in their parish's celebration of Zhnyva, "the harvest," a holy day similar to Thanksgiving. (Courtesy of Oksana Doroshkevich Hiser.)

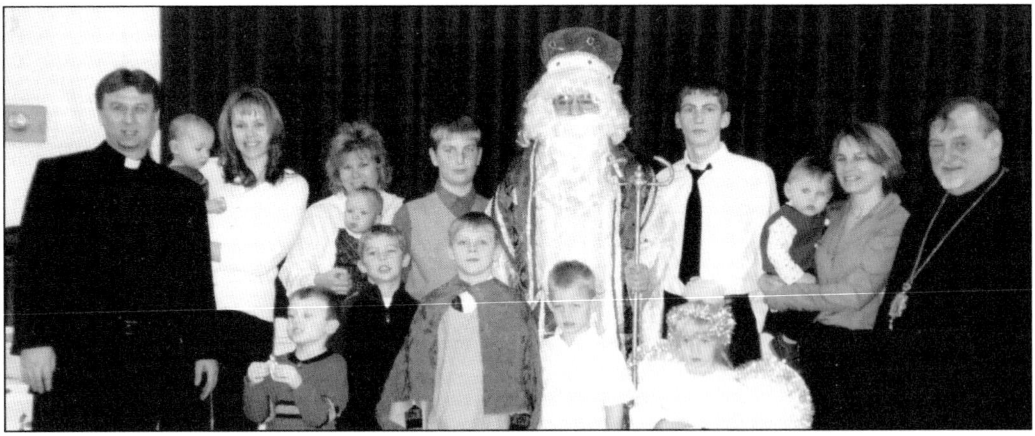

ST. NICHOLAS. One of the most highly revered saints in the Eastern Church, St. Nicholas is the patron saint of children and sailors. It is an annual tradition in many western Pennsylvania Ukrainian churches to hold a St. Nicholas program in his honor demonstrating charity, faithfulness, and love. Metropolitan Constantine (far right) of the Ukrainian Orthodox Church visits St. Nicholas Ukrainian Orthodox Church in Monessen during this event in 2002. (Courtesy of Anna Mae Selembo.)

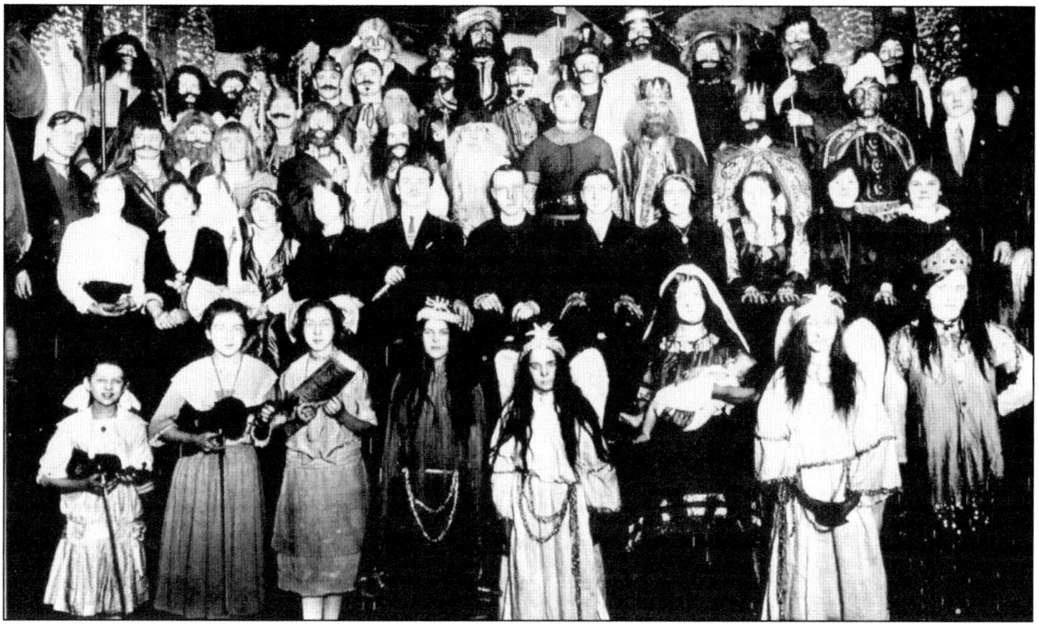

VERTEP. A standardized pageant of the Christian Nativity, *vertep* or *yalynka* has been performed by Ukrainians since the late 16th century. Church school students at St. John the Baptist Ukrainian Catholic Church on Pittsburgh's South Side perform in 1915 in the photograph above. Children from St. John the Baptist Ukrainian Catholic Church in McKees Rocks continue the vertep tradition around 1978 in the photograph below. (Above, courtesy of St. John Ukrainian Catholic Church, South Side; below, courtesy of St. John Ukrainian Catholic Church, McKees Rocks.)

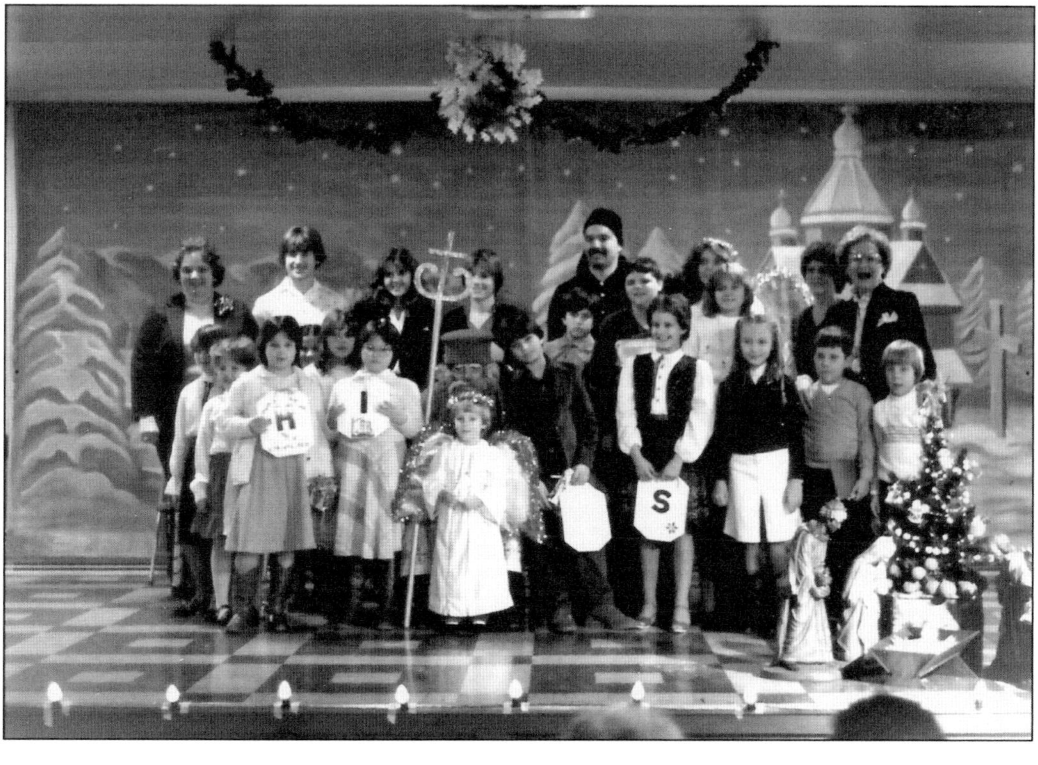

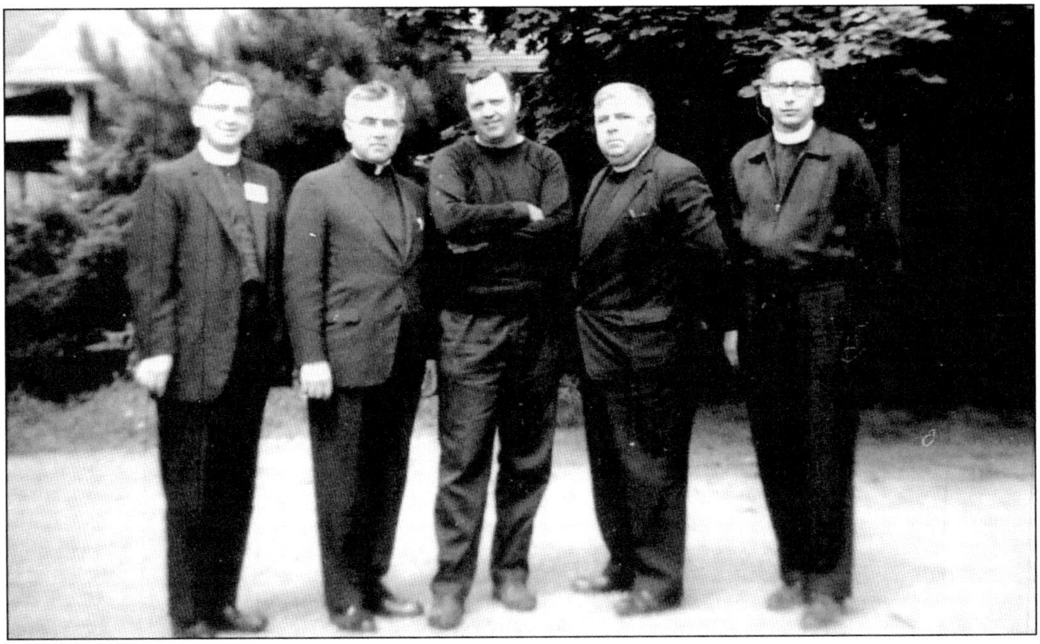

Camp Konokwee and Teenage Conference. The Western Pennsylvania Region of the Ukrainian Orthodox League began sponsoring encampments for teenagers known as Teenage Conference in 1958. When the All Saints Camp in Emlenton was dedicated in 1978, the Diocesan Church School encampment was established. Primarily religious in nature, these encampments retain a strong Ukrainian flavor by including folk dances and songs, language, and culture, with encampment yearbooks named *Tabir*, "camp," and *Vatra*, "campfire." (Courtesy of LAVRSHH.)

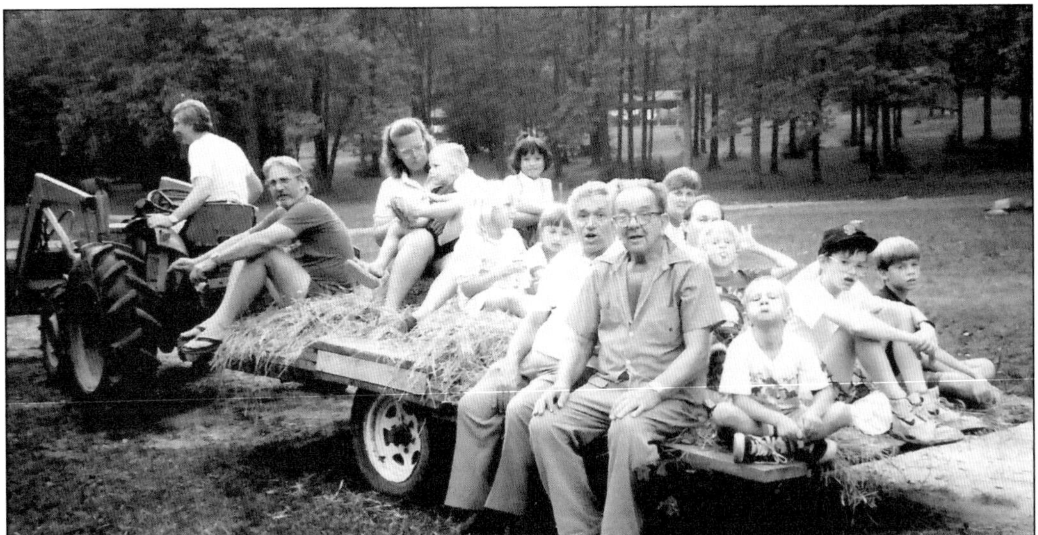

Family Fest at All Saints Camp. Participants in All Saints Ukrainian Orthodox Church Camp's Family Fest Weekend enjoy a hayride over Labor Day weekend in 1989. The camp is located on 97 acres of land along the Allegheny River just outside of Emlenton along the Allegheny River and is home to the Diocesan Church School Camp, Teenage Conference, and Mommy and Me/Daddy and Me encampments. (Courtesy of Oksana Byczkalo.)

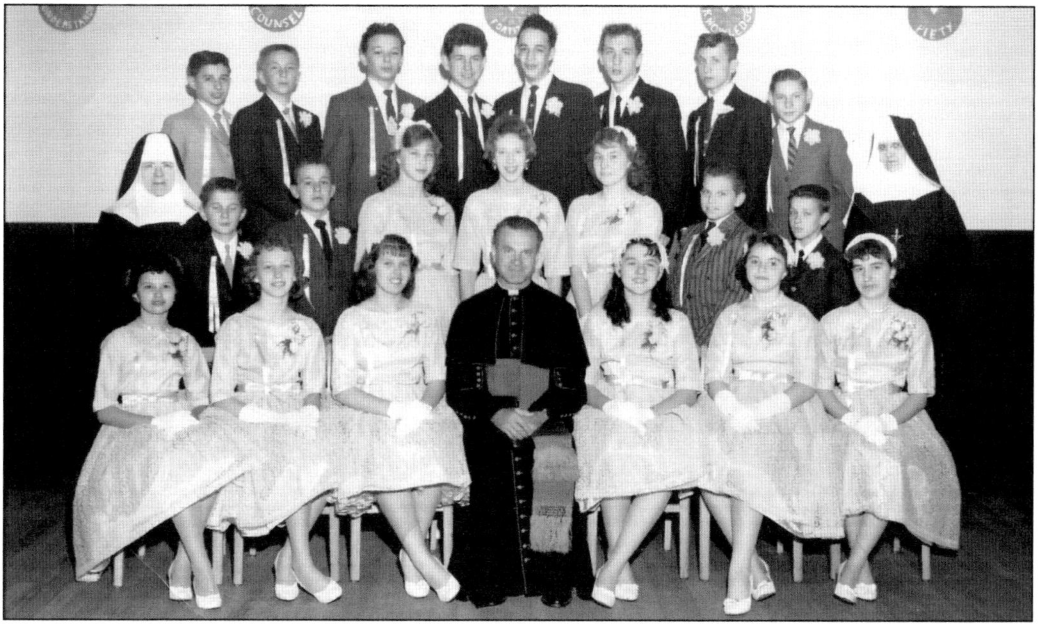

ST. JOHN THE BAPTIST SCHOOL. In 1933, the parish of St. John the Baptist Ukrainian Catholic Church on Pittsburgh's South Side established an all-day school for first-graders. In each of the next seven years, an additional grade was added, and the first graduates completed their studies in 1941. Graduates from 1960 pose at the end of the school year. (Courtesy of Debra Meyer-Kincak.)

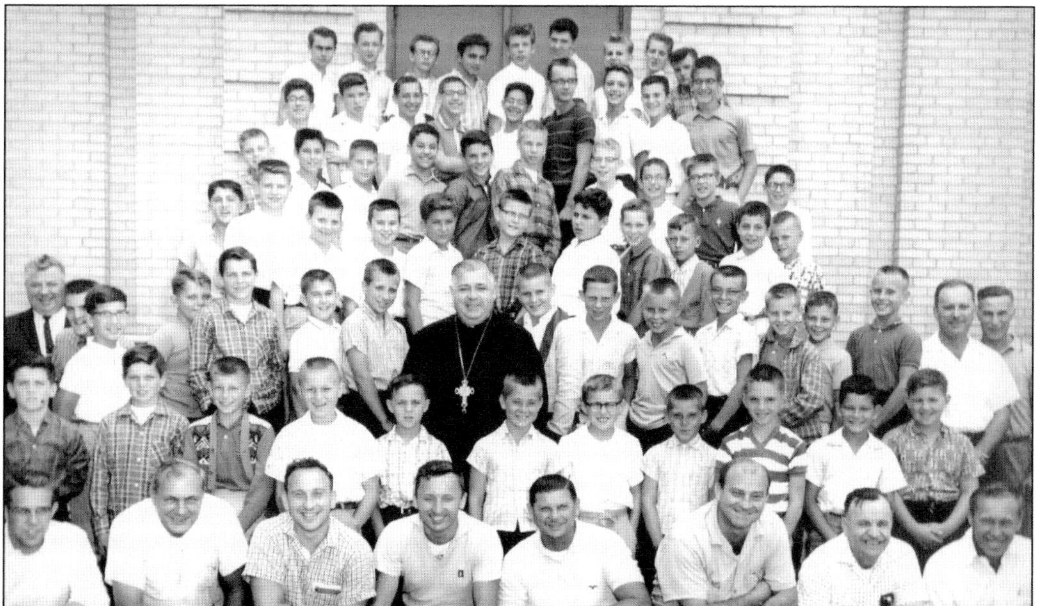

ALTAR BOY CONFERENCE. The Western Pennsylvania Region of the Ukrainian Orthodox League united parishes of the Ukrainian Orthodox Church of the United States of America through a variety of events. One of these was a retreat held in Carnegie in 1961 for altar boys from the region for the purposes of additional instruction, fellowship, and fun. (Courtesy of MASPPUOGCCC.)

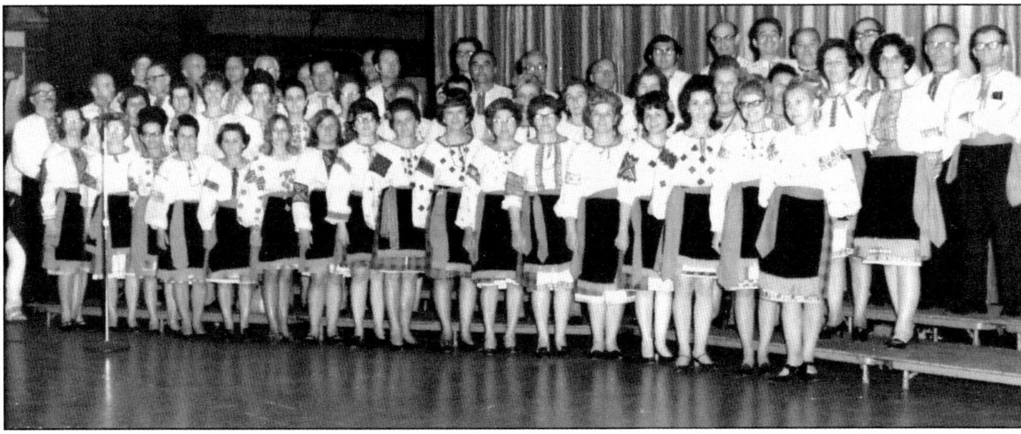

THE LEAGUE OF UKRAINIAN CATHOLICS. The League of Ukrainian Catholics (LUC) is an officially sanctioned lay organization of the Ukrainian Catholic Church and sponsors educational and social activities for the spiritual enlightenment of its members. It has branches in many western Pennsylvania Ukrainian Catholic churches. Here its combined choir is ready for a performance in this early-1970s photograph. (Courtesy of Nickolas C. Kotow.)

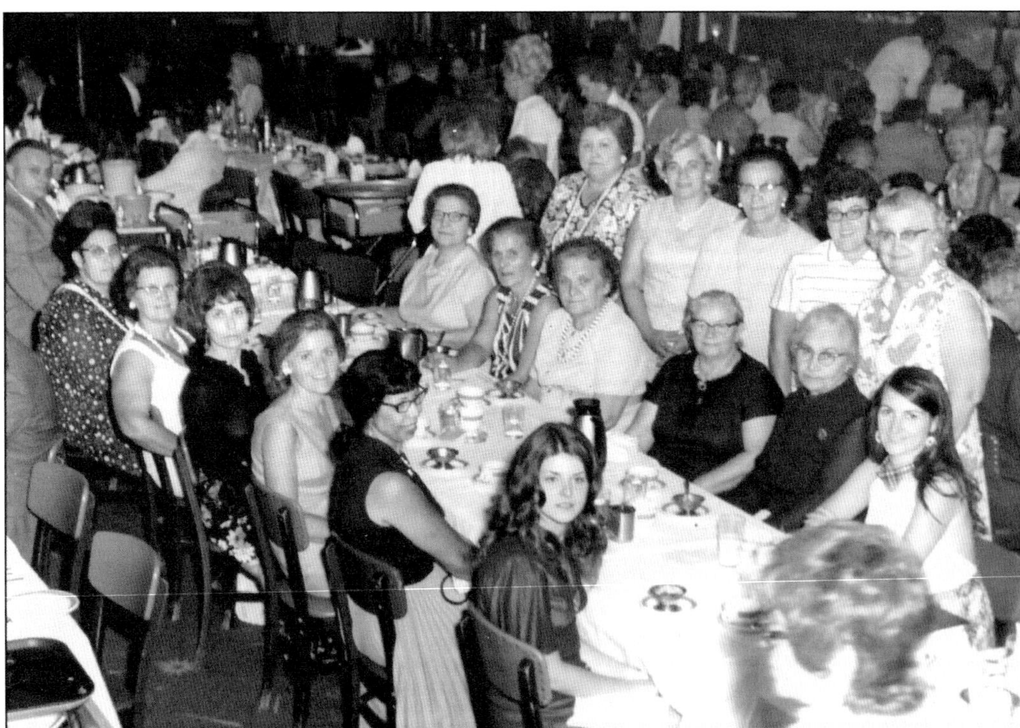

UKRAINIAN ORTHODOX LEAGUE CONVENTION. An official lay organization of the Ukrainian Orthodox Church of the United States of America, the Ukrainian Orthodox League (UOL) sponsors educational, spiritual, and cultural activities for its members. It holds an annual convention, many of which have taken place in western Pennsylvania, including this one in 1967, which shows the delegation from the Slickville parish. (Courtesy of Holy Ghost Ukrainian Orthodox Church.)

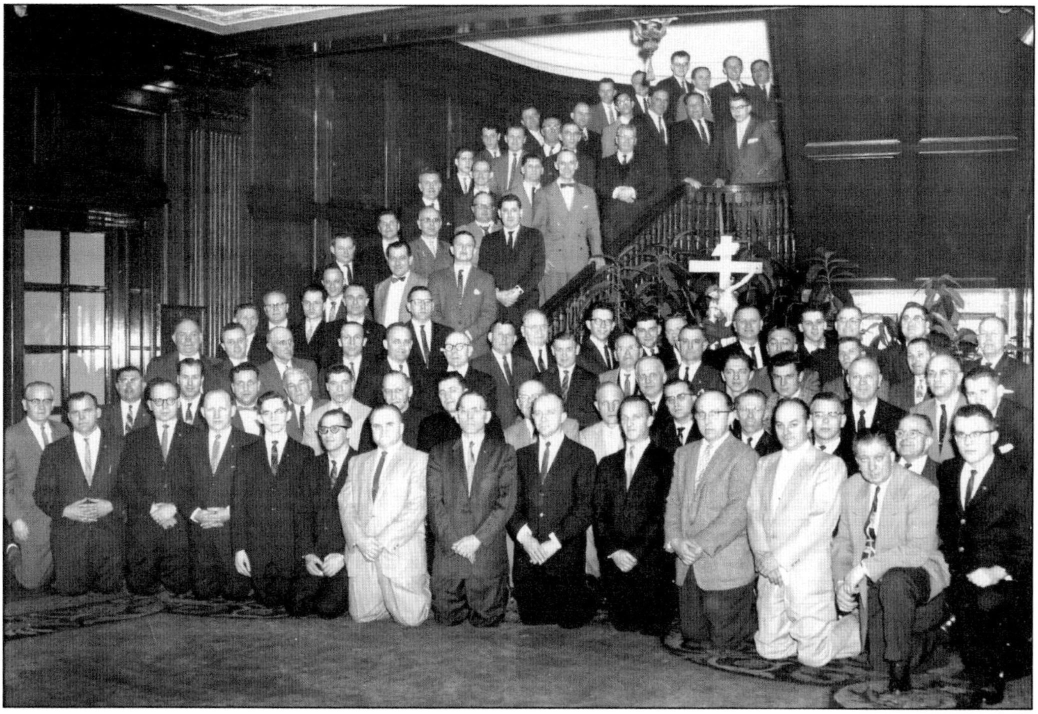

Day of Recollection. Members of the Ukrainian Catholic Church gathered for this religious retreat held at the St. Francis Retreat House in Pittsburgh in 1960. (Courtesy of Joan Fedora.)

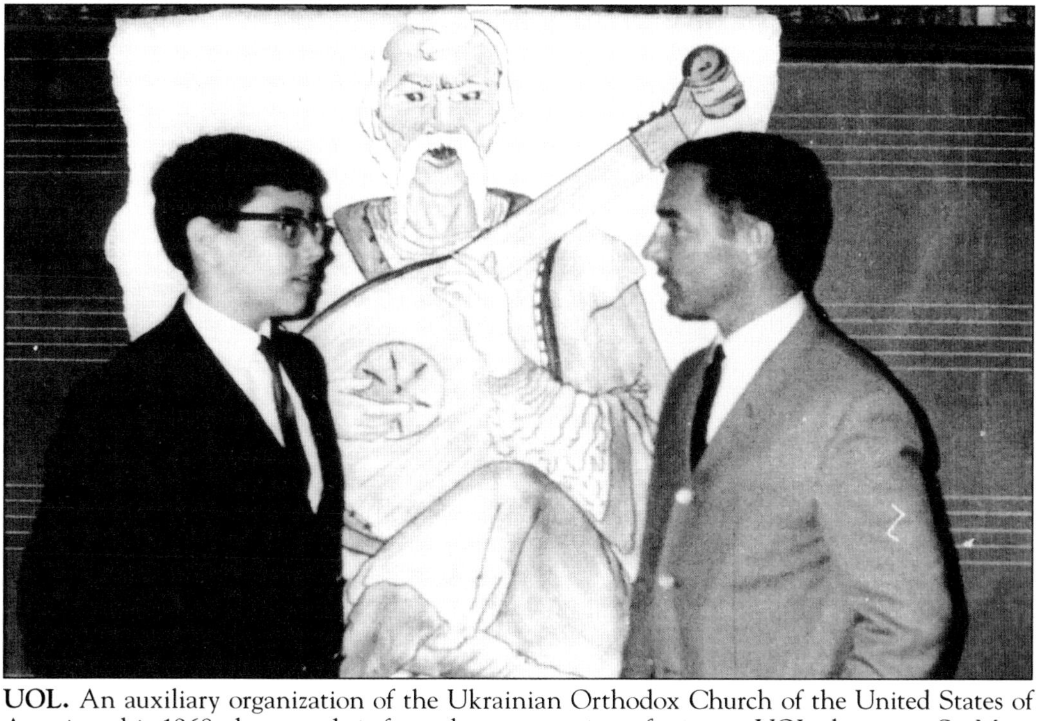

UOL. An auxiliary organization of the Ukrainian Orthodox Church of the United States of America, this 1968 photograph is from the presentation of a junior UOL chapter at St. Mary Ukrainian Orthodox Church in McKees Rocks. (Courtesy of LAVRSHH.)

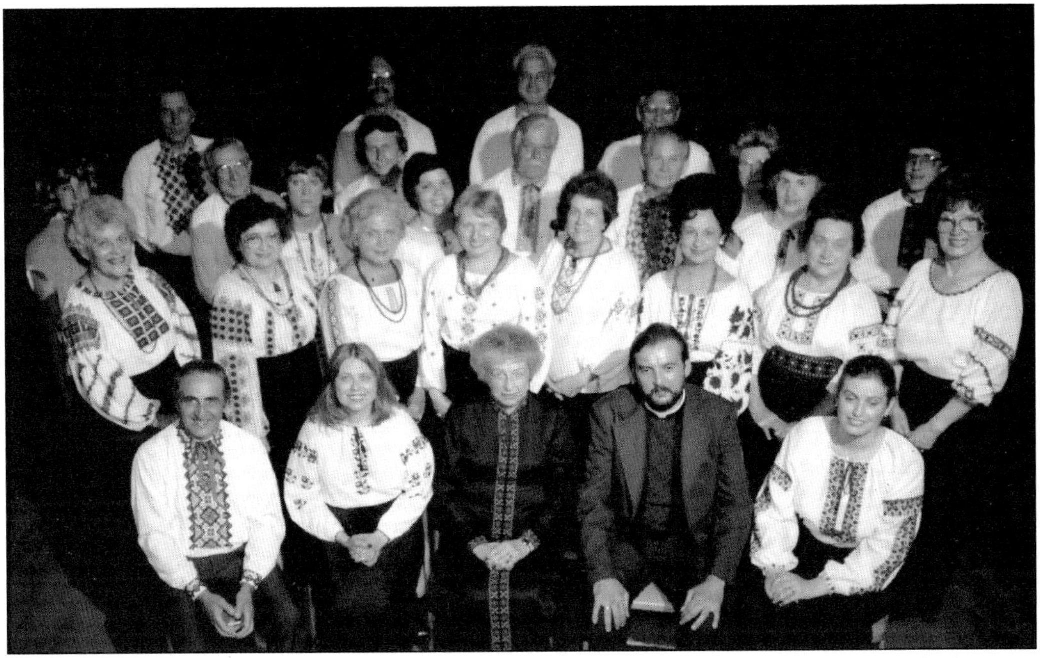

WESTERN PENNSYLVANIA REGIONAL CHOIR. The UOL sponsored a choir composed of singers from parishes of the Ukrainian Orthodox Church of the United States of America throughout western Pennsylvania. The choir performed at church and Ukrainian community events from the 1950s through the 1990s. (Courtesy of Marianne Carmack.)

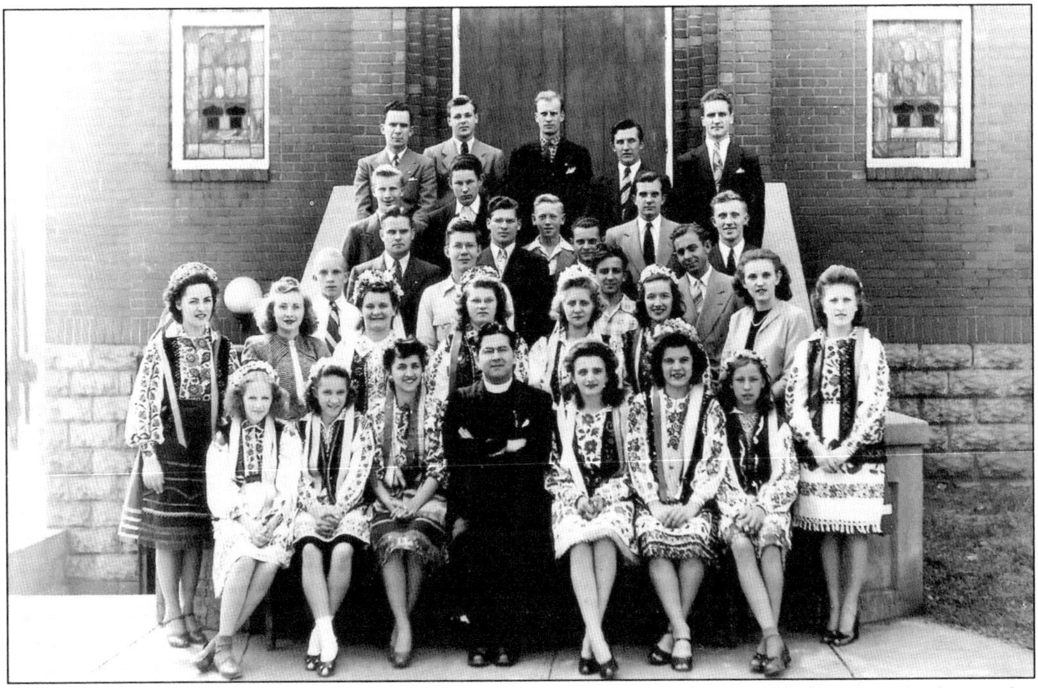

THE LYSENKO UKRAINIAN ORTHODOX CHOIR OF ARNOLD. This 1940s photograph shows the choir named in honor of legendary "Father of Ukrainian Classical Music," Ukrainian composer Mykola Lysenko. (Courtesy of LAVRSHH.)

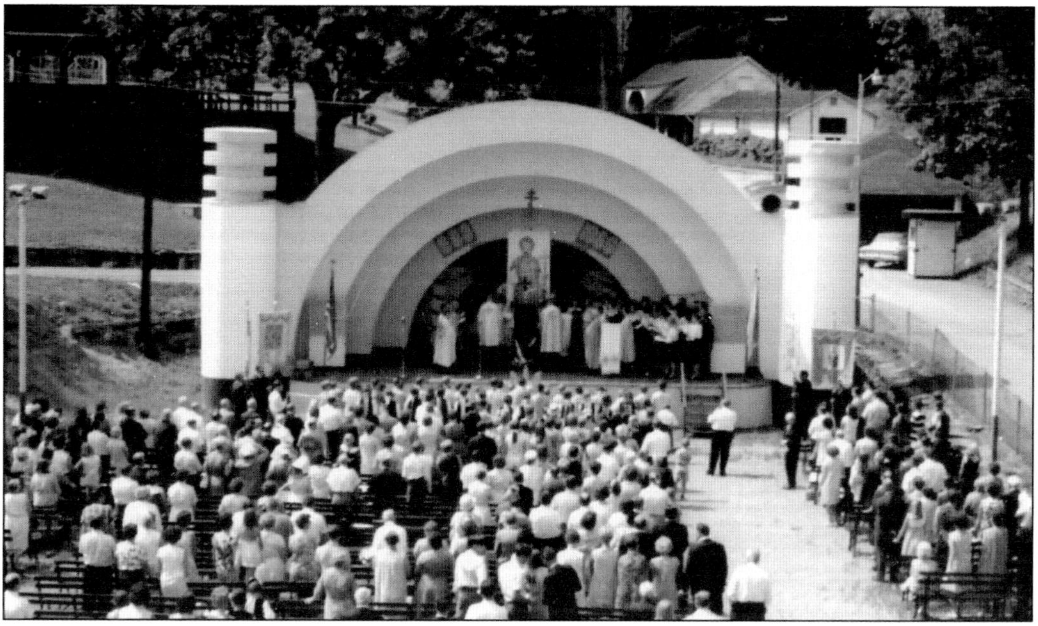

UKRAINIAN DAY AT WEST VIEW PARK. West View Park was located in Pittsburgh's North Hills and was a popular place for rides and picnics. Many Ukrainian events were held there, including this commemoration of the 980th anniversary of Christianity in Ukraine sponsored by the Western Pennsylvania Deanery of the Ukrainian Orthodox Church of the United States of America. (Courtesy of LAVRSHH.)

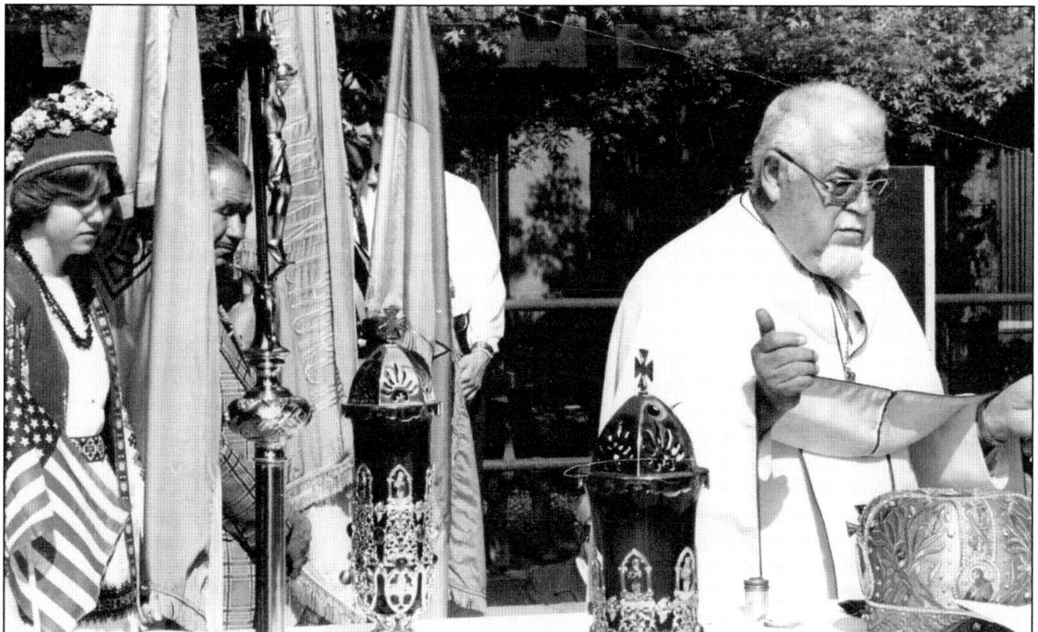

BLESSING. By tradition, Ukrainian events begin with an invocation of esteemed clergy. During the 1978 Convention of the UNA held in Pittsburgh, Fr. Andrew Beck prays for the success of the convention and the health of its participants. Other national conventions of the UNA were held in Pittsburgh in 1900, 1946, and 1994. (Courtesy of MASPPUOGCCC.)

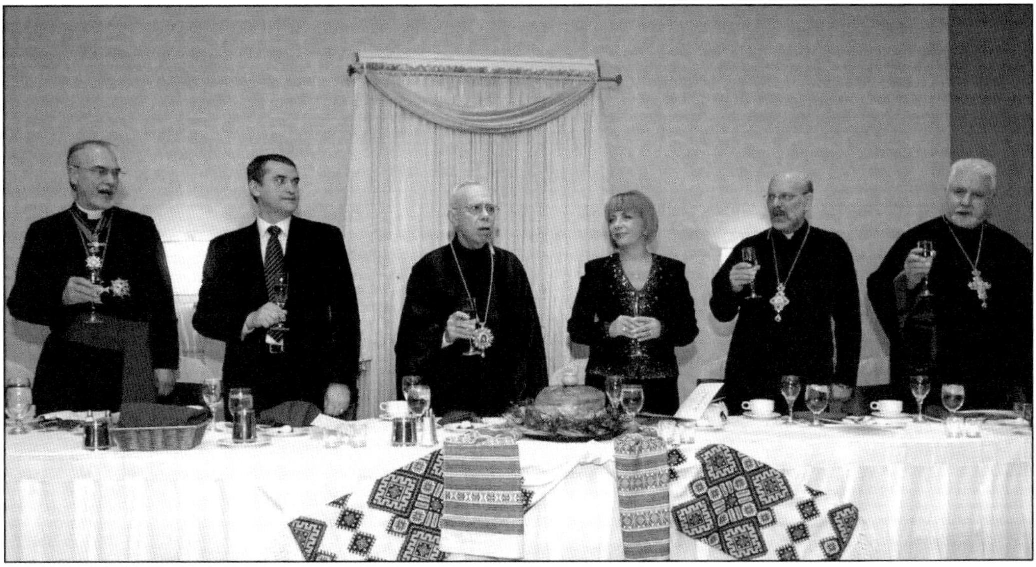

THE BISHOP'S CHARITY BALL. An annual event since 1989, the Ukrainian Catholic Church's Diocese of St. Josaphat sponsors the Bishops' Charity Ball to raise funds for church projects. In 2008, first lady of Ukraine Kateryna Yushchenko received an award from Bishop Robert Moskal in honor of the humanitarian work she performs through her foundation, Ukraine 3000. His Excellency Dr. Oleh Shamshur, ambassador to the United States of America from Ukraine, participates in the ceremonies as Bishop Moskal raises a toast in Kateryna Yushchenko's honor. (Courtesy of Michael Haritan.)

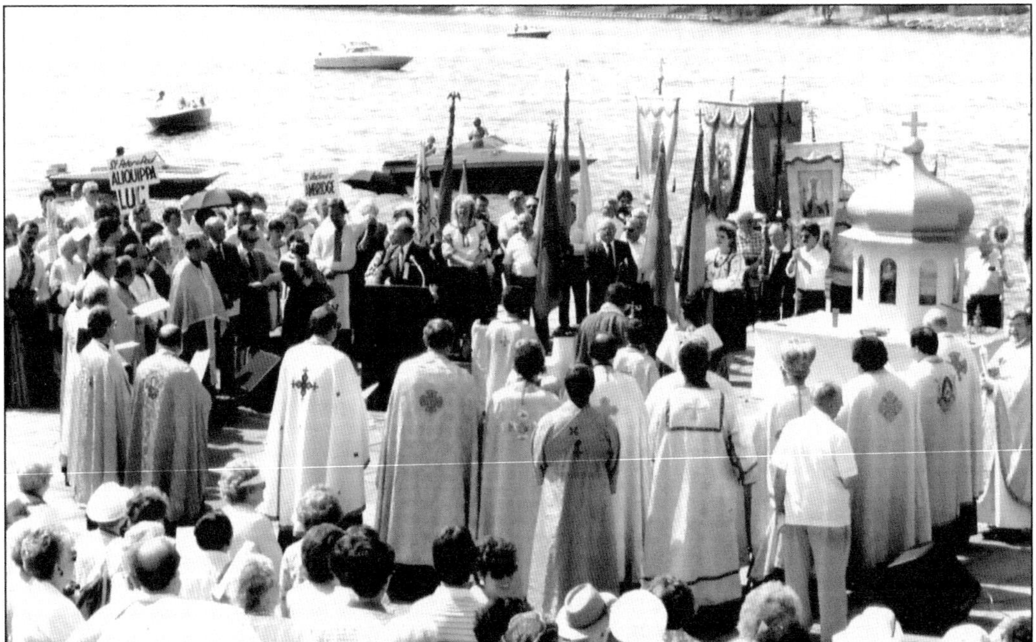

MILLENNIUM. Ukrainians from all over western Pennsylvania gathered in Pittsburgh's Point State Park for a solemn commemoration and blessing of the river in July 1988 to commemorate the millennium year of Christianity in Ukraine. (Courtesy of Michael Haritan.)

Three

Preserving and Growing a Rich Heritage

Ukrainian Style

Ukrainians are an artistic people with a rich cultural arts heritage. The many regional peoples and cultures inhabiting Ukrainian lands led to the development of varied forms of folk arts, including dances, embroidery, *pysanky*, folk songs, pottery, painting, and folk costume, with charming linguistic nuances reflected in the various Ukrainian dialects. A good portion of Ukrainian immigrants to western Pennsylvania arrived from rural towns and villages, where they had practiced these arts, and bringing them to their new land further developed them and made them part of the American culture.

During the first 40 years of Ukrainian immigration to western Pennsylvania, ethnic identity was preserved and further developed by the fraternal insurance associations and the Ukrainian churches. After Ukraine's 1918 declaration of independence, an explosion of Ukrainian artistic expression took place in Ukraine and in diaspora communities throughout the United States. Choirs, dance and drama groups, sports leagues, women's associations, and language schools sprang up in virtually every Ukrainian community. Many of these were sponsored directly by the Ukrainian churches and were given a home for such activities by supportive clergy and parish boards.

At the same time, new community organizations arose such as citizens' clubs, which were founded to help Ukrainian immigrants adapt to life in the United States. These clubs took on an increasingly social nature over the years, sponsoring dances, cultural workshops, as well as providing venues for social interaction and expression.

Following World War II, further attempts at creating a self-sustaining community were made through the formation of heritage schools, financial institutions, and quasi-political organizations. Food festivals featuring Ukrainian dishes such as *kovbasa* (spiced sausage), *halushky* (cabbage and noodles), *varenyky* (pierogies), *holubtsi* (cabbage rolls), and *borshch* (beet soup) gave real flavor to being Ukrainian.

The long-awaited dream among Ukrainians worldwide came true in 1991 with the dissolution of the USSR and the declaration of Ukrainian independence, confirmed overwhelmingly by popular referendum. Ukrainians were free to travel abroad, and visiting dance and choral groups became regular items on the community's social calendar.

The Ukrainians of western Pennsylvania have focused on preserving and growing a rich heritage, mixing various elements, continuing to evolve—not merely remaining a construct of the past. Despite the necessary and at times vehement protestations that they were not Russians or Poles, their Ukrainian identity has always been one based on being "pro" Ukrainian and not "anti" anything or anyone. They are international-global, yet unique and regional; Ukrainian and American at the same time. They insist that they are not better than anyone, but at the same time that they are no less.

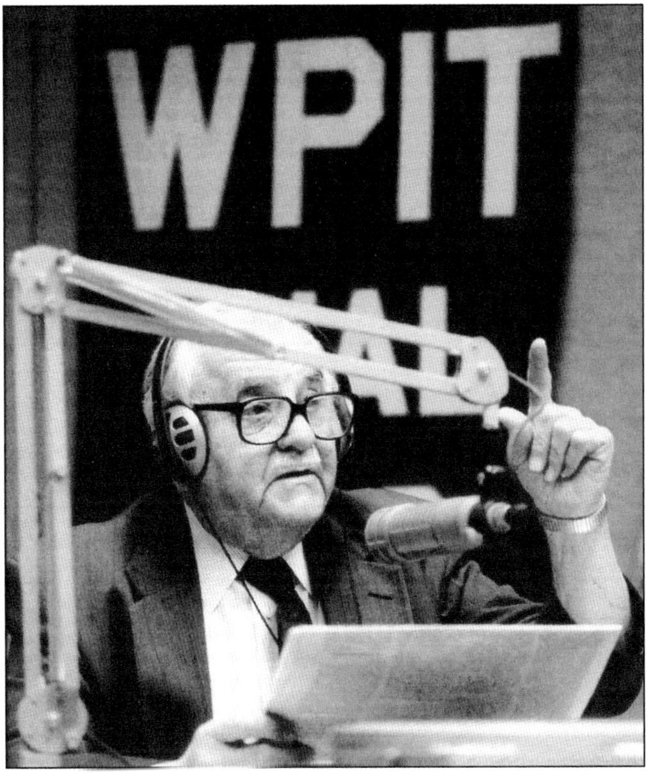

UVAHA! (ATTENTION). The Ukrainian Radio Program has been heard on WPIT-AM 730 Sundays from 1:00 to 2:00 p.m. since Michael Komichak became the host in 1950, taking over a Ukrainian radio show hosted by Nick Arseny, which aired from Greensburg. Michael Komichak has aired a new program every Sunday since, making him arguably the longest-running host of an ethnic radio program in the United States. The program is a mix of music, news from Ukraine, announcements of local Ukrainian community events, and interviews. An after-church Sunday tradition in the community, the show can also be heard on the internet. Michael Komichak has hosted a Sunday serenade of Ukrainian music at times over the years as well. (Courtesy of Michael Komichak.)

Programme

11:00 a. m. — Holy Field Mass at Fabian's Park
The Choir under the direction of John Dyrkacz will sing responses to the Holy Mass

1:00 p. m. — Dinner served

2:00 p. m. — Dancing at the Pavilion
Featuring Johnny Melvin and his Orchestra

4:00 p. m. — Choral Competition

1. Choir of the Holy Virgin Church, Arnold, Pa.
Directed by Reverend G. Pavlovsky

(a) Over the Vast Plains; Canticle .... K. Stetzenko
(b) The Cossack Set Out beyond the Danube .... G. Davidowsky
(c) The Canoe .... G. Pavlovsky

2. Lyssenko Choir of Ambridge, Pa.
Directed by Reverend E. Korolyshyn

(a) Chant of St. George .... J. Jacinevich
(b) Ulianka Cut the Silken Grass .... M. Stupnicky
(c) The Evening .... M. Hayvoronsky
(d) A Violin is Playing in the Street .... A. Koshetz

3. Hayvoronsky Choir of Pittsburgh, Pa.
Directed by Melvin Zelechivsky

(a) My Thoughts .... I. Vorobkevitch
(b) Cossack Rides to War .... M. Hayvoronsky
(c) The Village is in Sight .... I. Yaroslavenko
(d) Ducks .... N. Leontovitch

5:00 p. m. — Ukrainian Folk Dances, by School of V. Avramenko, Monessen, Pa.
Directed by Mr. Nick Arseny

5:30 p. m. to ? ? — Dancing at the Pavilion
Featuring Johnny Melvin and his Orchestra

CONCERT PROGRAM. The program for Ukrainian Day in Arnold featured a choral competition among Ukrainian groups from Ambridge, Arnold, and Pittsburgh. The works of some of the best-known Ukrainian composers including Aleksander Koshetz, Maksym Hayvoronsky, and Mykola Leontovich were included in this 1930s-era program as was a performance by the Avramenko Dance School of Monessen. (Courtesy of Steve Pituch.)

FUND-RAISERS. Ukrainian communities across the United States found various ways to raise funds for the establishment of the Harvard University Ukrainian Research Institute (HURI), and western Pennsylvanians did their part with this grand concert in 1972. Other causes supported by the community include the Shevchenko Scientific Society, Ukrainian Free Academy of Sciences, Ukrainian Free University, Ukrainian Helsinki Monitoring Group Fund, and the World Congress of Free Ukrainians, among many others. (Courtesy of Yaroslaw Hodowanec.)

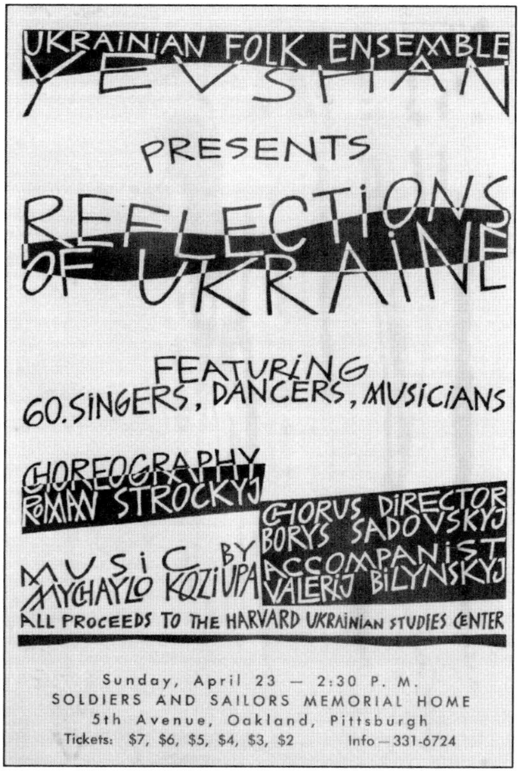

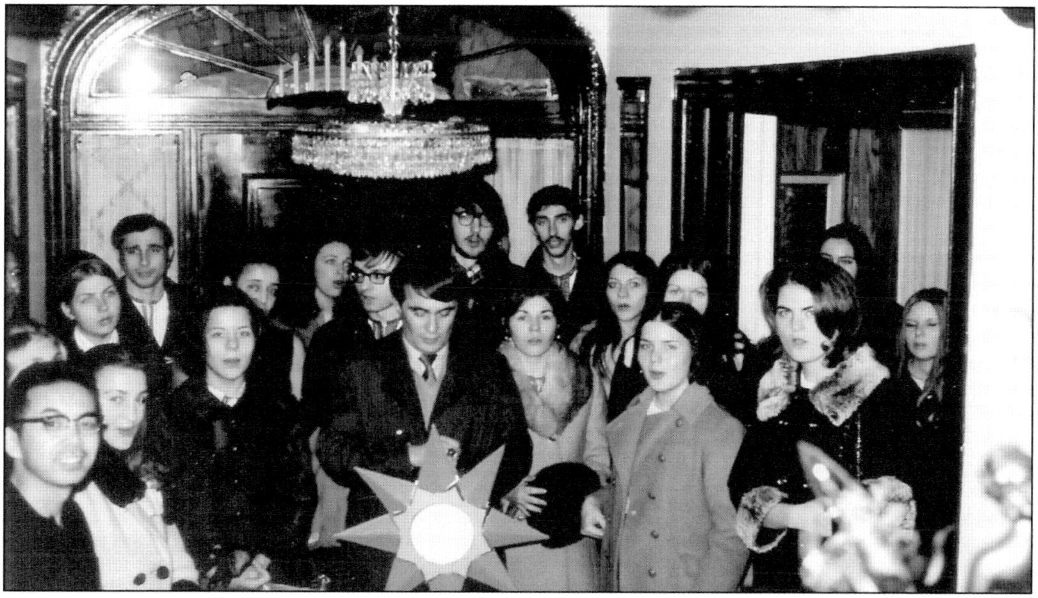

KOLYADKY. Members of the youth group TUM (Ukrainian acronym translating to society of Ukrainian youth) go from house to house singing traditional Ukrainian Christmas carols in this 1970 photograph. An annual tradition dating back to the earliest days of Christianity in Ukraine, carolers sing news of the Christ child's birth and bring wishes of health, wealth, and happiness to the homes of Ukrainians throughout the area joining their hosts in partaking of the bountiful Ukrainian Christmas Day meal. (Courtesy of Yaroslaw Hodowanec.)

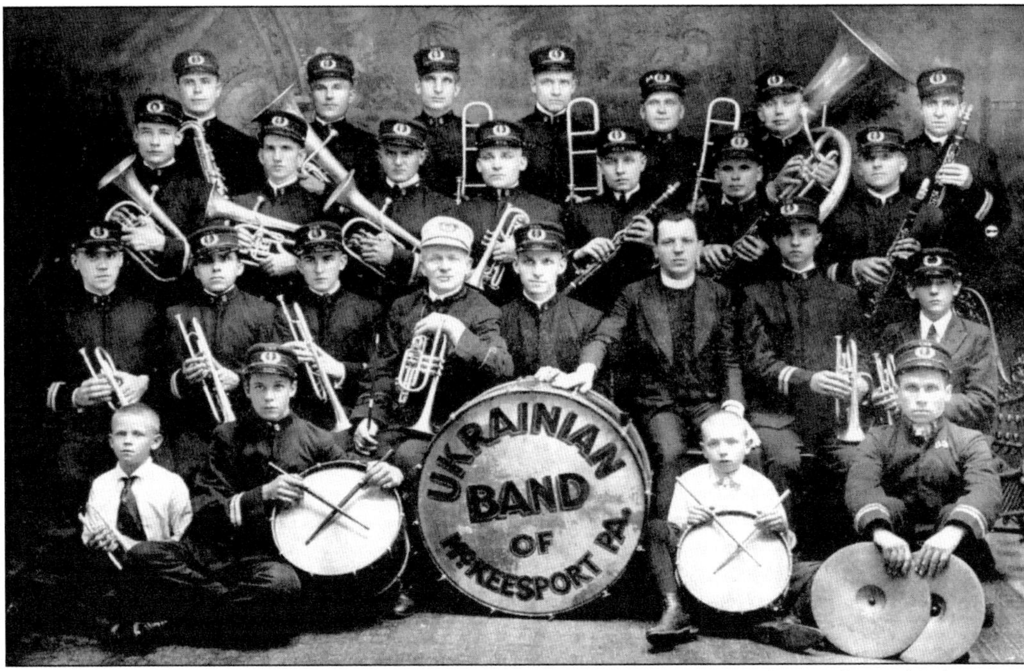

UKRAINIAN BANDS. Many Ukrainian communities in western Pennsylvania hosted Ukrainian bands, which played a mix of traditional Ukrainian music and popular American standards. The photograph above was taken in 1919 in McKeesport and the photograph below in the 1920s in Monessen. (Above, courtesy of St. John the Baptist Ukrainian Catholic Church, McKeesport; below, courtesy of Daria Pishko Komichak.)

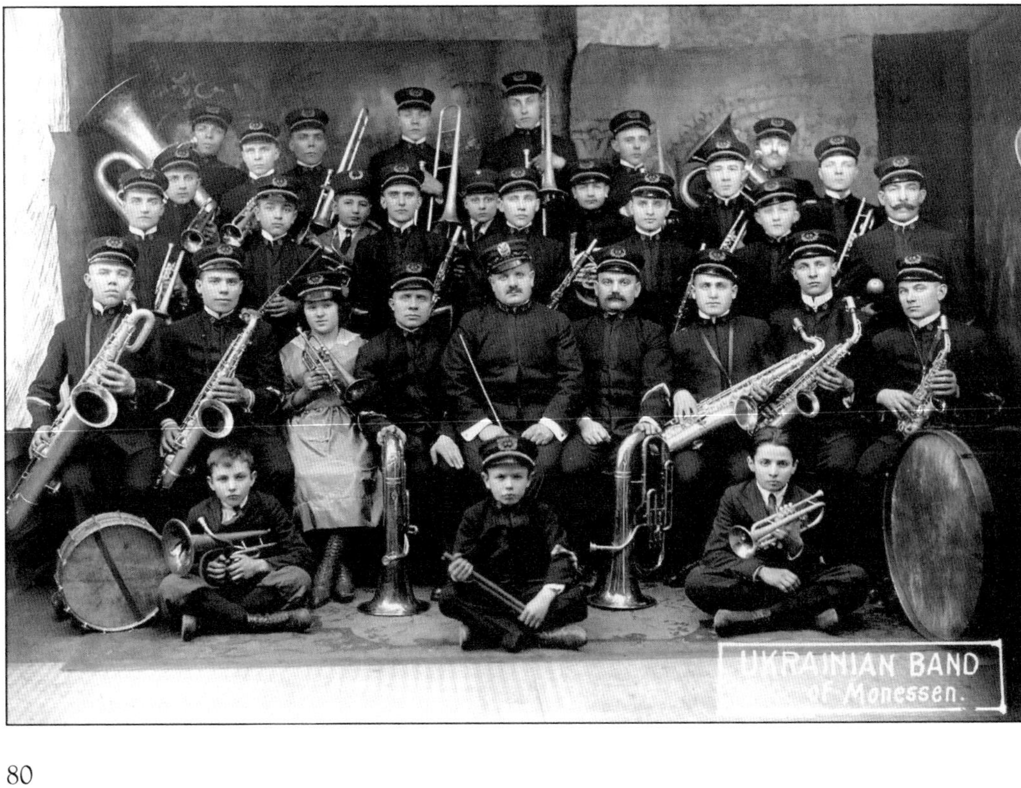

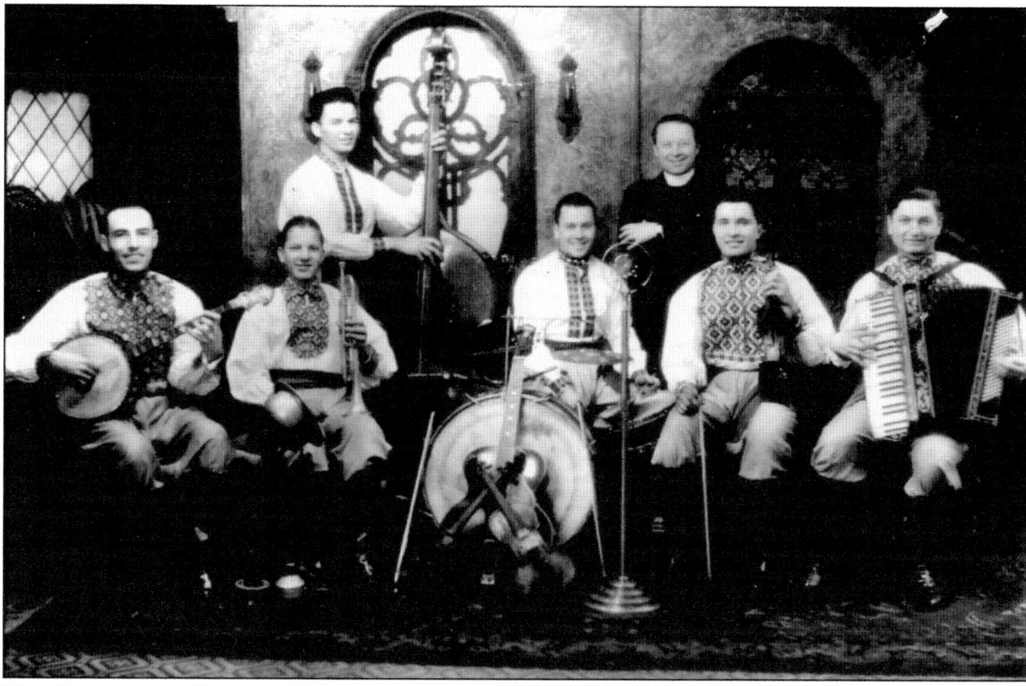

THE UKRAINIAN RHYTHM ACES OF ALIQUIPPA. A well-known Ukrainian band in the 1930s, the Ukrainian Rhythm Aces of Aliquippa's leader was community-activist Chester Manasterski and performances were held at community events and weddings. (Courtesy of MASPPUOGCCC.)

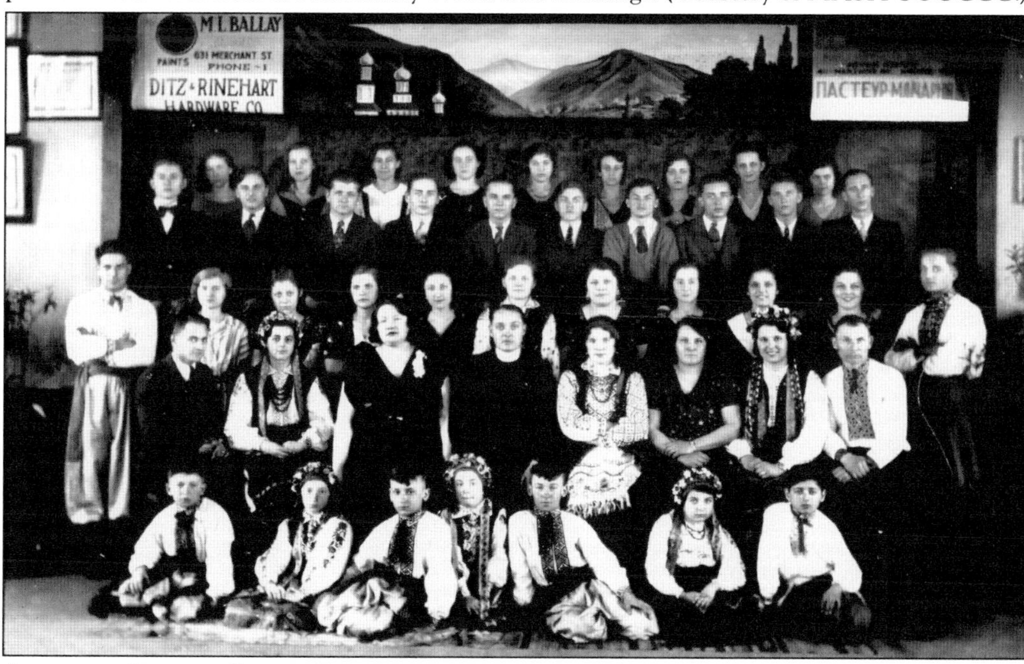

AMBRIDGE DRAMA GROUP. Dramatic groups were popular in Ukrainian churches in the early to mid-20th century. This photograph from the late 1920s shows Ambridge's drama group posing before a backdrop of a Ukrainian village with advertisements from Ukrainian businesses surrounding it. (Courtesy of St. Vladimir Ukrainian Orthodox Church.)

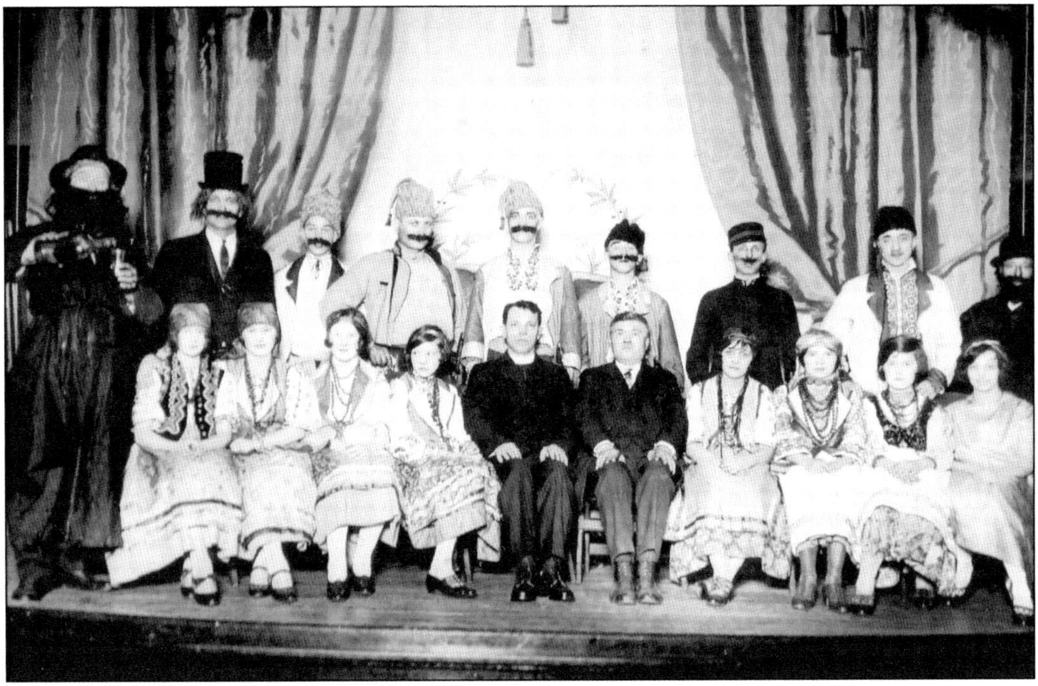

McKEESPORT DRAMA GROUP. The plays performed by these drama groups were generally ones depicting life in the homeland. Stories of kozak exploits were among favorites. (Courtesy of Melanie Hutskow.)

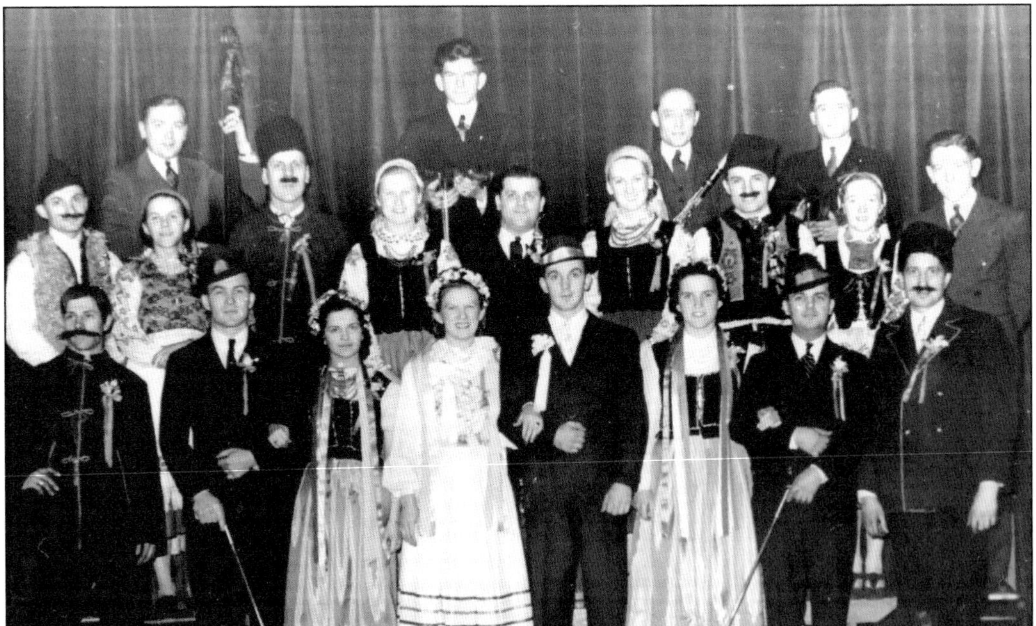

FORD CITY DRAMA GROUP. Dramatic groups were so popular at the time that packets containing scripts, costumes, and other tools necessary for staging these shows could be bought all in one piece. Some churches funded the construction of their parish halls by charging admission to these shows. (Courtesy of Pat Morovich.)

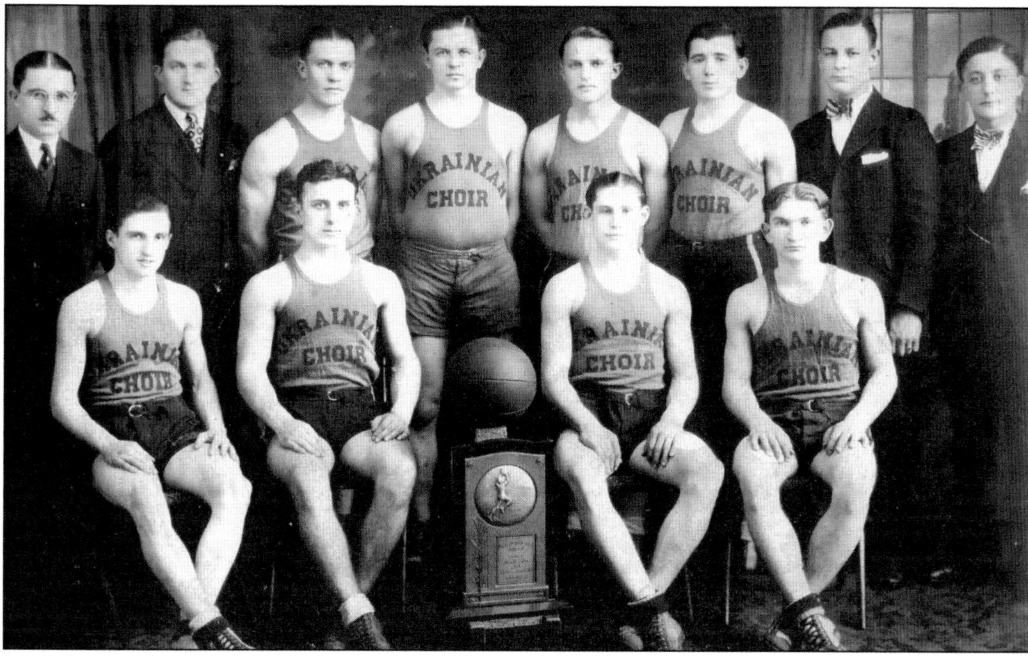

McKees Rocks Basketball. Sports leagues were popular in Ukrainian communities in the early 20th century. Basketball was popular in the 1920s and 1930s, as shown by this 1929 photograph from McKees Rocks. In the 1950s and 1960s, bowling leagues replaced other sports in terms of popularity. (Courtesy of St. Mary Ukrainian Orthodox Church.)

BASKET-BALL EDITORIAL

1939—Season

ARNOLD Ukrainian Athletic Club's Basketball team completed a highly successful season.

They were crowned Area No. 5 and the Western Regional Champions of the U. Y. L. of N. A. only to lose the National Title to the Chester Penn'a. Ukrainians at closing seconds by a hard fought battle, both teams with their title's at stake, gave their best performance.

Campaigning in the Western Pennsylvania, the center of some of the Country's best Basket-Ball Clubs, the Arnold team compiled a fine record — winning 30 games and losing 11.

In competition against Ukrainian teams from Pennsylvania, Ohio and Canada the team won 11 games, lost 2.

Although five (5) first years men were carried on the squad, records prove their ability for the next season and many years to come.

This team scored 1887 points, an average of 46 points per game.

Our goal and motto next season:

Nothig less than the NATIONAL TITLE FOR ARNOLD.

Arnold Basketball Program. The Ukrainian Youth League of North America was a major sponsor of the Ukrainian sports leagues. They provided an athletic outlet primarily for the young men of the community, as well as venues for social interaction. (Courtesy of Steve Pituch.)

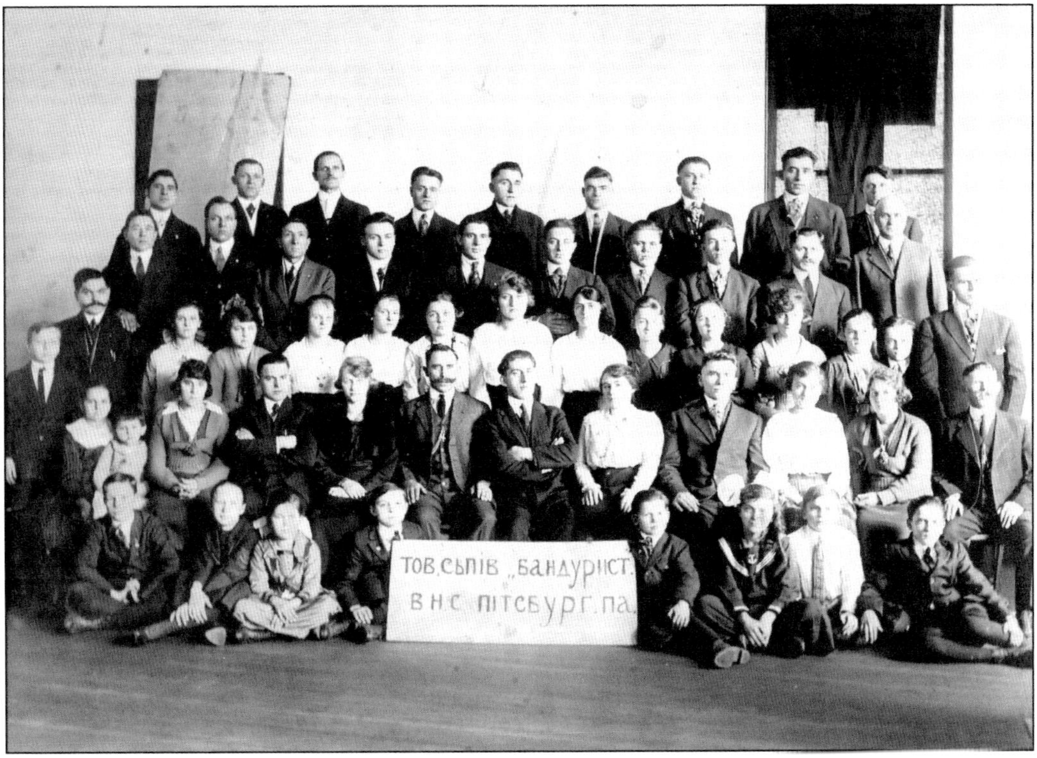

A Family Affair. Ukrainian community events usually involved all ages, uniting families and communities. This 1920s photograph from Pittsburgh's North Side shows the chorus "Bandurist." (Courtesy of St. George Ukrainian Catholic Church.)

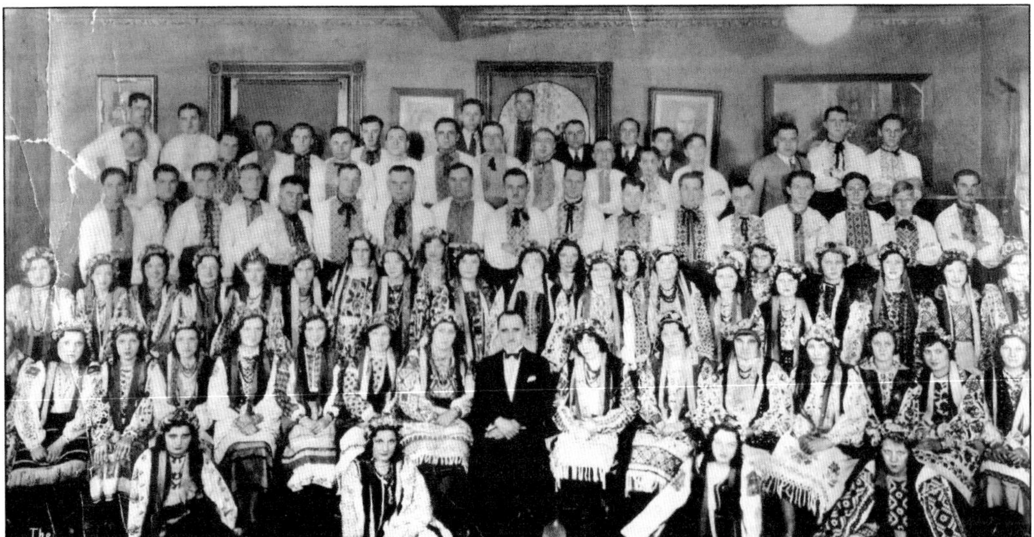

The Ukrainian National Choir of Constantin Orlyk. Adult choirs performing at community events featured such Ukrainian folk songs as "Chueysh, Brate Miy" (Hear, My Brother) and "Reve ta Stohne" from a Shevchenko poem and for which Carnegie choirs were particularly noted, among many others. (Courtesy of Marianne Carmack.)

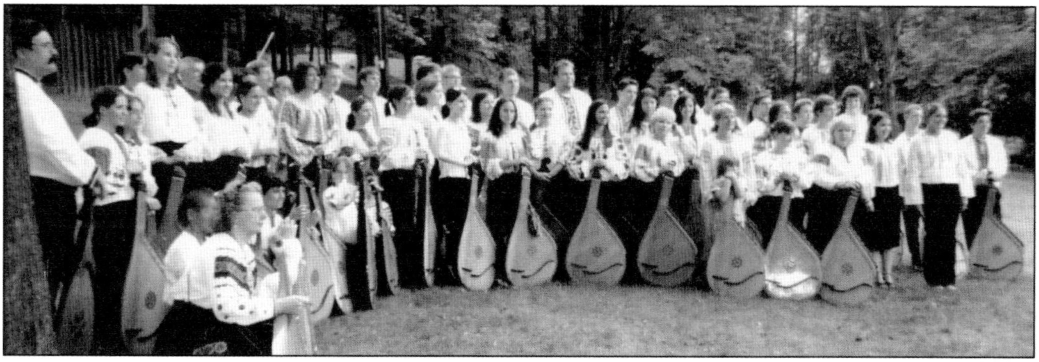

BANDURA CAMP. The Ukrainian Bandurist Chorus, a 20-member all-male musical ensemble founded in Ukraine in 1918, has sponsored a two-week encampment held at All Saints Ukrainian Orthodox Church Camp since 1979. Students receive instruction in playing the *bandura*, a 60-stringed instrument, which unifies acoustic principles of the lute and the harp, and was first noted in a sixth century Greek chronicle. (Courtesy of George Honchar.)

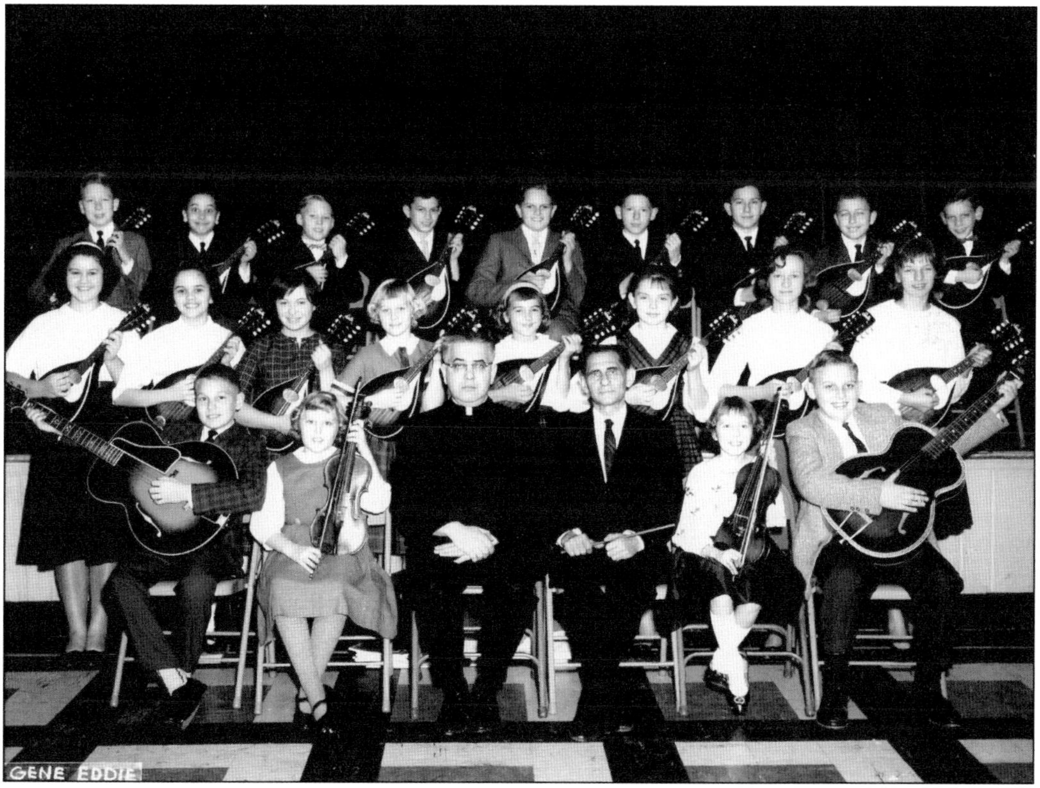

CENTERING LIFE AROUND THE CHURCH. To a great extent, the lives of many western Pennsylvania Ukrainians have been centered around activities connected to their churches. This 1950s mandolin orchestra from McKees Rocks provides an example. (Courtesy of Maria Byczkalo Orient.)

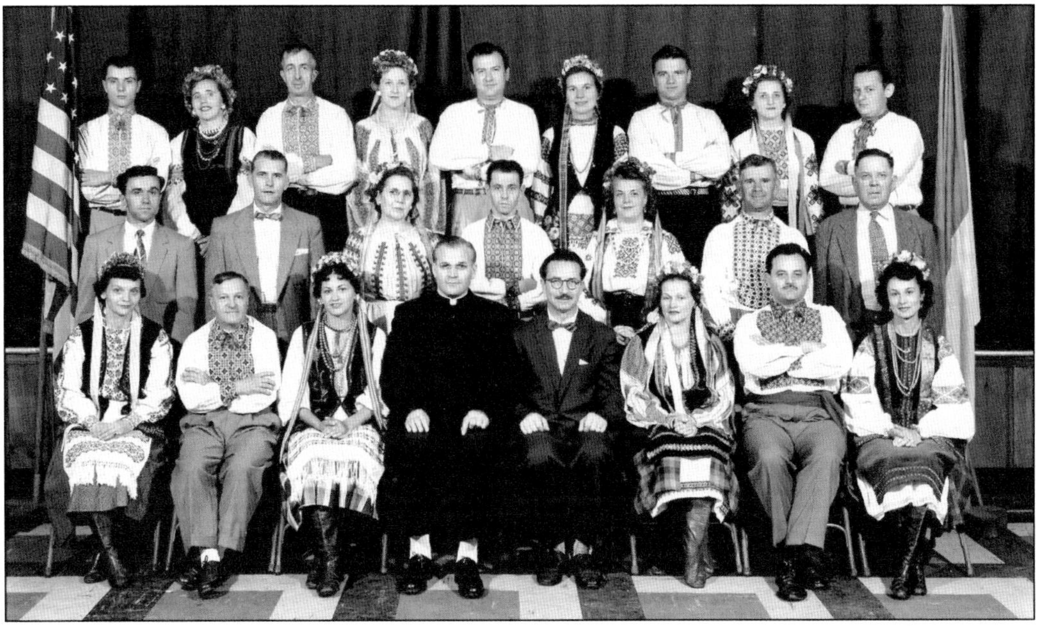

The Church Choir. Choirs in Ukrainian churches sing a cappella in four-part harmony as they provide the responses that a *dyak*, cantor, or the congregation might give. The church choir of St. Mary Ukrainian Orthodox Church in McKees Rocks (above) poses with their spiritual father and dyak in this 1950s photograph. Members of SS. Peter and Paul Ukrainian Orthodox Greek Catholic Church in Carnegie pose with their instructor B. M. Hoptiak in 1940 (below). (Above, courtesy of Oksana Byczkalo; below, courtesy of MASPPUOGCCC.)

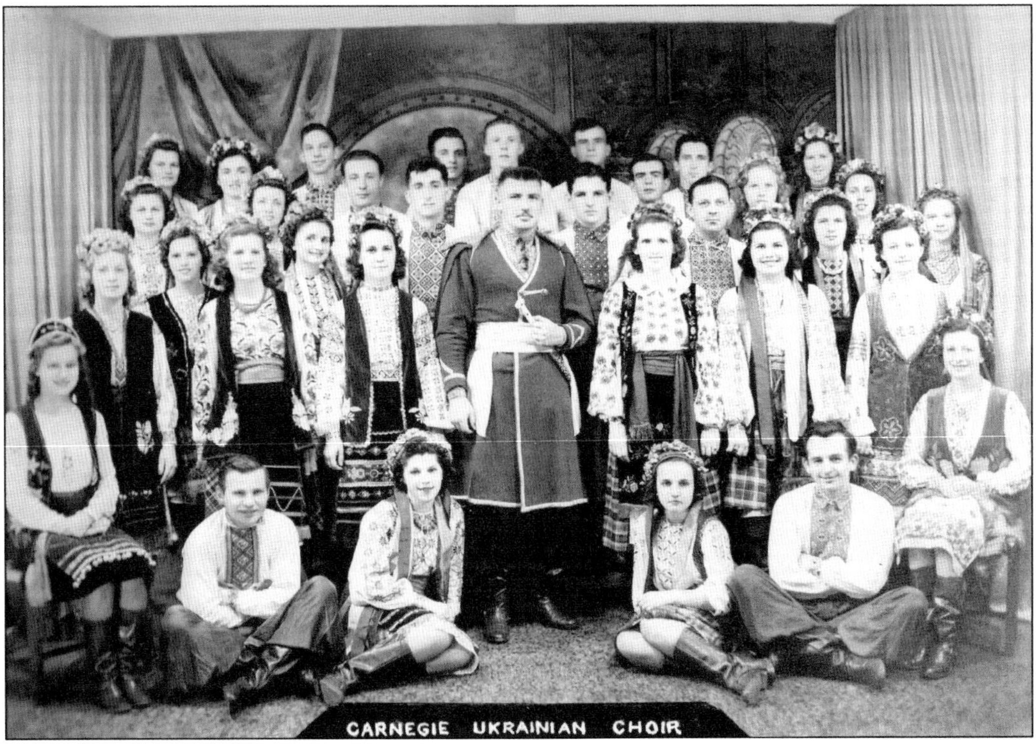

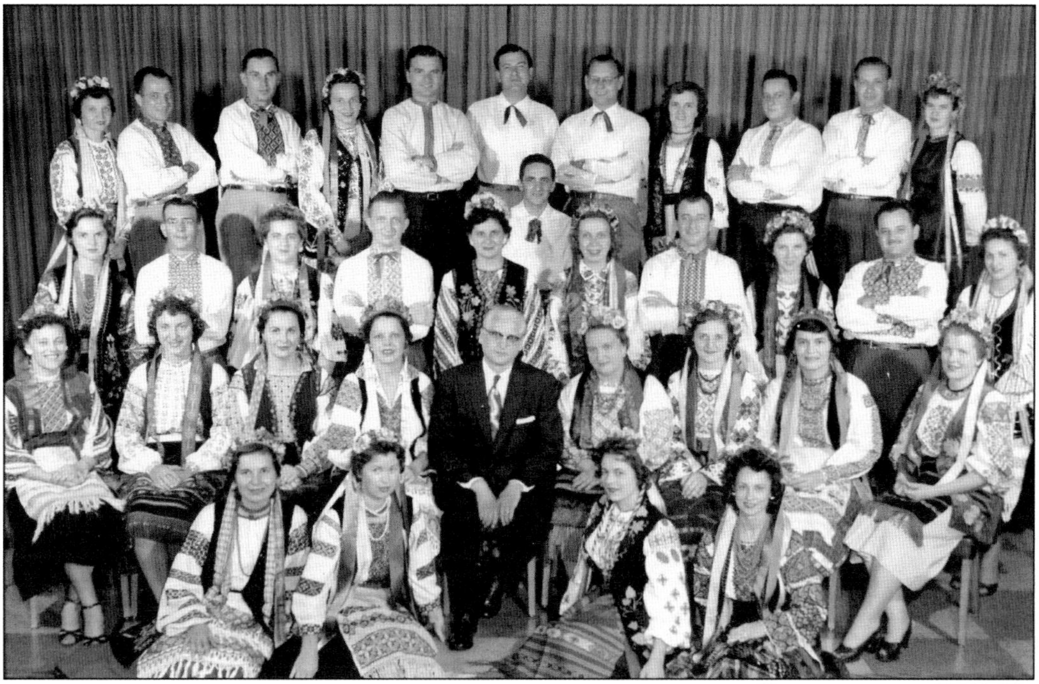

THE UYLNA CHOIR. Members of the western Pennsylvania branch of the Ukrainian Youth League of North America prepare for the national organization's 1955 convention, which was held in Pittsburgh. (Courtesy of MASPPUOGCCC.)

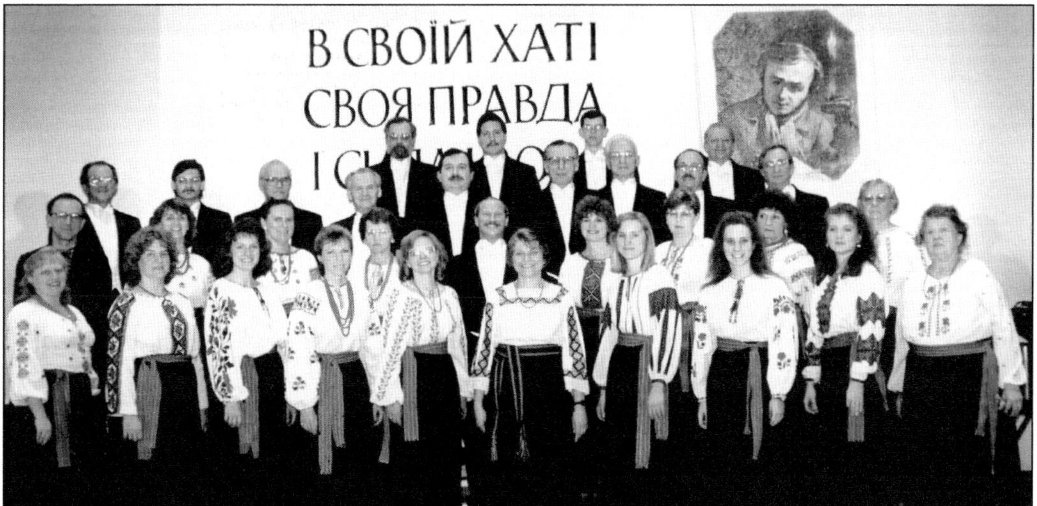

THE UKRAINIAN CULTURAL TRUST CHOIR. Started by director Dorothy Waslo in 1991, the choir has found a regular place on the community's social calendar with its annual Christmas and Lenten concerts. Each year two concerts of each type are held in different churches throughout the region—one for Catholic Christmas and Easter, which coincide with the American holidays, and the second for Orthodox Christmas and Easter. One of the choir's most requested numbers is "Shchedryk," the melody used in the "Carol of the Bells." "Shchedryk" was written by Ukrainian composer Mykola Leatorych in 1916 and is actually a New Year's carol—a song of tidings, good news, and prosperity brought by the warbling of a bird. (Courtesy of Melanie Hutskow.)

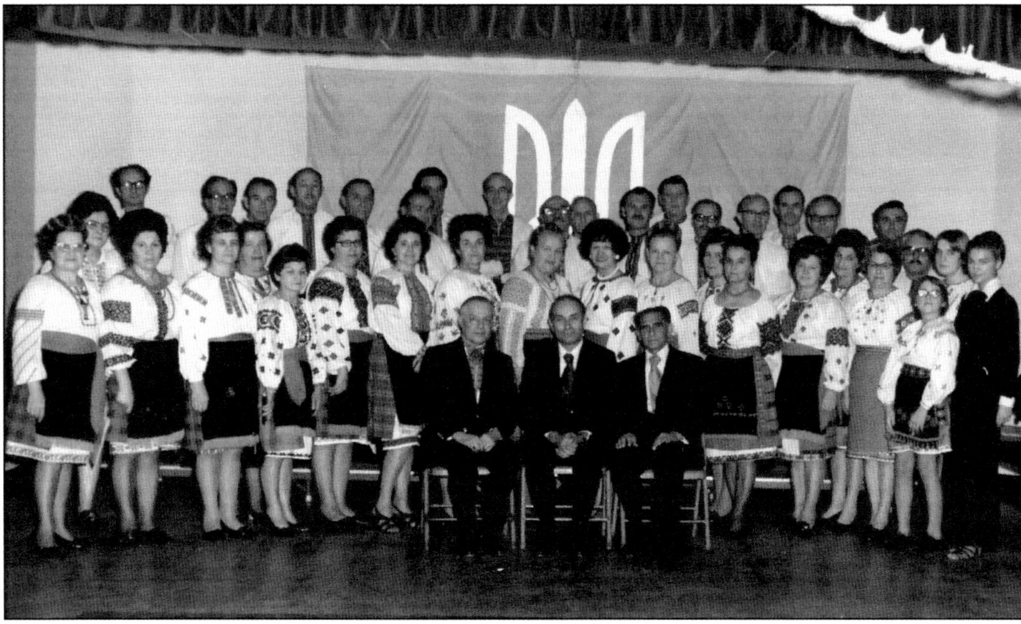

THE SELFRELIANCE CHOIR. The Selfreliance Association of American Ukrainians was founded following World War II in order to assist Ukrainian immigrants in adapting to life in the United States. In addition to providing social settlement services, the organization sponsored a choir and is the sponsor for the Ukrainian Selfreliance of Western Pennsylvania Federal Credit Union. (Courtesy of USWPFCU.)

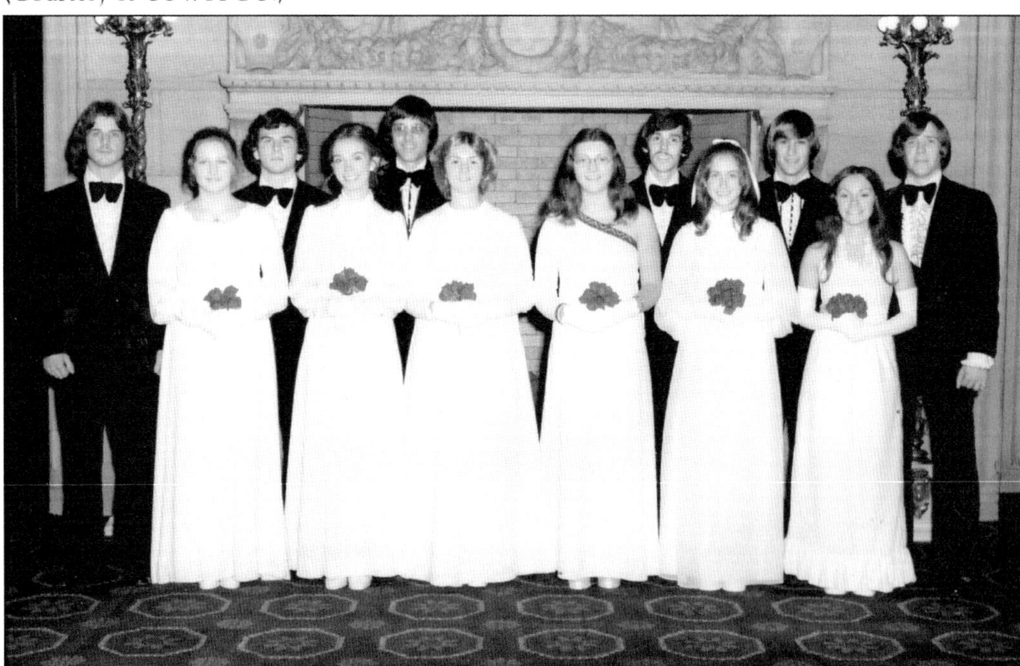

DEBUTANTES. Debutantes have been presented to western Pennsylvania Ukrainian society at the Ukrainian Technological Society (UTS) dinner dance held yearly in late November since 1970. (Courtesy of Luba Hlutkowsky.)

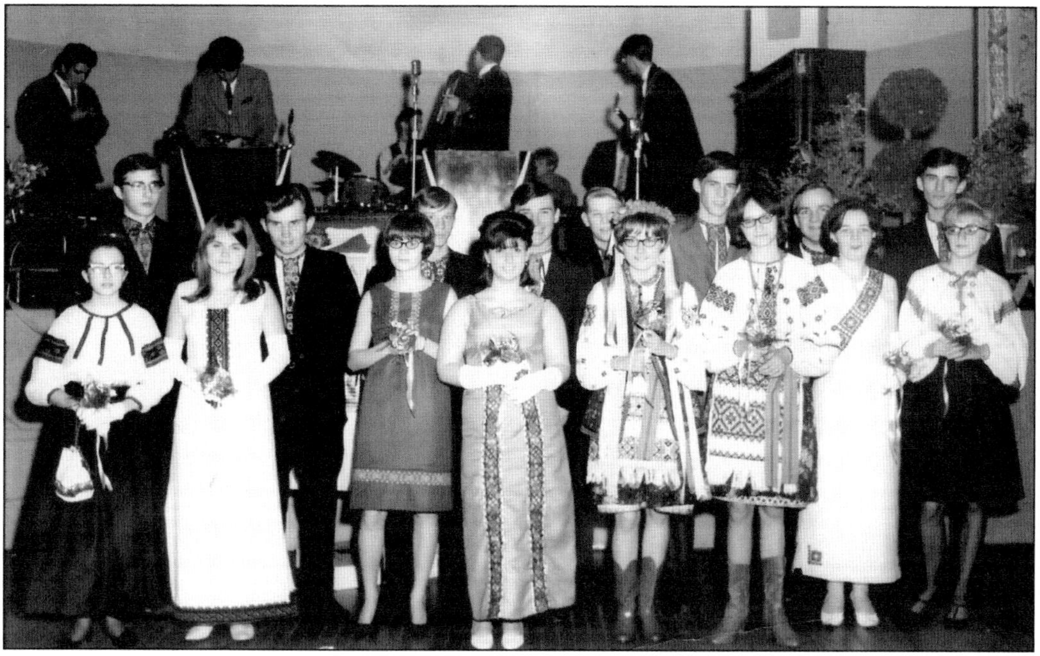

THE EMBROIDERED EVENING. Known in Ukrainian as Vyshyvanni Vechornytsi, this annual social event presents an opportunity for Ukrainians to show off their intricately designed embroidered outfits. This photograph was taken at the first event sponsored by the Ukrainian National Women's League of North America in 1965. (Courtesy of Mary Zaliszczuk.)

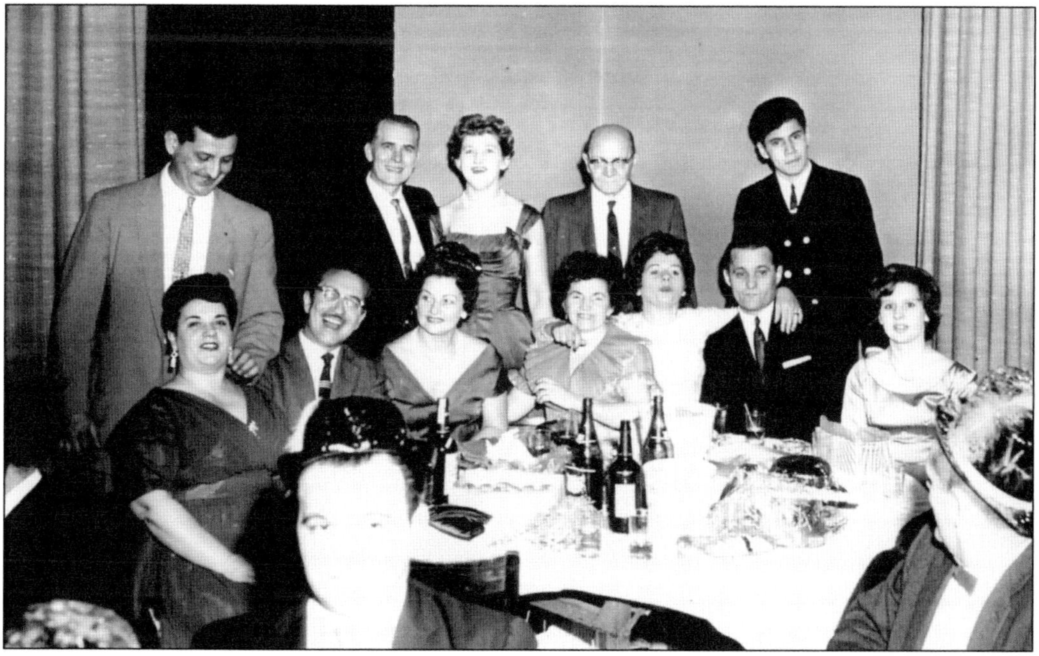

THE MALANKA. Not only do many Ukrainians celebrate Christmas 13 days after most of their American neighbors, they also celebrate New Year's Day on January 14. The Malanka dance has been a tradition for years and commemorates the feast day of St. Melania. (Courtesy of Katherine Kiray.)

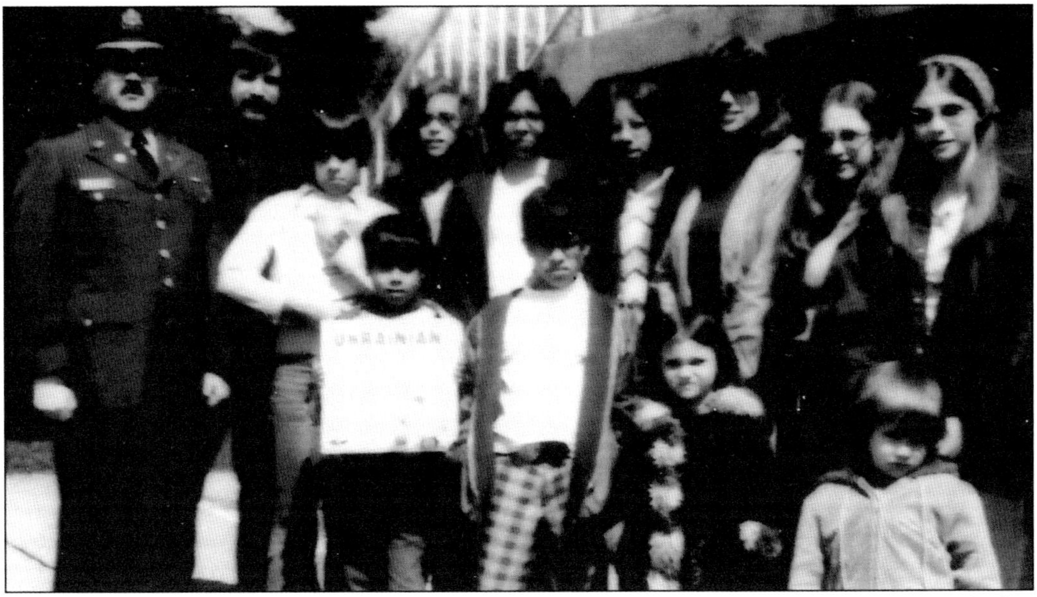

LEARNING THE UKRAINIAN LANGUAGE. Students from Holy Ghost Ukrainian Orthodox Church in Slickville had the opportunity to study the language of their forebears at the U.S. Army Reserve Unit in Greensburg from September 1975 to May 1976. The first thing a student of the Ukrainian language needs to learn is the Cyrillic alphabet—the Ukrainian variant of which has 33 letters, some of which are similar to the English and Greek alphabets, all phonetically based. (Courtesy of Stephen P. Hallick-Holutiak Jr.)

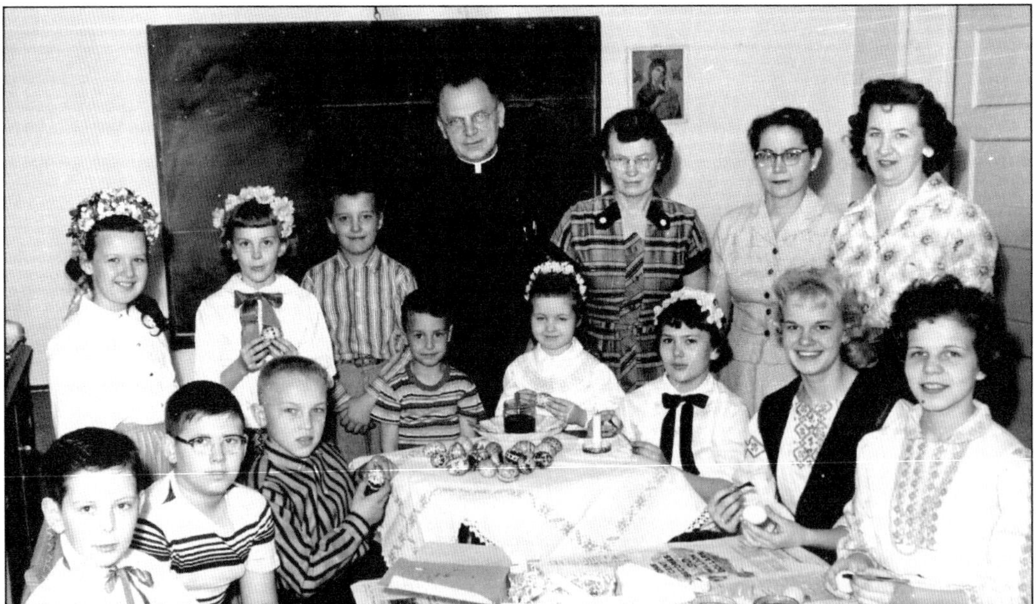

MONESSEN PYSANKY. Classes in the making of Ukrainian pysanky (Easter eggs) were another aspect of cultural life in Ukrainian communities throughout western Pennsylvania. In this 1950s photograph from Monessen, *Pani* "Mrs." Yarosh provides instruction to parish youth. (Courtesy of Helen Guzensky.)

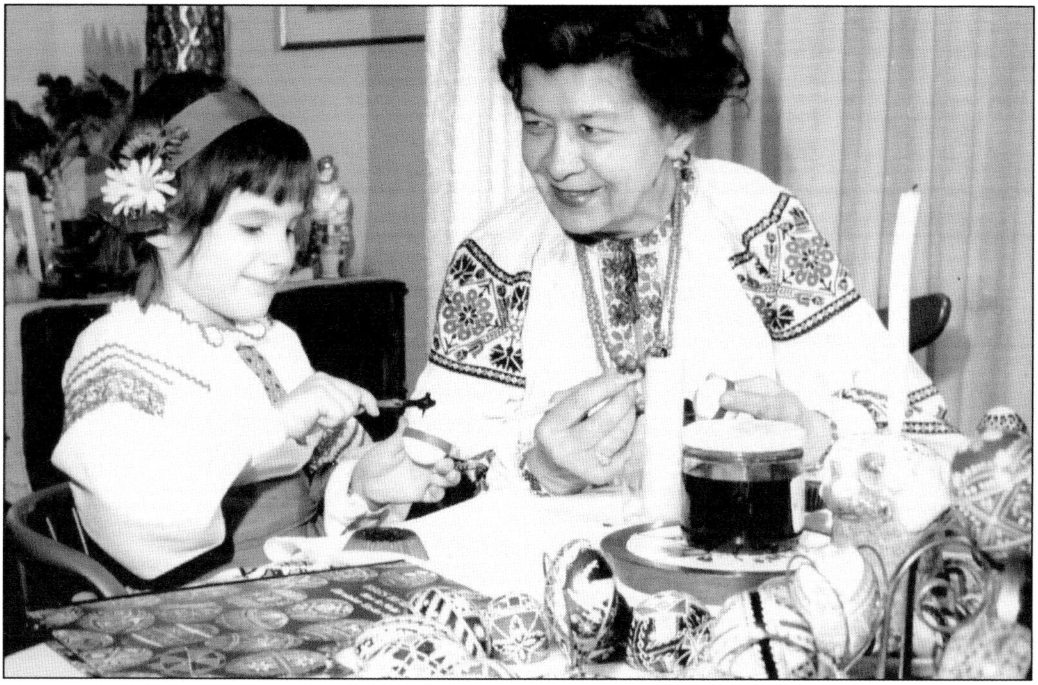

PASSING ALONG A TRADITION. In the top photograph, Pani Tillie Beck demonstrates how to hold the stylus, which is used to apply hot wax to a raw chicken egg in order to turn it into a Ukrainian Easter egg or *pysanka*. The word *pysanka* comes from the Ukrainian *pysaty* or "to write." Starting with the lightest color and continuing through progressively darker colors, wax is applied in a batik-style process covering that which the artist wishes to remain a certain color. Once the final background color is applied, the wax is removed and the egg varnished revealing a unique hand-made creation. They represent in symbols gifts of strength, prosperity, good fortune, fertility, and life, and remind one of Christ's resurrection and the gift of eternal life. Ukrainians in western Pennsylvania and throughout the United States preserved this ancient Ukrainian tradition, which was suppressed by the Soviet government for its Christian symbolism. The bottom photograph, from 1958, shows children at St. Mary Ukrainian Orthodox Church in McKees Rocks being taught by Joanne Staroschak, who traveled to Ukraine several times after the fall of communism to assist in reintroducing this custom. (Above, courtesy of MASPPUOGCCC; below, courtesy of Joanne Staroschak.)

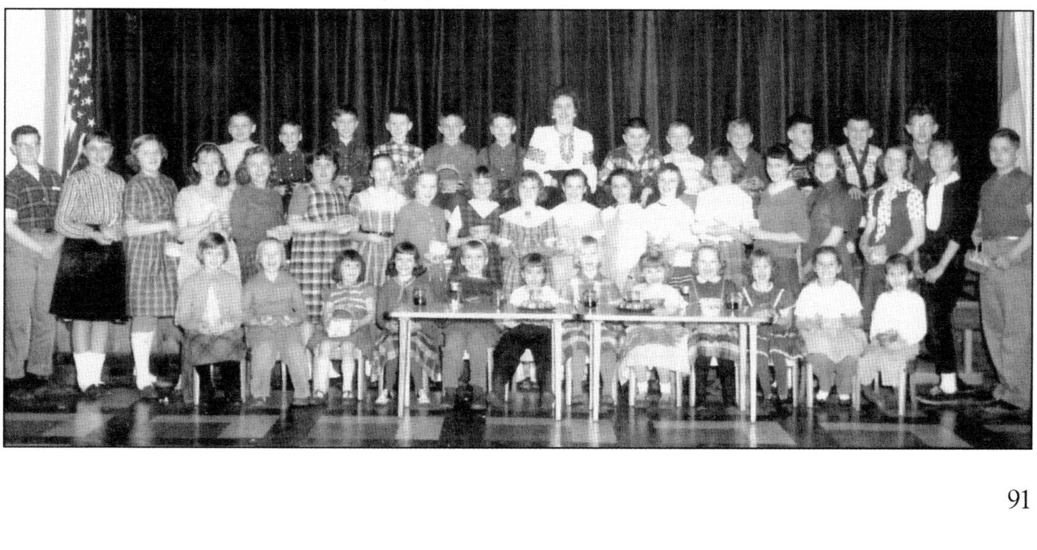

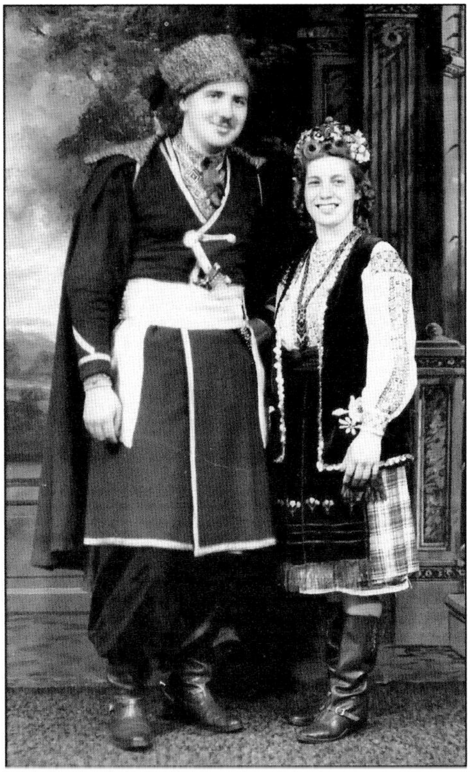

VASILE AVRAMENKO. Ukrainian ballet master Vasile Avramenko poses with a student from Carnegie. Avramenko was instrumental in standardizing Ukrainian folk dance as well as in establishing Ukrainian folk dance/ballet troupes throughout western Pennsylvania and the United States in the 1920s and 1930s, which were named in his honor. (Courtesy of MASPPUOGCCC.)

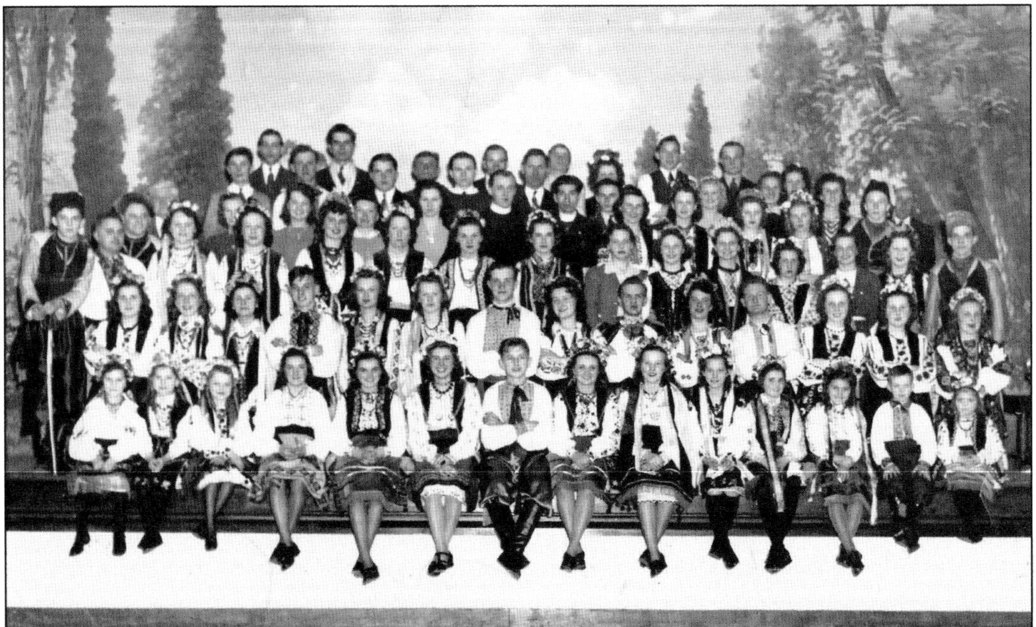

MONESSEN DANCERS. Students from Avramenko's dance troupes in Butler, Carnegie, McKees Rocks, Monessen, and Sharon gather to commemorate the birth of Taras Shevchenko in this 1941 photograph. Their instructor was Nick Arseny, and they were accompanied by a choir directed by Stephen Musiychuk. (Courtesy of Daria Pishko Komichak.)

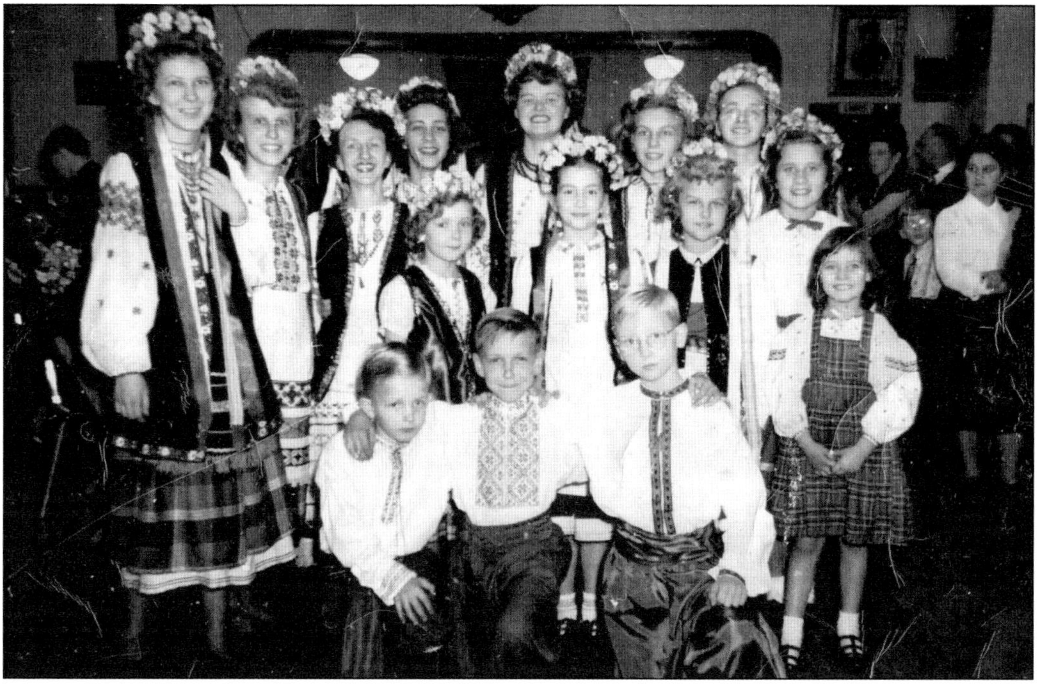

JEANNETTE DANCERS. The most popular form of attire for Ukrainian folk dance groups was the Kyivan style, as Kyiv is the country's capital. The boys wear *sharovary* pants, and the girls each sport a *vinok* on their heads with long, flowing ribbons. (Courtesy of Anna Mae Selembo.)

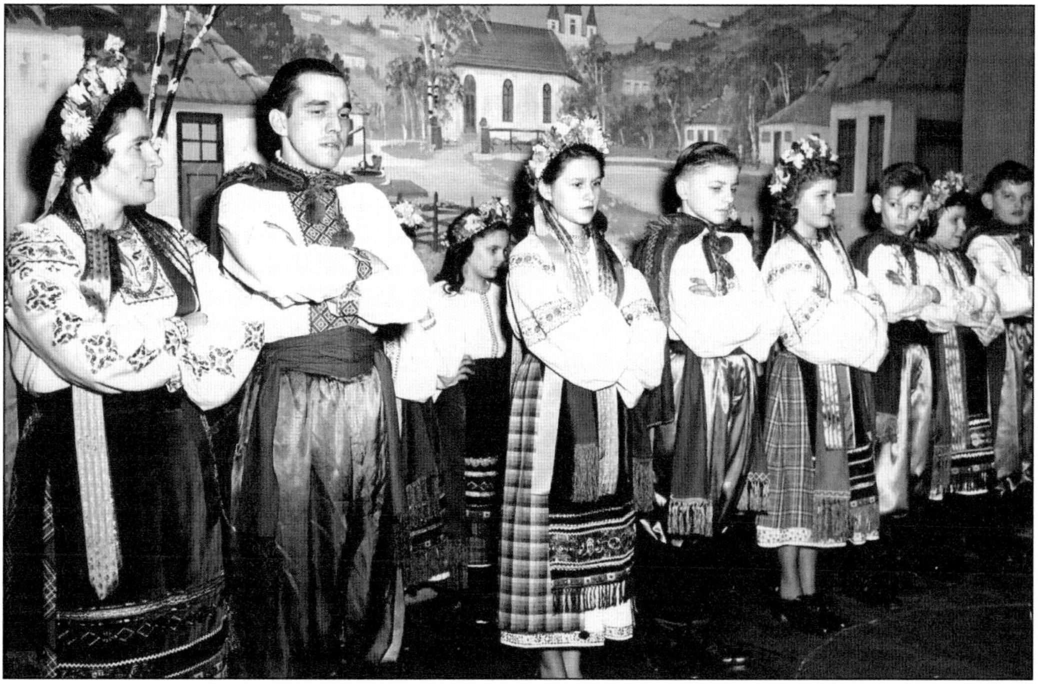

LYNDORA DANCERS. Performing on a stage with a backdrop of a Ukrainian village is the mixed-age dance troupe from SS. Peter and Paul Ukrainian Orthodox Church in Lyndora in the 1950s. (Courtesy of Barb Pupi.)

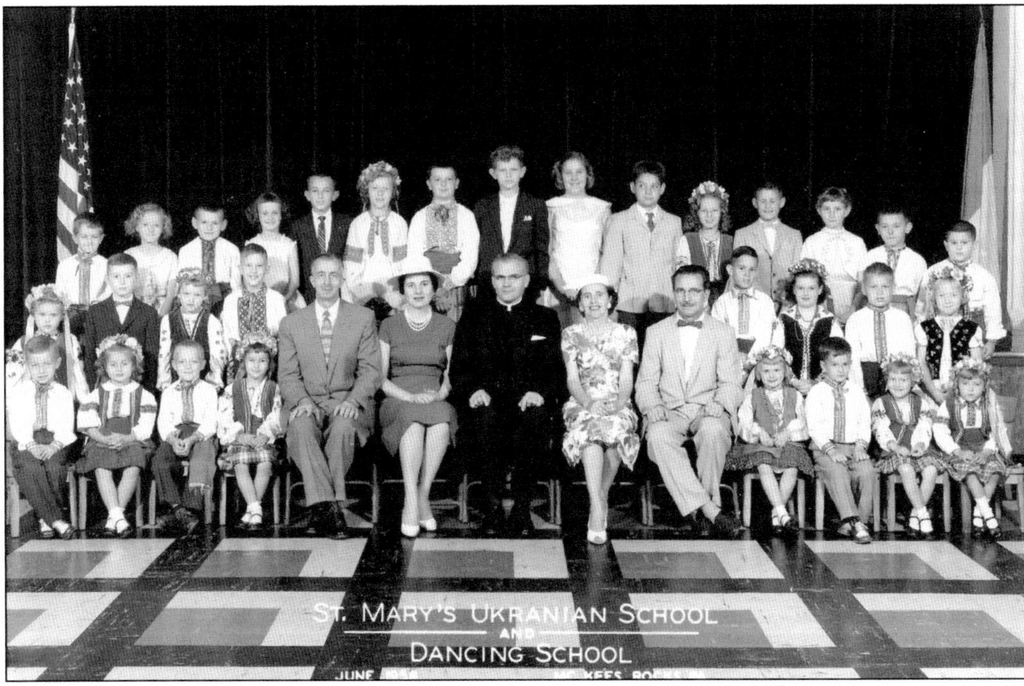

McKEES ROCKS DANCERS. Learning dances with names such as *hopak*, *metelytsya*, *vesnyanky*, *kozachok*, and *hutsulka*, children from St. Mary Ukrainian Orthodox Church in McKees Rocks stop for a photograph in the 1950s. (Courtesy of St. Mary Ukrainian Orthodox Church.)

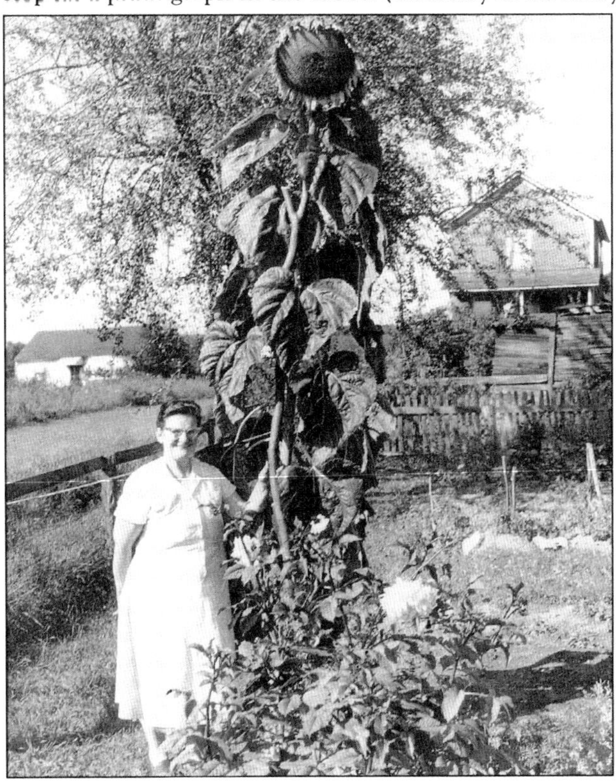

SUNFLOWERS. A veritable symbol of the fertility and bounty of the steppes of Ukraine, cultivation of the sunflower is essential to the economy of contemporary Ukraine. In this 1942 photograph, a proud Ukrainian American stands next to her prize-winning sunflower in her yard in Nanty Glo. (Courtesy of Irene Nestor.)

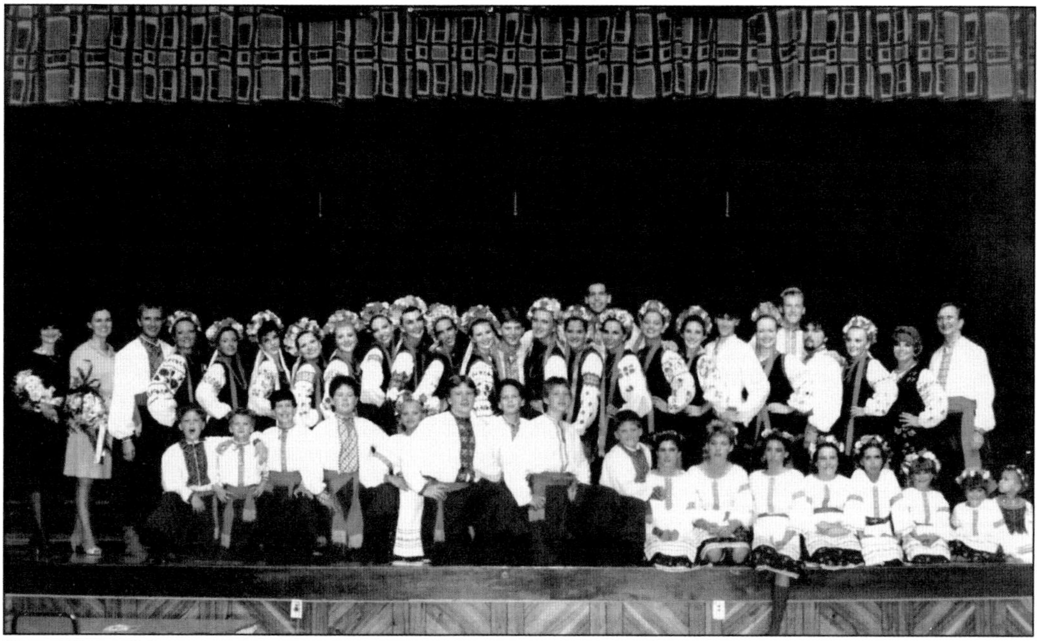

The Kyiv Ukrainian Dance Ensemble. SS. Peter and Paul Ukrainian Orthodox Greek Catholic Church in Carnegie has sponsored Ukrainian folk dance groups throughout its history dating back to the early 1900s. After various reorganizations and names, it adopted the name Kyiv in 1984 under the direction of Beverly Kapeluck and has attracted students from throughout western Pennsylvania, performing to this day. This July 1987 photograph was taken following a performance at the 40th Annual Convention of the UOL. (Courtesy of MASPPUOGCCC.)

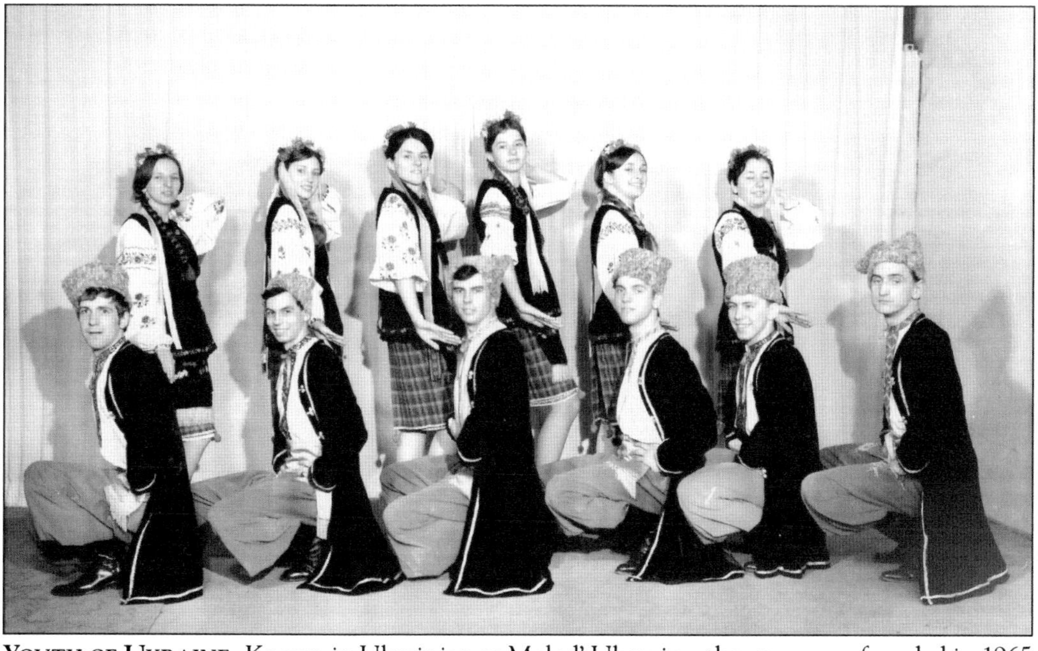

Youth of Ukraine. Known in Ukrainian as Molod' Ukrayiny, the group was founded in 1965 and performed extensively in the 1960s and 1970s including at the Pittsburgh Folk Festival. It was renamed the Poltava Dance Company in 1967. (Courtesy of Luba Hlutkowsky.)

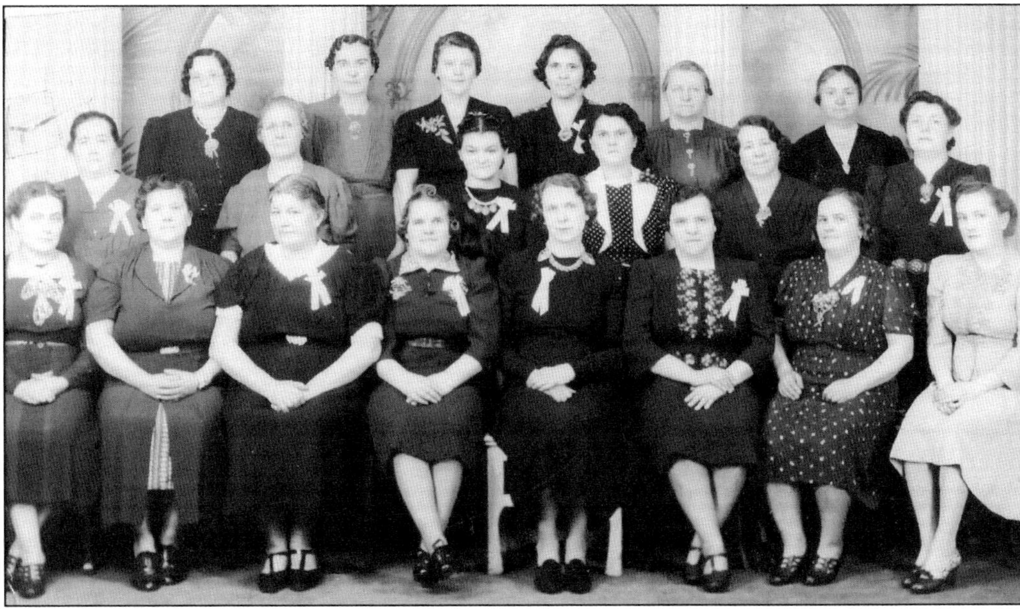

UKRAINIAN NATIONAL WOMEN'S LEAGUE OF NORTH AMERICA, BRANCH 27. The Ukrainian National Women's League of North America (UNWLA) was created in 1925, and branch 27 was founded in Pittsburgh in 1929 in honor of Olha Bassarab. UNWLA branches generally followed a calendar of events set up to commemorate significant Ukrainian cultural events and to support Ukrainian organizations. This photograph was taken in the 1940s. (Courtesy of Katherine Kiray.)

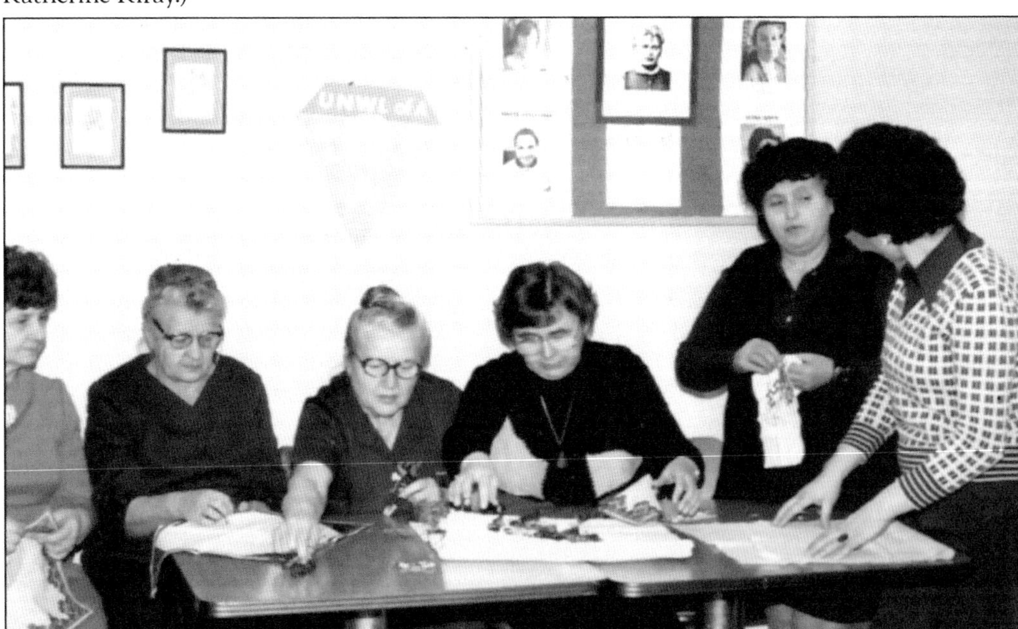

SOYUZ UKRAINOK. Best known by its Ukrainian variant, one of the main goals of UNWLA is to preserve and promote Ukrainian cultural arts. In this 1976 photograph, members conduct a workshop on Ukrainian embroidery, which is most easily differentiated from other cultures' embroidery by its intricate geometrical and floral patterns. (Courtesy of Marika Zaliszczuk.)

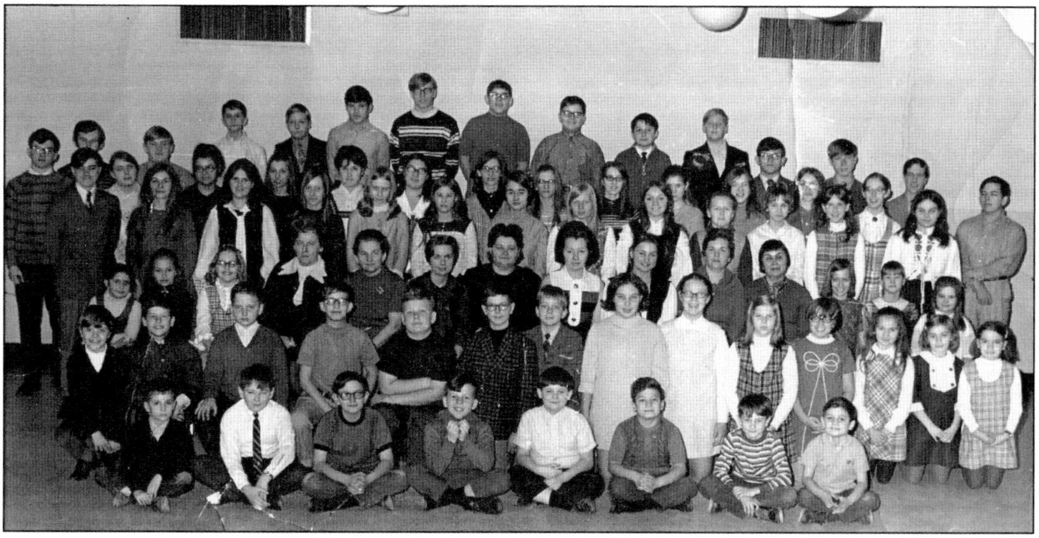

RIDNA SHKOLA. Students of the Ridna Shkola School of Ukrainian Studies of Pittsburgh pose for a group photograph during its founding year in 1969. The Ridna Shkola (native school) system consists of dozens of schools throughout the United States with classes usually held on Saturdays, and provides instruction in Ukrainian language, culture, history, and traditions. (Courtesy of Dana Krupnyk.)

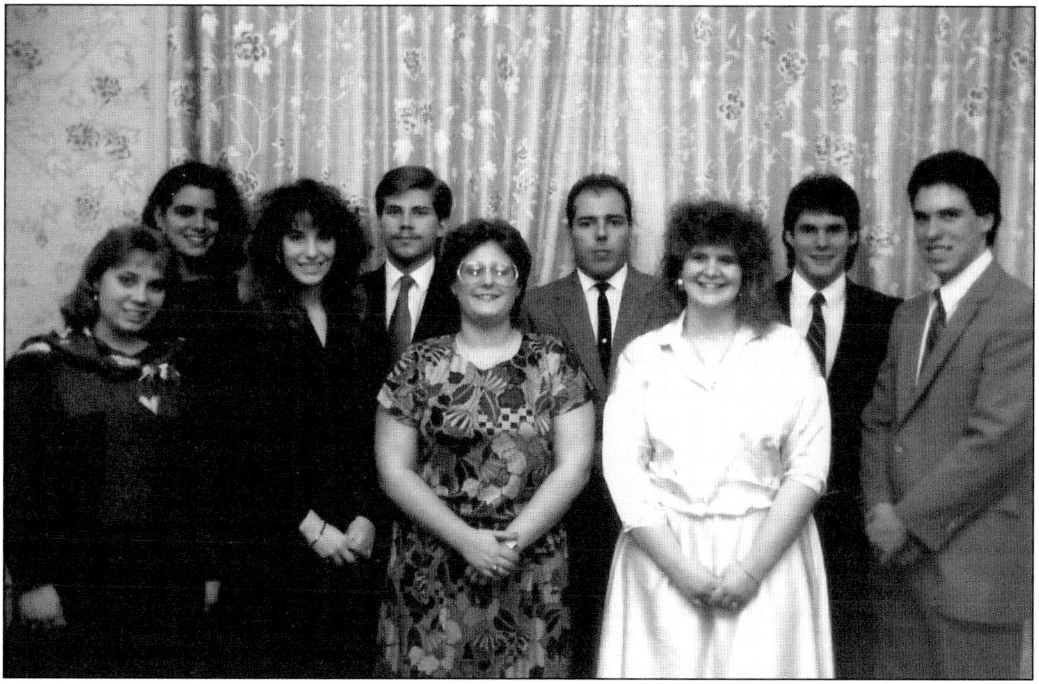

SCHOLARSHIPS. UTS started a scholarship program in 1973 to promote higher education among community members. To date, UTS has presented awards totaling $154,000 in 351 scholarships to 243 students. This photograph was taken following the 1987 awards program. (Courtesy of Nickolas C. Kotow.)

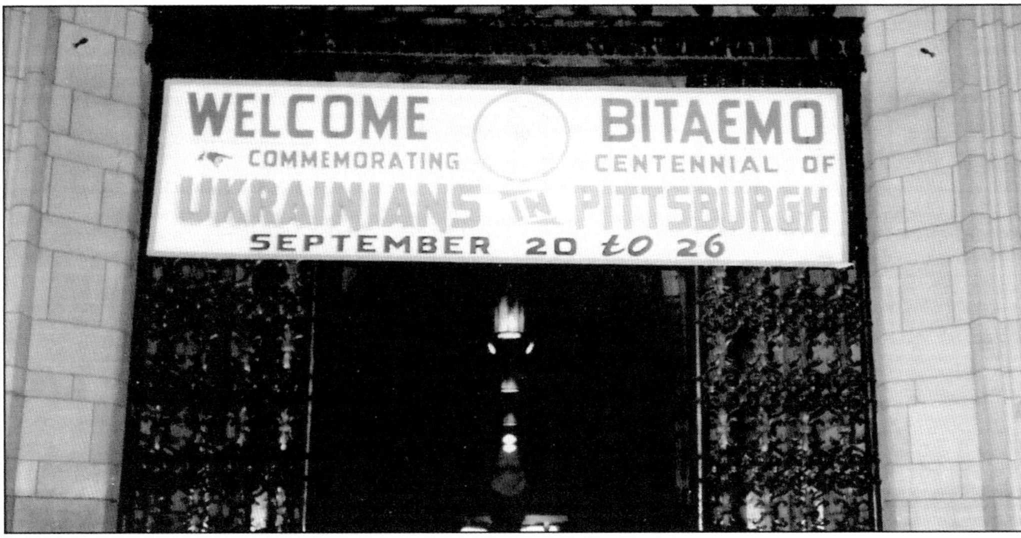

COMMEMORATING THE CENTENNIAL OF UKRAINIAN IMMIGRATION. One of the best-remembered events in the history of the Ukrainian American community of western Pennsylvania is the Pittsburgh Ukrainian Festival, held yearly at the end of September from 1982 through 2002 at the University of Pittsburgh's Cathedral of Learning in Oakland. The festival began as a fund-raiser for construction of the Ukrainian Nationality Room, located on the third floor of the cathedral. Seed money was provided by LUC and the Western Pennsylvania Region of the UOL for this combination food, entertainment, cultural, and educational festival. Over its 20-year span, the festival proved to be one of the most successful attempts to coordinate activities among the far-flung Ukrainian communities of western Pennsylvania and received a write-up in the August 2001 issue of *Better Homes and Gardens Hometown Cooking* magazine as one of the country's best ethnic festivals. The photograph above shows a banner hung in the Commons Room of the Cathedral of Learning and the photograph below shows Allegheny County Commissioners presenting a proclamation honoring the centennial and the establishment of the festival. (Above courtesy of Nickolas C. Kotow; below, courtesy of Roman Kyshakevych.)

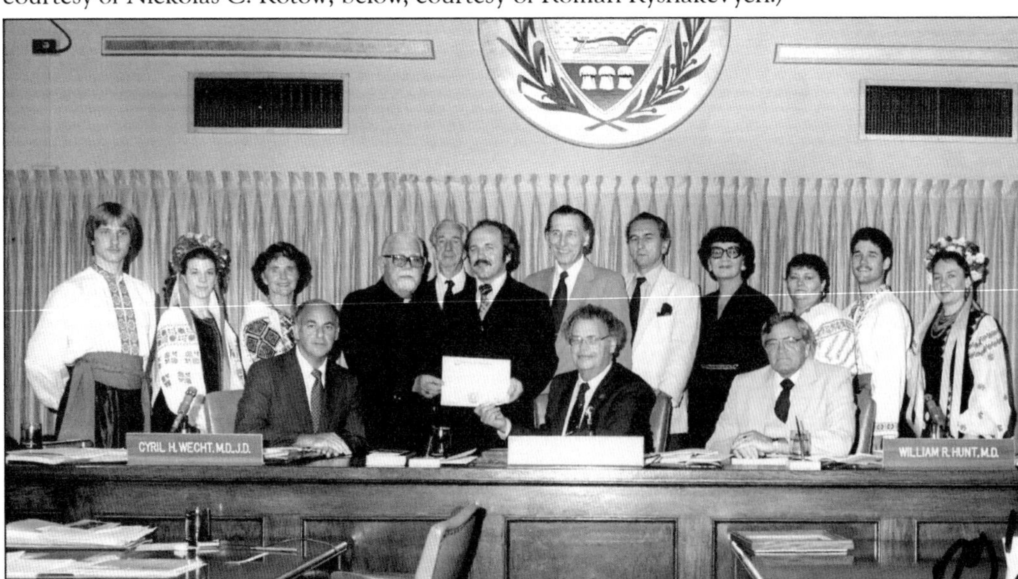

GERDANY. A festival artist demonstrates the art of Ukrainian *gerdany*, or beaded necklaces. A must-have for any Ukrainian woman, these necklaces range from simple chokers to elaborate long chains. (Courtesy of Nickolas C. Kotow.)

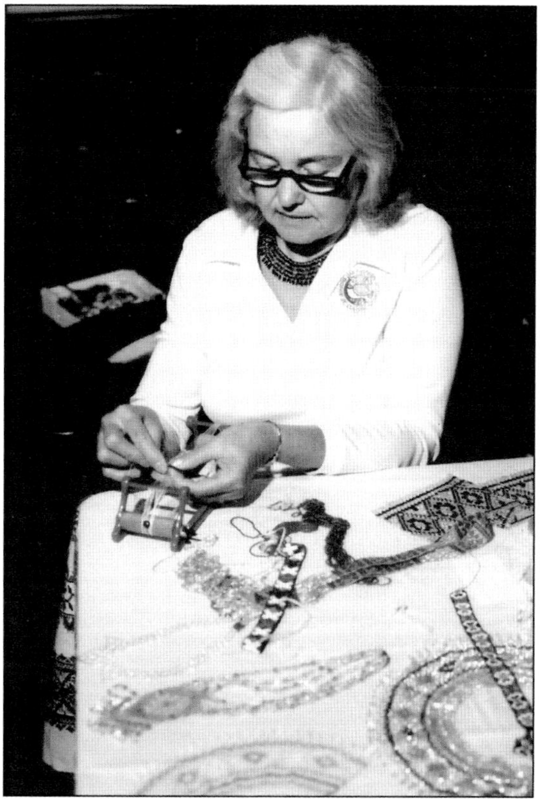

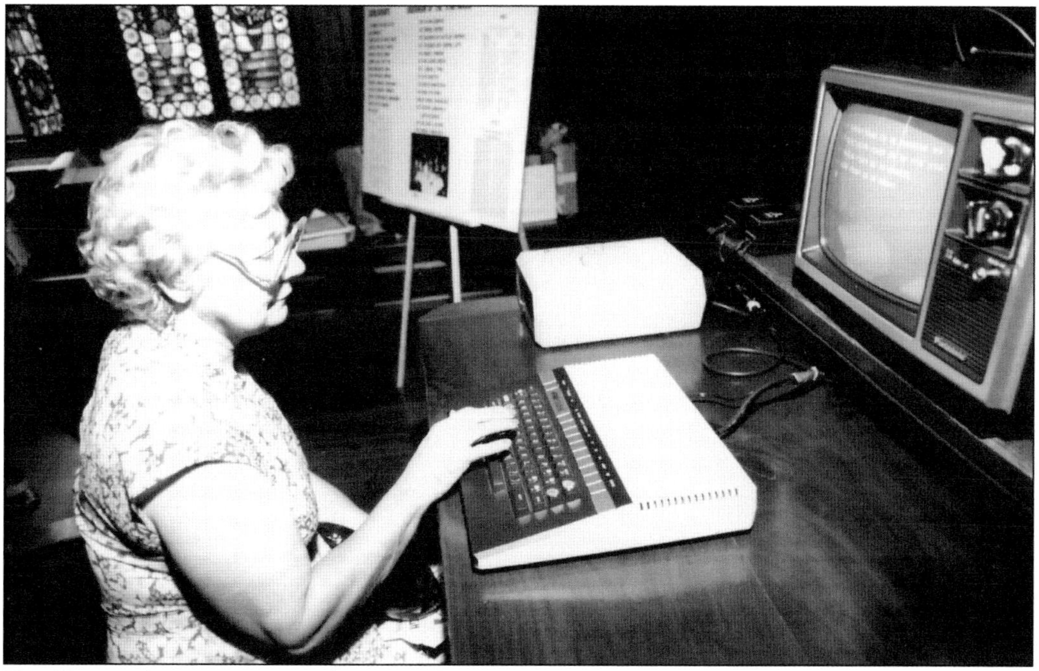

THE KOZAK QUIZ. Visitors to the 1984 Ukrainian festival could test their knowledge of Ukrainian history and culture using the latest in computer technology. (Courtesy of Nickolas C. Kotow.)

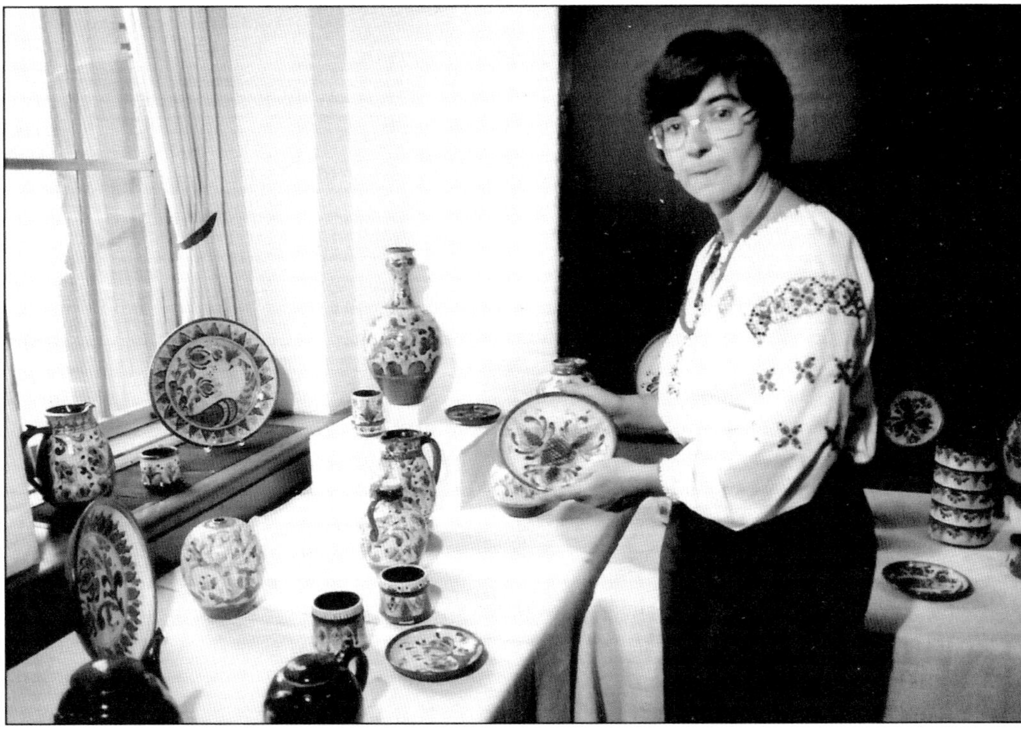

CERAMICS. Artist Natalia Kormeliuk was a regular at the festival demonstrating traditional ceramic arts, which gave festivalgoers an appreciation for the technique that went into the crafts they so eagerly bought. (Courtesy of Nickolas C. Kotow.)

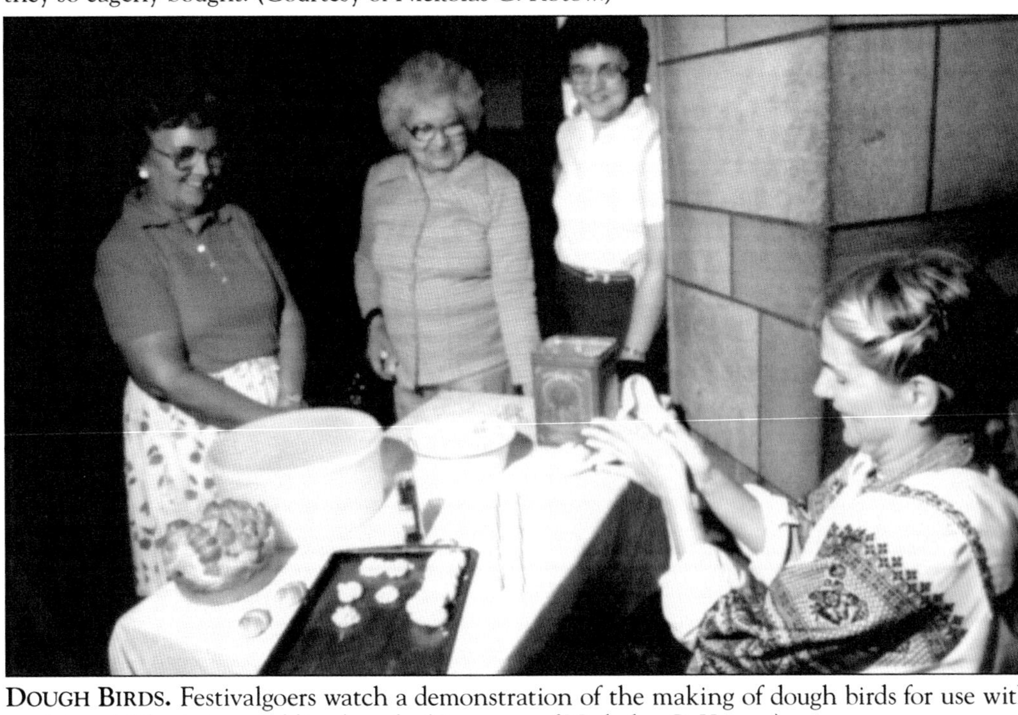

DOUGH BIRDS. Festivalgoers watch a demonstration of the making of dough birds for use with traditional Ukrainian wedding breads. (Courtesy of Nickolas C. Kotow.)

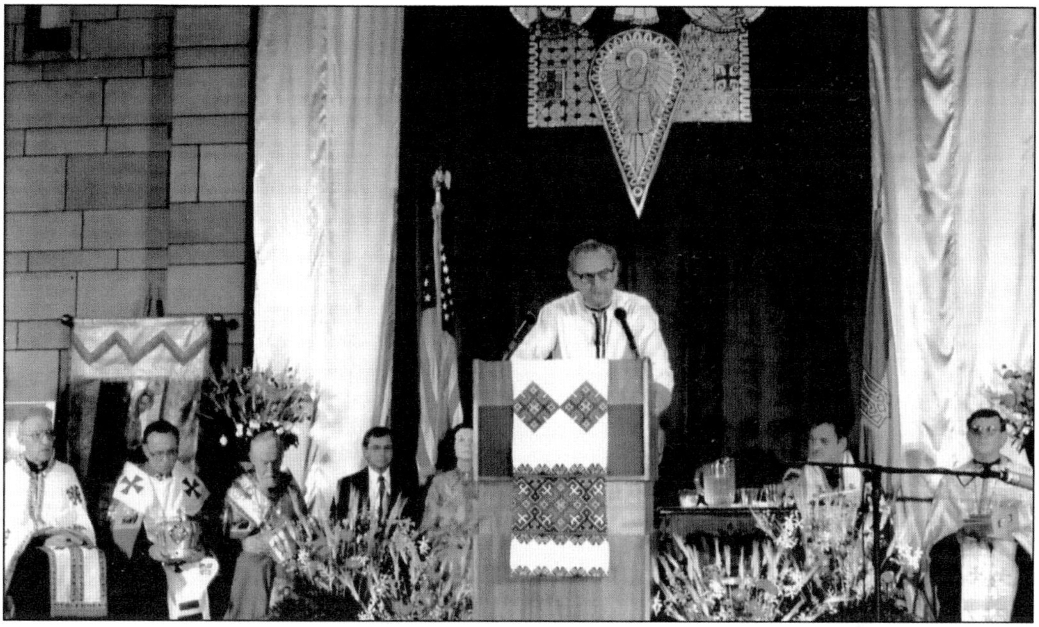

UKRAINIAN NATIONALITY ROOM DEDICATION. The goal of the Pittsburgh Ukrainian Festival was met with the 1990 completion of the Ukrainian Nationality Room, one of 27 such classrooms located in the University of Pittsburgh's Cathedral of Learning. Dr. George Kyshakevych was the driving force behind obtaining permission from the university to construct the room and led a community-wide effort to raise funds to cover its construction. (Courtesy of Michael Haritan.)

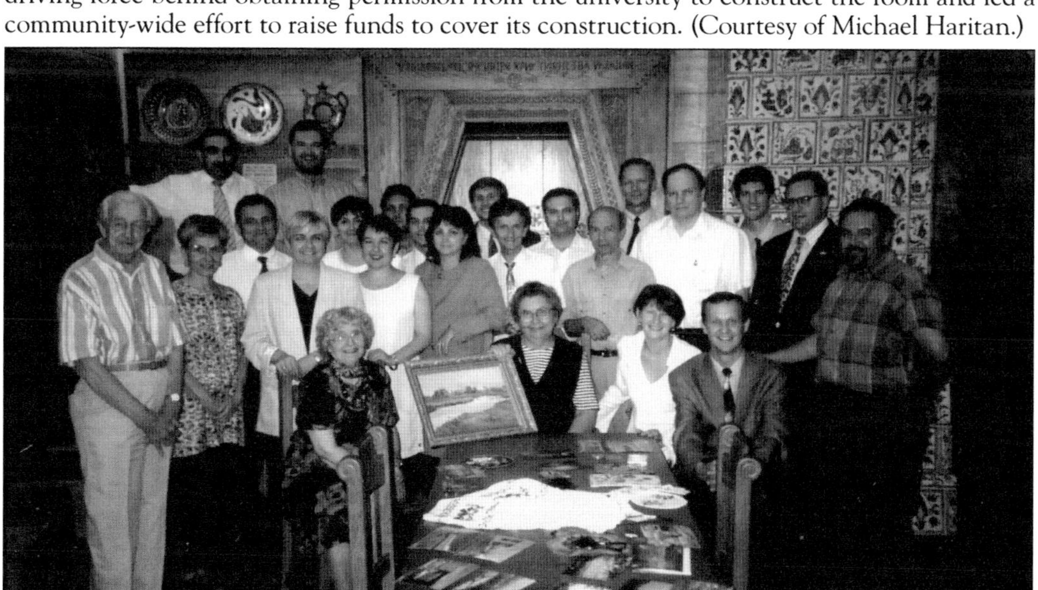

"WHEN A GUEST ENTERS THE HOUSE, GOD ENTERS THE HOME." The Ukrainian Room at Pitt, as it is colloquially known, is a must-see for Ukrainian visitors to the area, as demonstrated by members of the Ukrainian community as they receive a delegation of visitors from Ukraine in July 1997. It was modeled after an 18th-century residence of the Ukrainian nobility. Ukrainian wooden architecture is on display in the hand-carved beams, ceiling, and door. A copper bas relief depicting the history of Ukraine, a porcelain tile oven, and intricate metalwork are other features of this room. (Courtesy of UCHI.)

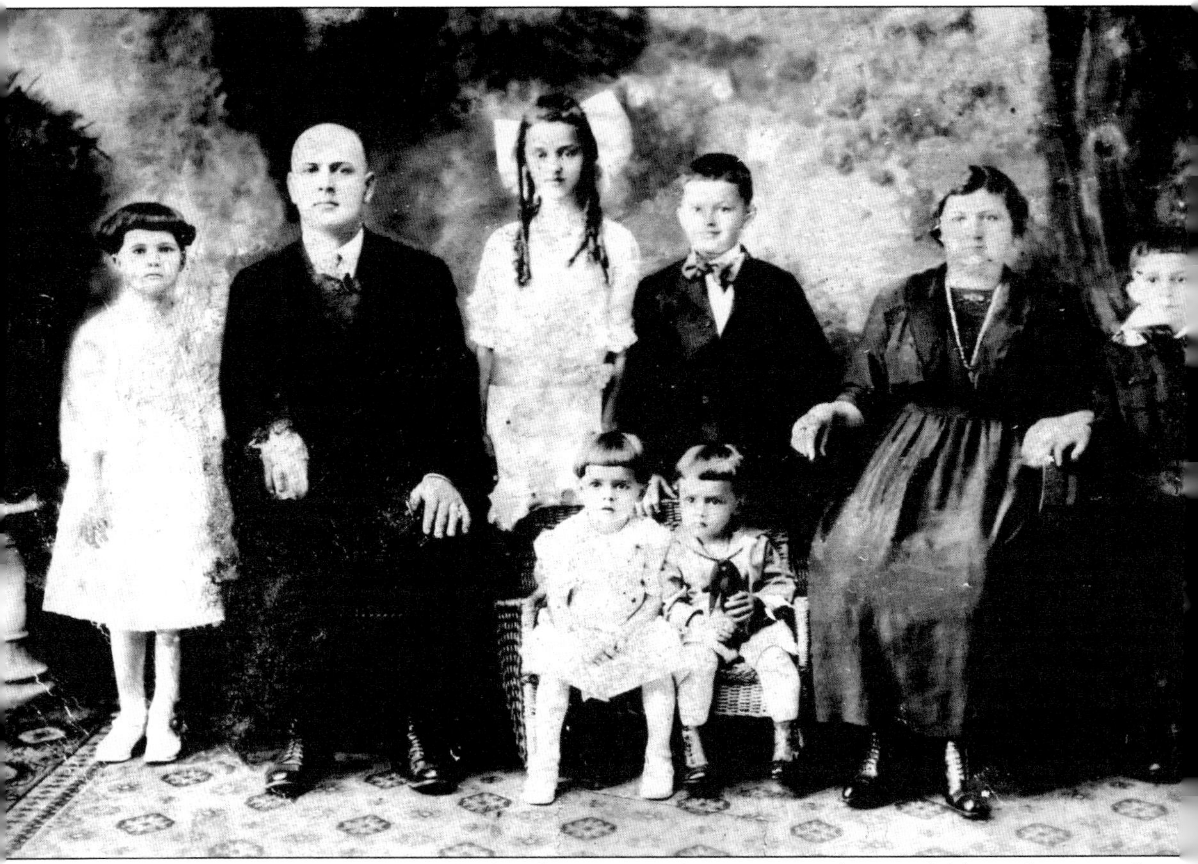

THE SHEVCHENKO LADY. Mildred Fall Kyrimes of McKees Rocks is a lifelong devotee of Ukrainian poet Taras Shevchenko and has proudly declaimed his poetry at community gatherings throughout the years. Pictured on the far left next to her father, she wrote this poem in honor of her father and all forefathers throughout Ukrainian communities in western Pennsylvania. "His name was John Fall. / He was a resident of McKees Rocks, / A member of St. Mary's Ukrainian Orthodox Church. / He was my father. / He came to America in 1903 at age 16, / He reared a family of six children. / Self-taught, he rose from laborer to chief inspector of diesel passenger engines. / He was my father. / Like a cobbler, he repaired our shoes. / Like a barber, he gave us haircuts. / Like a carpenter, he built cupboards, made benches, and repaired our furniture. / He was my father. / Like our neighbors, we were all very poor. / He reminded us that our poverty was never an excuse for immorality, lawlessness, or irresponsibility! / He was my father. / He made us proud of our Ukrainian heritage. / He introduced us to Shevchenko's poetry. / He taught us Ukrainian folk songs. / He was my father. / I thank God for my father, John Fall / and for all those other Ukrainian fathers, who organized parishes and built those beautiful churches. / Who also built those impressive halls for comradery, concerts, dances, dramas, and countless Ukrainian independence rallies. / Who joined together in brotherhoods, providing insurance, funds, publications, and other services / as they continued to support their families and rear their children according to God's precepts. / May their memory be eternal." (Photograph courtesy of Carol Kyrimes; poem courtesy of Library and Archives Division, Senator John Heinz History Center.)

Four

Ukrainian Ingredients in the Melting Pot

An Exotic Blend

Ukrainians in western Pennsylvania do not have a strong history of segregating themselves into distinct ethnic neighborhoods and have always been somewhat integrated into the general community. In addition to the towns represented in this book, the *40th Anniversary Jubilee Book of the UNA*, published in 1936, identified these other western Pennsylvania towns with organized Ukrainian communities: Bentleyville, Butler, Canonsburg, Derry, Donora, Etna, Export, Forbes Road, Homer, Houtzdale, Iselin, Leechburg, Lundy's Lane, Smoke Run, Titusville, Vandergrift, and Yatesboro. There are surely more communities with a history of organized Ukrainian life that this publication has not been able to identify.

Additionally, the vast geographical dispersion of Ukrainians in western Pennsylvania diluted their numbers and prevented the phenomenon of a "Ukrainiantown." Distinct areas with significant Ukrainian populations did develop, particularly in the early days. Many of these communities still have significant Ukrainian American populations, and recently arrived Ukrainian immigrants have followed them there.

Some evidence of this integration is that many Ukrainian Americans in western Pennsylvania have occupied roles in local government. In his 1990 study *Ukrainians in American Politics*, Stephen P. Hallick-Holutiak Jr. identified 26 successful officeholders, who held positions over the years in the towns of Ambridge, Arnold, Carnegie, Ford City, Lyndora, McKees Rocks, Monessen, Stowe, and Wilmerding. His study points out that most of them served on school boards and as mayors or council people in primarily smaller municipalities.

Another manifestation of integration regards Ukrainian surnames and their orthographic variations, retentions, and changes. Again, Stephen Hallick-Holutiak, in initial research for his 1994 study *Dictionary of Ukrainian Surnames in the USA*, found that only about 8 percent of Ukrainian surnames collected in western Pennsylvania had been changed deliberately. Career advancement, prejudice, simplification, and a desire to become "American" were given as reasons. Additional Americanization of surnames includes double letter equivalents, adjustment of vowels and diphthongs, loss of the soft sign, and the simplification of consonant clusters.

Geography, intermarriage, and confusion over identity have posed challenges for organized Ukrainian communities over the years. The long struggle for independence and recognition unified a diverse community, and the transition to an established, more cosmopolitan identity has occurred. An increasingly closer connection with the non-Ukrainian community has developed and Ukrainians in western Pennsylvania can now fully share their culture with an ever more interested American public. Universities, nonprofit groups, hobbyists, businesspeople, students, and others are taking a greater interest in Ukraine and its people, and the landscape of western Pennsylvania shows this.

In the end, the many Ukrainian communities of western Pennsylvania demonstrate a strong tradition of preserving the past while planning for the future. They have added quite a few Ukrainian ingredients to the melting pot of western Pennsylvania, and their flavor can easily be tasted throughout the region.

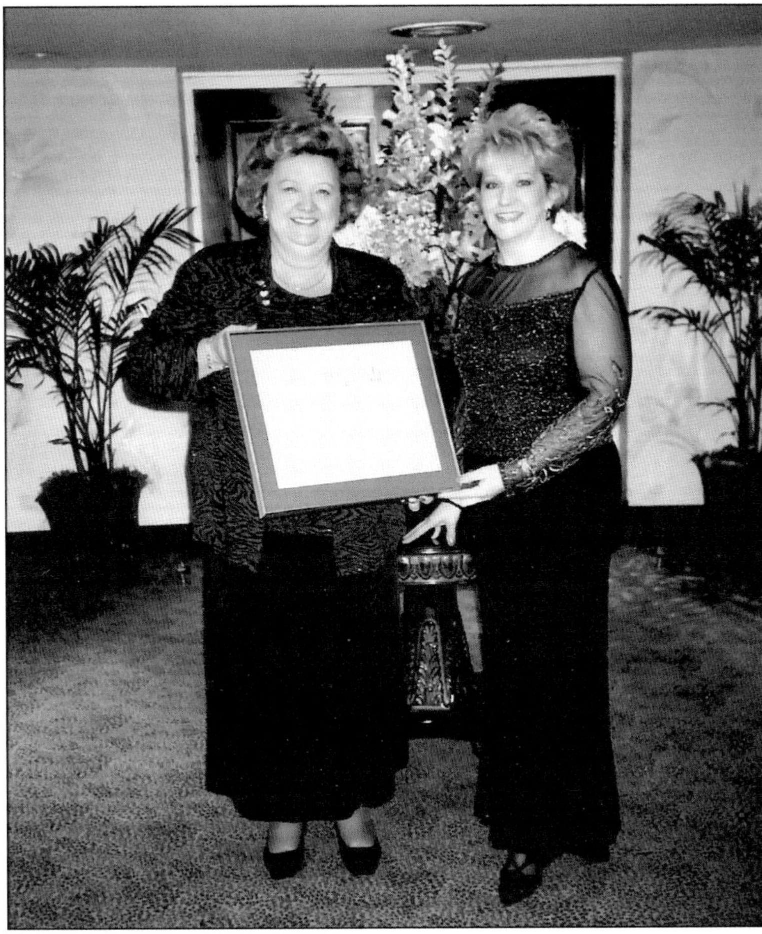

UKRAINIAN OF THE YEAR. UTS president Debra Walenchok presents the society's annual Ukrainian of the Year Award to Nadia Komarnyckyi McConnell, president of the US-Ukraine Foundation, in November 2003 at the Churchill Valley Country Club. UTS was founded in 1970 as a society of Ukrainian professionals in western Pennsylvania. It presents this award to local, national, or international figures based on technological or professional accomplishments, contributions to the perpetuation of Ukrainian heritage, and/or humanitarian achievements. Awardees include Stepan Chemych; Michael Maynosz; Metropolitan Mstyslav of the Ukrainian Orthodox Church of the United States of America; Patriarch Joseph I–Cardinal Slipyj of the Ukrainian Catholic Church; Michael Komichak; Very Rev. George Hnatko; Sydir Michael Tymiak; Osyp Zinkevych; Chester Manasterski; Nadia Svitlychna; George Kyshakevych, DMD; Kateryna Dowbenko and Luba Hlutkowsky; Very Rev. Wasyl Dzydzora; Michael Korchynsky; Theodore Hrycyk; Tatiana Kyshakevych, Ph.D.; Metro Staroschak; Wasyl Jaszczun, Ph.D.; Rt. Rev. Andrew Beck; Olga S. Manasterski; Marta Pisetska Farley; Hon. Leonid Makarovych Kravchuk; Ulana M. Diachuk; Andrew S. Gregorovich; John Smith; Nickolas C. Kotow; Danylo Husar Struk, Ph.D.; Lubomyr T. Romankiw, Ph.D.; Michael John Jula; Joanne Staroschak; Hon. Bohdan A. Futey; Bohdan Hryshchyshyn; Nadia Komarnyckyj McConnell; Mitred Archpriest Michael Poloway; Hon. Viktor Andriyovych Yushchenko; Taras G. Szmagala; Michael Kutsenkow, MD; and Daniel W. Pituch, DMD, MD. The UTS also presents a Friendship Award to a non-Ukrainian person or entity in recognition of service to Ukraine and/or Ukrainians. Awardees include Gail Shrott; the Norwin Pennsylvania Chapter of Rotary Club International; Andrew N. Farley; and Marlies Backhaus Murphy, MA. (Courtesy of UCHI.)

UKRAINIAN TOPONYMS. Toponyms are place names, and in his *Slavic Toponymic Atlas of the United States*, Stephen P. Hallick-Holutiak Jr. identified seven Ukrainian toponyms in western Pennsylvania. The first photograph is an honorary title bestowed by the Borough of McKees Rocks for the block in front of St. Mary Ukrainian Orthodox Church marking the church's 100th anniversary. The second shows Odessa Place, which is located in the Lincoln-Lemington neighborhood of the city of Pittsburgh. The street was originally named Odessa Alley and was adopted from popular usage of Jewish immigrants from the Ukrainian city of Odessa—a seaport located on the Black Sea. Maliniak Street, Sarniak Avenue, and Skurkay Avenue in Monessen are all located in an area once known as Sarniak Farms. Other Ukrainian toponyms in western Pennsylvania, such as Ukrainian Street in Monessen, the Mazeppa Furnace (a blast furnace used in the iron industry in the mid-1800s) in the abandoned village of Mazeppa Post Office near Mercer; and Odessa, a small town north of Clearfield, have since been renamed. (Courtesy of UCHI.)

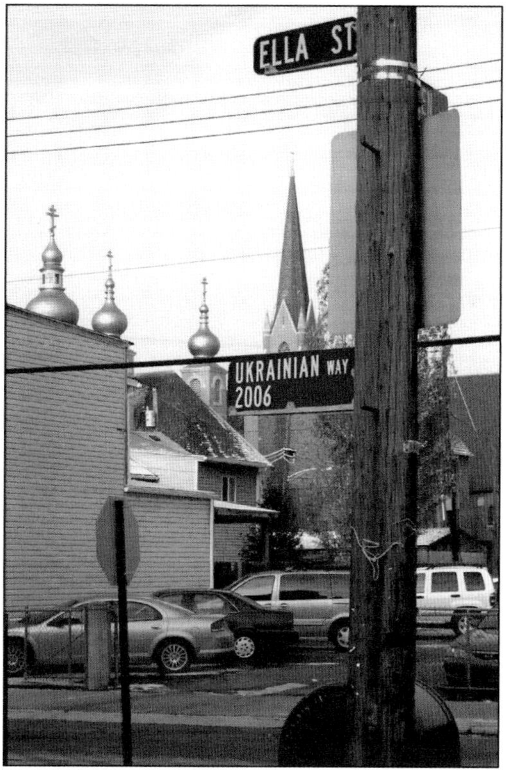

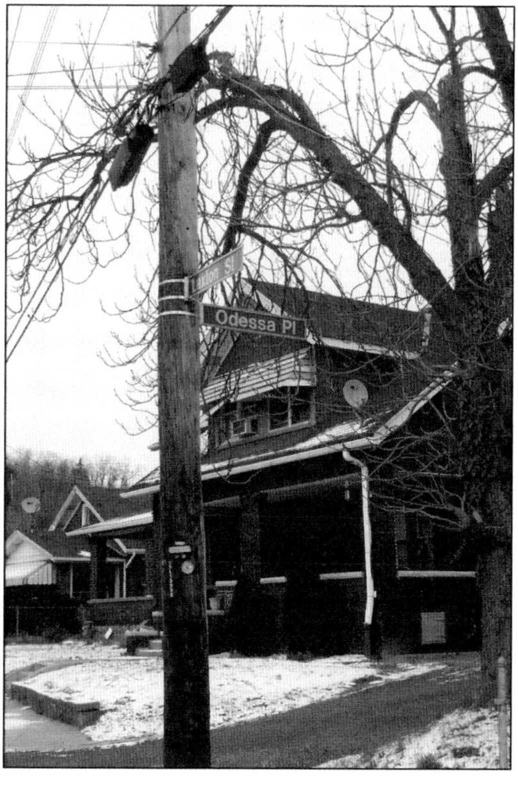

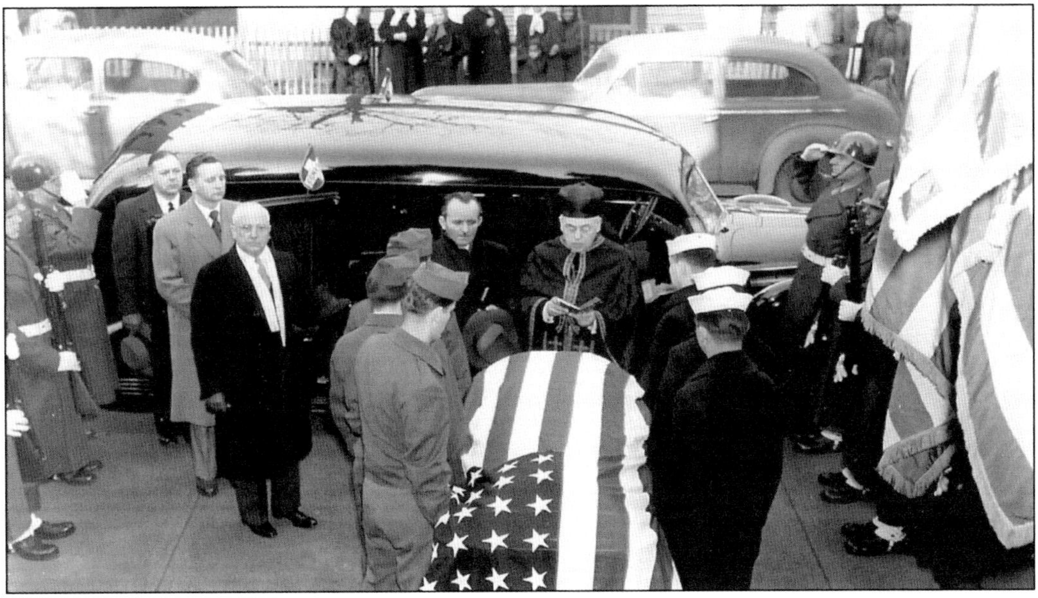

World War II. Ukrainians across western Pennsylvania took part in the war effort, and many gave their lives. Pvt. George Popivchak, a paratrooper of the 507th Parachute Infantry 82D "All American" Airborne Division, was killed at Normandy at age 24. The parish of St. John the Baptist Ukrainian Catholic Church in McKeesport reported the deaths of 10 of its sons in the war, and every Ukrainian parish reports the active involvement of its parishioners in the war effort. (Courtesy of Mark F. Popivchak.)

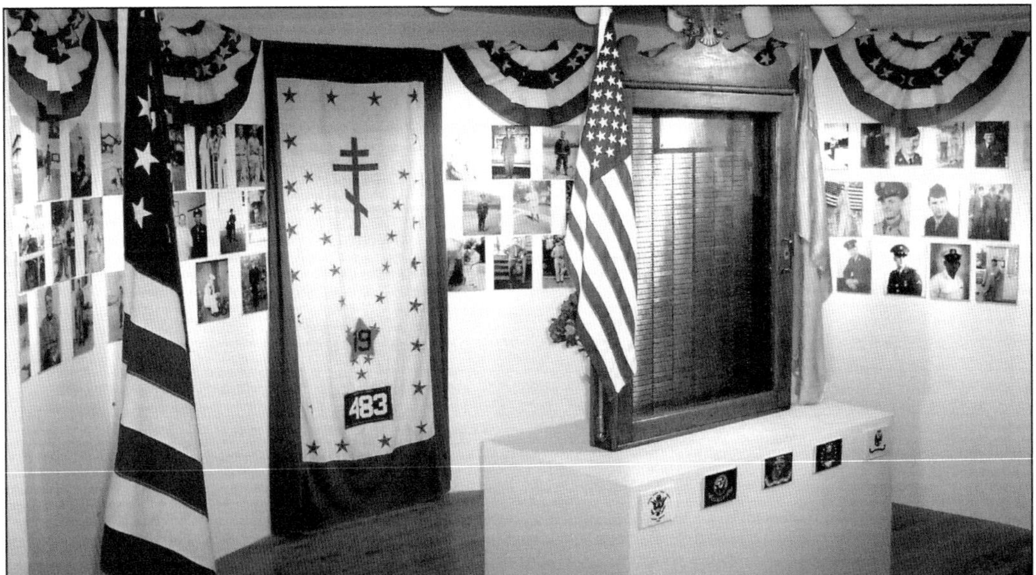

Remembering. This display from the museum of SS. Peter and Paul Ukrainian Orthodox Greek Catholic Church in Carnegie honors the efforts of parishioners, who served the United States in World War II. In the foreground is a memorial with brass plates listing some of the names of parishioners who served in the war. The flag in the background hung in the church throughout much of the war, and notes that 483 parish members served and 19 died. Photographs of some of the parish's servicemen are reproduced along the walls. (Courtesy of UCHI.)

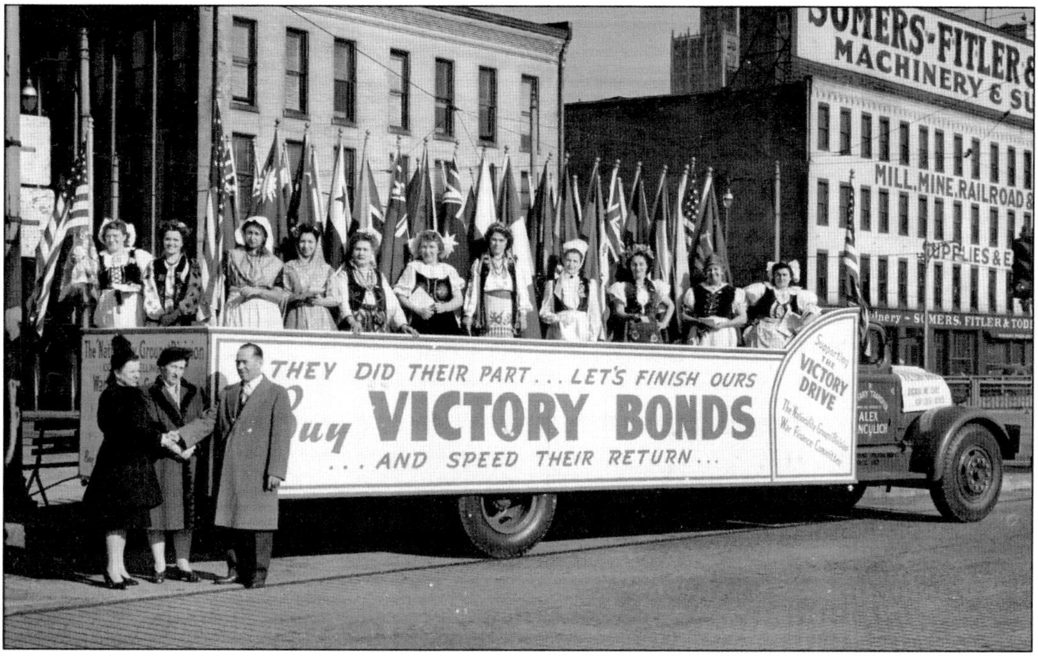

Doing Their Part. Two young western Pennsylvania Ukrainian women stand alongside those of other ethnic groups in this truck, which traveled the streets of the city of Pittsburgh encouraging residents to buy war bonds, which were used to finance the U.S. war effort. (Courtesy of Katherine Kiray.)

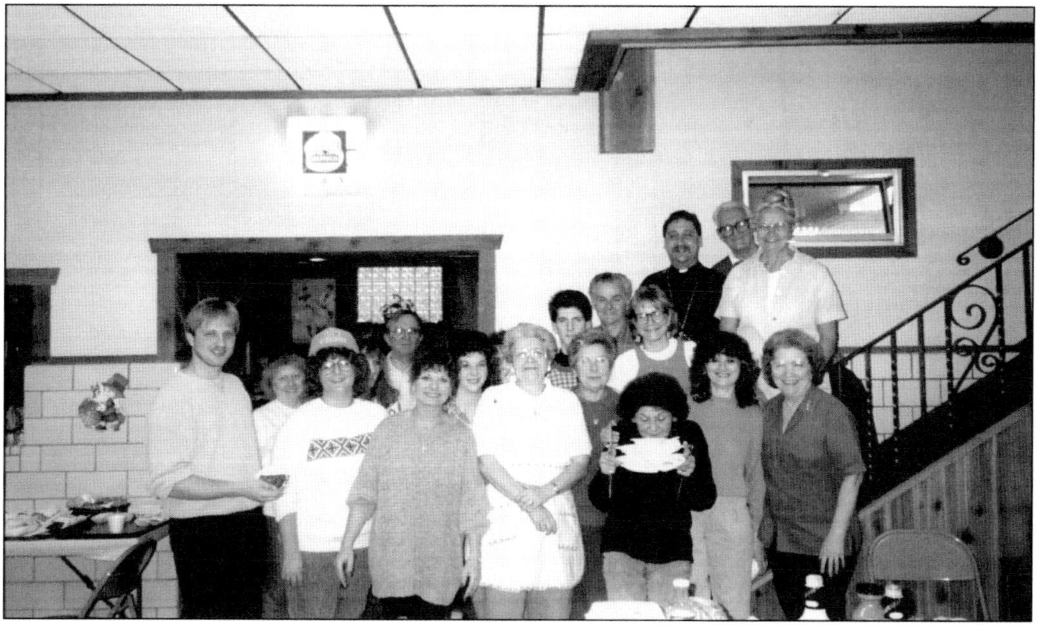

Thanksgiving Outreach. Members of SS. Peter and Paul's in Carnegie began hosting a Thanksgiving dinner for the community in 1989 to provide fellowship and a place to enjoy the holiday for those less fortunate. An annual event since then, many nonparishioners assist in the preparation, serving, and delivering of meals to homes for the elderly and those who cannot leave their homes. (Courtesy of MASPPUOGCCC.)

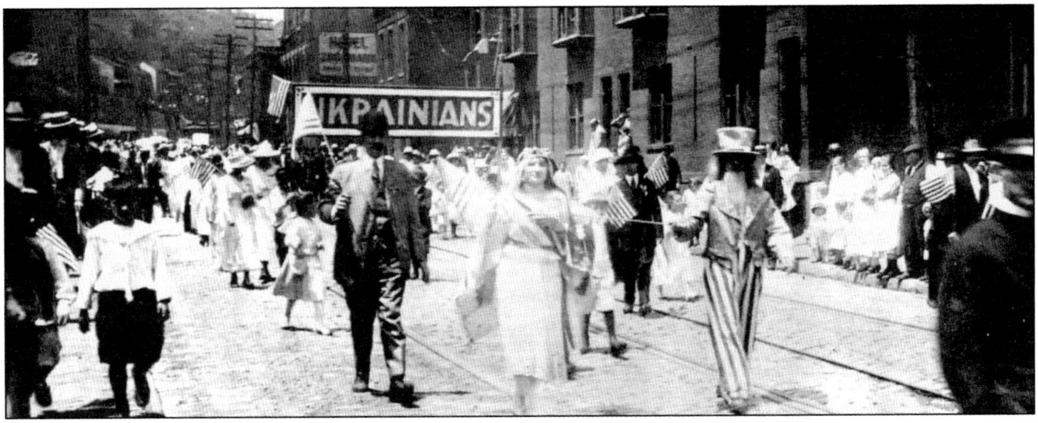

PATRIOTISM. Ukrainians from Pittsburgh's South Side neighborhood march in a parade down Carson Street in this photograph taken shortly after World War I. (Courtesy of St. John the Baptist Ukrainian Catholic Church.)

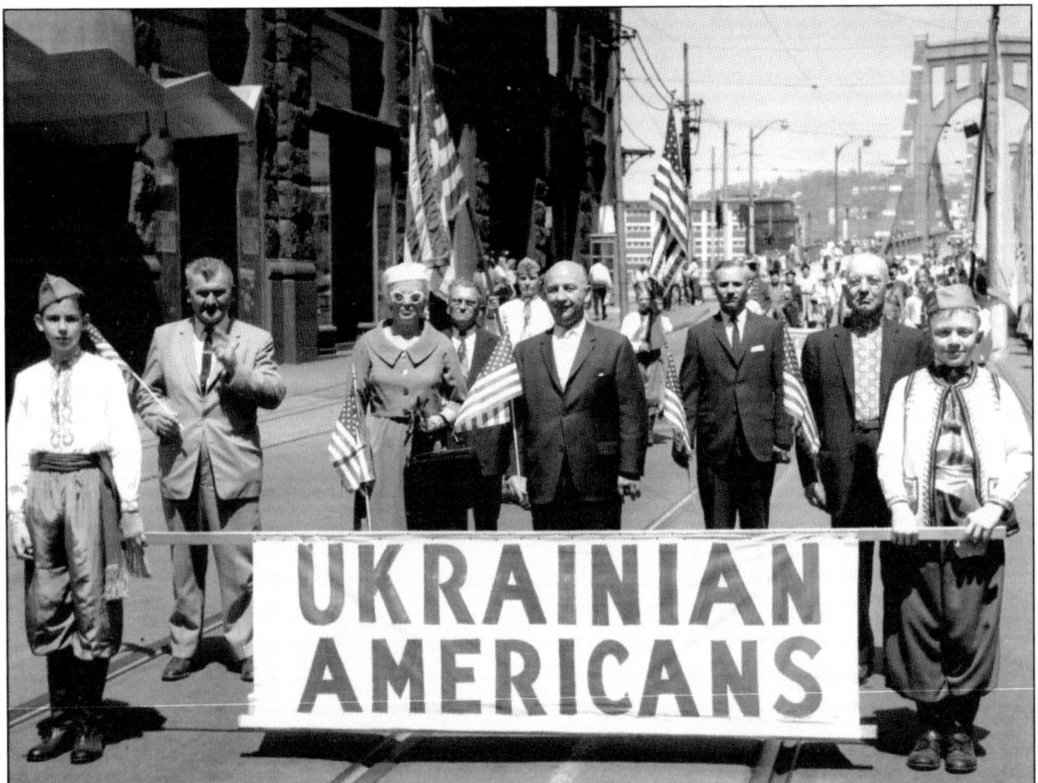

LOYALTY DAY. Originally known as Americanization Day, this official U.S. holiday started in 1921 as a counter to the Communists' May 1 celebration of the Russian Revolution. It evolved into Loyalty Day by a congressional resolution in 1949. Western Pennsylvania Ukrainians take part in this May 4, 1962, parade, which took marchers from West Park in the city's North Side through downtown to the Pittsburgh City-County Building on Grant Street. Grand marshal for the parade was August R. Madera, commander of the Allegheny County Council Veterans of Foreign Wars (VFW). (Courtesy of Michael Komichak.)

Butler Bicentennial. Gregory and Pauline Pawluk ride the Ukrainian float during the city of Butler's Bicentennial Parade. Pauline presents the traditional Ukrainian greeting of bread and salt, while Gregory holds a sheaf of wheat, representing Ukraine's status as the "breadbasket of Europe." A large pysanka stands behind them. (Courtesy of George Pawluk.)

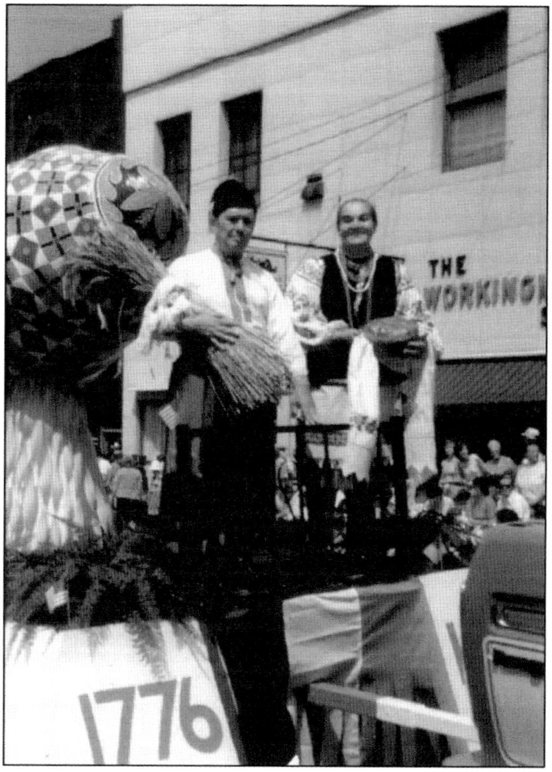

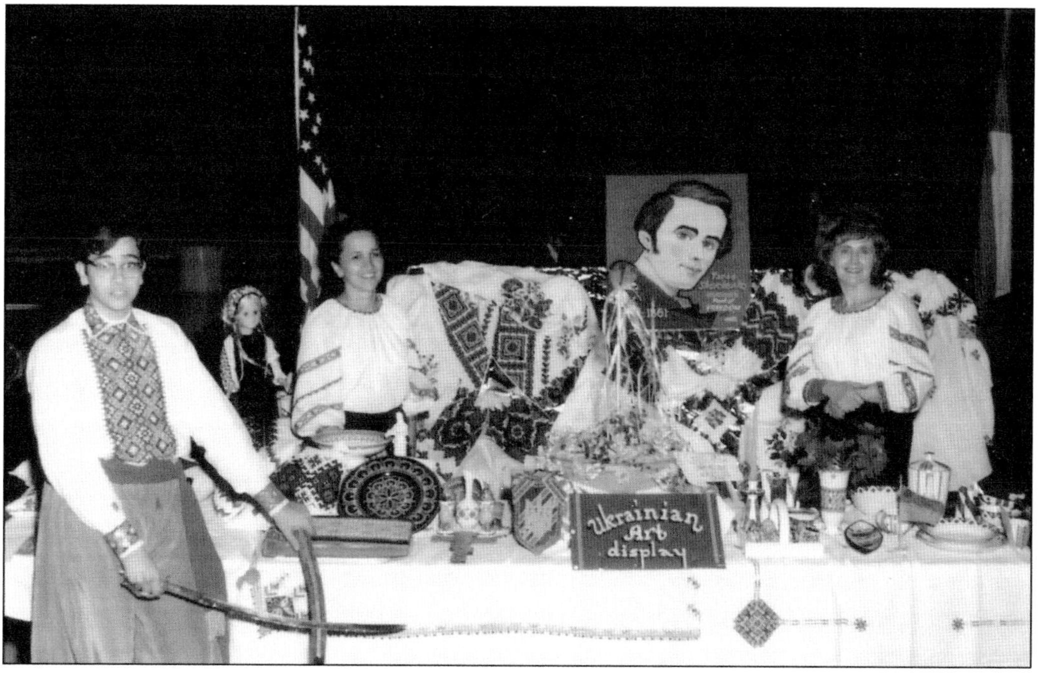

McKees Rocks Nationality Festival. Ukrainians from McKees Rocks proudly display cultural artifacts at this local festival of nationalities in 1969. (Courtesy of LAVRSHH.)

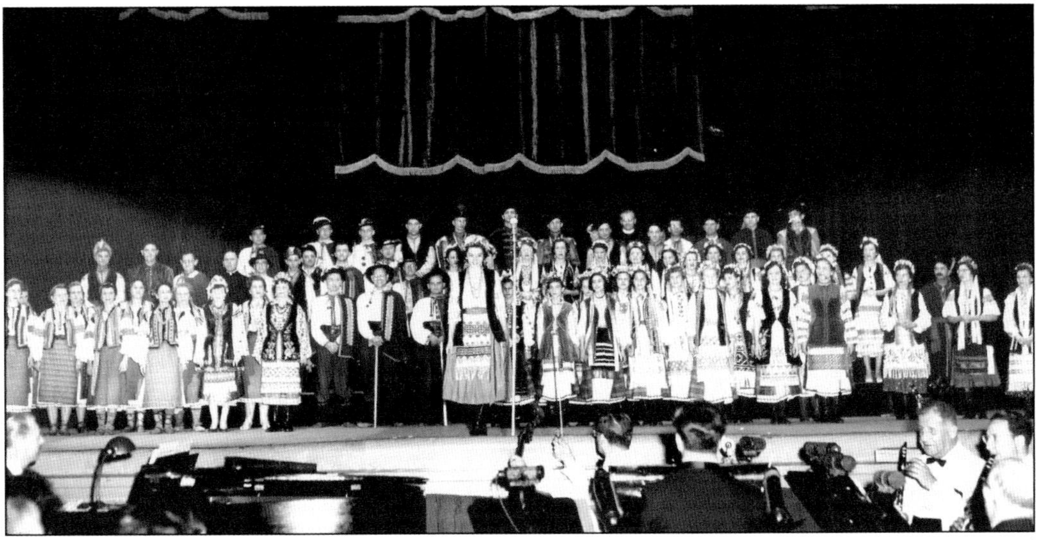

THE PITTSBURGH FOLK FESTIVAL. Ukrainians were one of seven original ethnic groups invited to participate in the first Pittsburgh Folk Festival, held at the Syria Mosque in Oakland in June 1956. The festival's purpose is to promote unity in diversity and is today preparing its 53rd festival with the representation of more than 25 ethnic groups. In the first photograph, Prof. Osyp Holowackyj, professional musician and *dyak* (teacher) at St. Mary Ukrainian Orthodox Church in McKees Rocks, conducts the Western Pennsylvania Regional Choir of the Ukrainian Orthodox League, which was accompanied by members of the Pittsburgh Symphony. The LUC has represented the Ukrainian community at the folk festival since 1957 in conjunction with the UNWLA Branch 27 and the Poltava Ukrainian Dance Company. The second photograph is of the Ukrainian cultural booth at a more recent festival. (Above, courtesy of MASPPUOGCCC; below, courtesy of Roman Kyshakevych.)

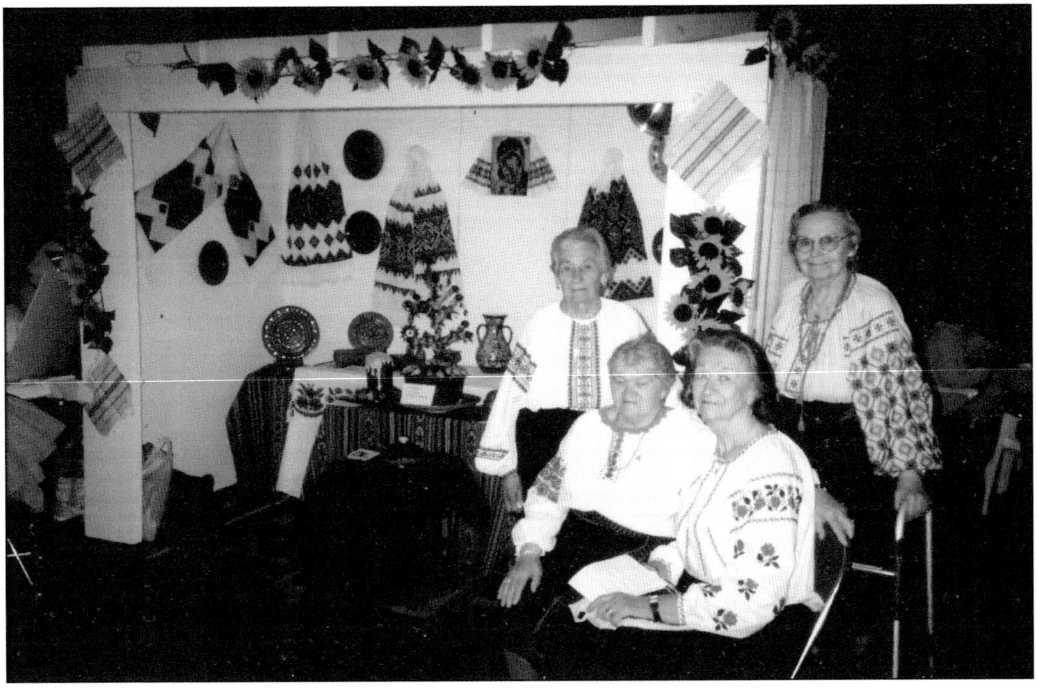

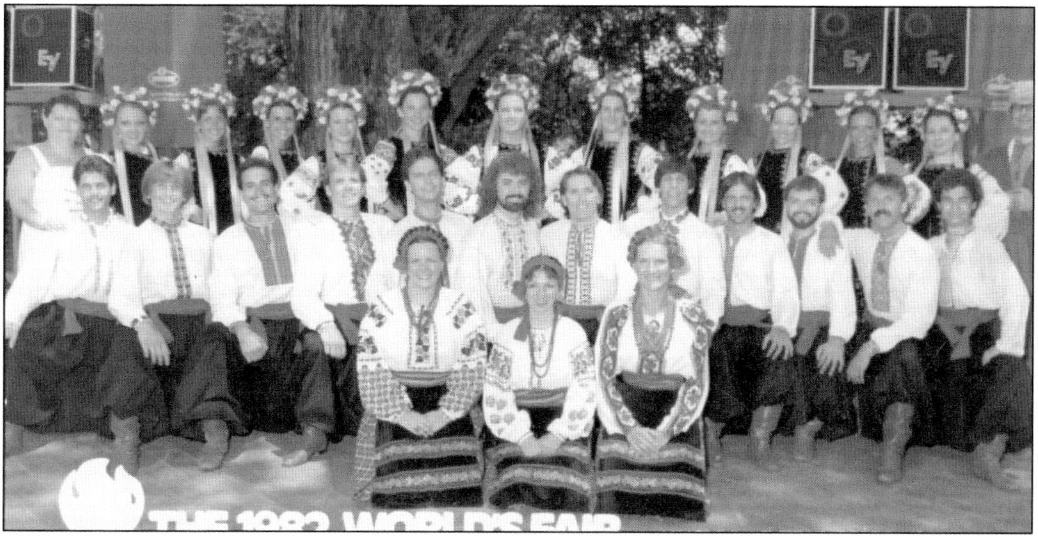

The 1982 World's Fair. The Poltava Ukrainian Dance Company was invited to perform at the 1982 World's Fair held in Knoxville, Tennessee. Posing with the company and its director Luba Hlutkowsky are the ladies of the vocal trio Veselka. (Courtesy of Luba Hlutkowsky.)

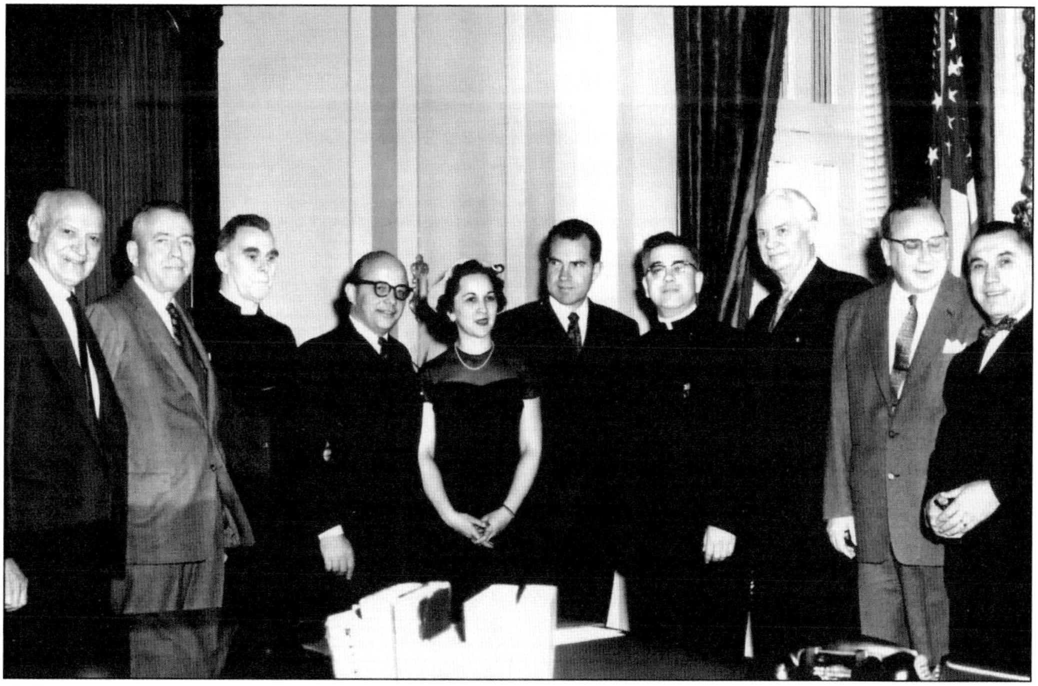

A Prayer before Congress. Fr. Stephen Hallick-Holutiak was invited to give the invocation at the U.S. Senate on January 22, 1958, on the occasion of the 40th anniversary of the proclamation of the independence of the UNR. In this photograph, he and his wife pose with then vice president Richard M. Nixon and other dignitaries at a reception that followed. (Courtesy of LAVRSHH.)

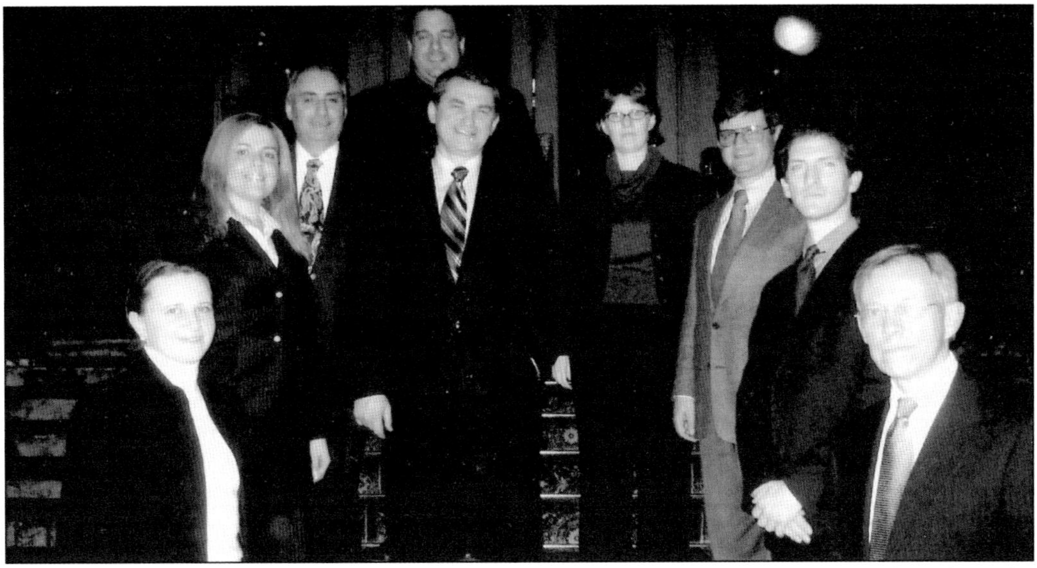

Visit of the Ukrainian Ambassador. His Excellency Dr. Oleh Shamshur (center), ambassador extraordinary and plenipotentiary to the United States from Ukraine, visited western Pennsylvania in March 2007 and poses in this photograph with board members of the Ukrainian Cultural and Humanitarian Institute (UCHI). The main purpose of his visit was to present information on the investment and business climate in Ukraine to the local business community and included meetings with local government officials and members of the Ukrainian community. (Courtesy of UCHI.)

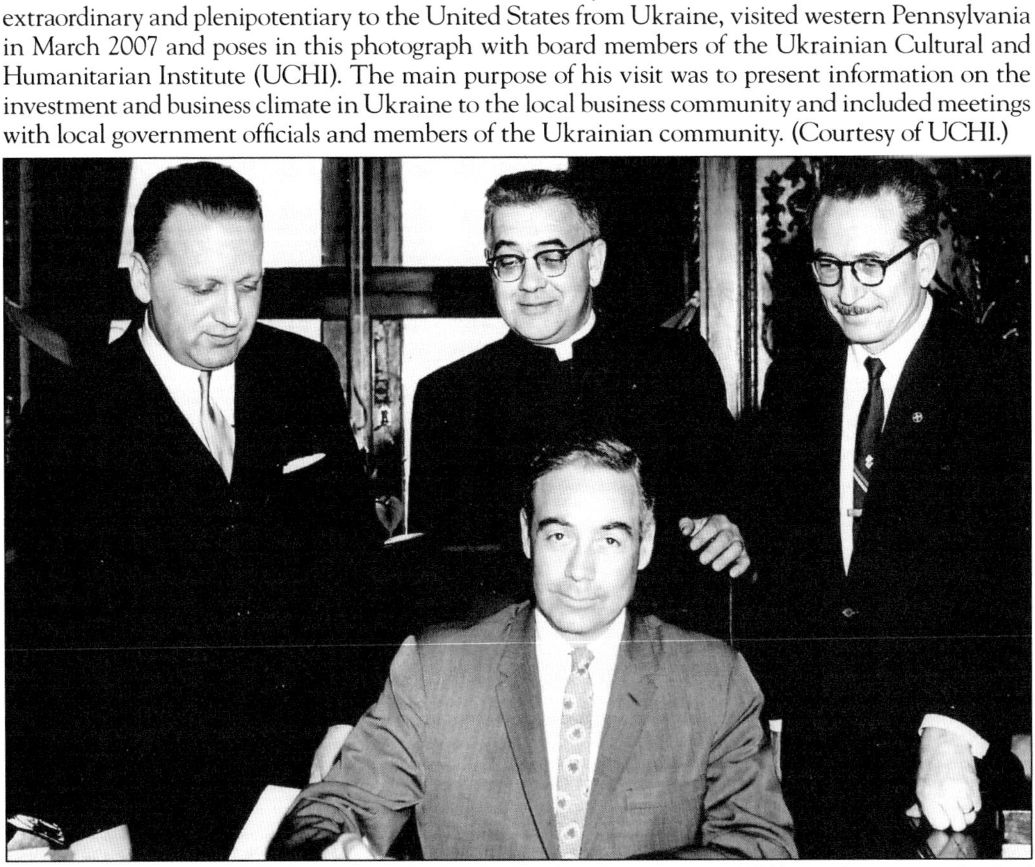

In the Halls of State Government. Pennsylvania governor William Scranton, flanked by representatives of Ukrainian communities from western Pennsylvania, signs a proclamation commemorating Ukrainian Independence Day in 1963. (Courtesy of LAVRSHH.)

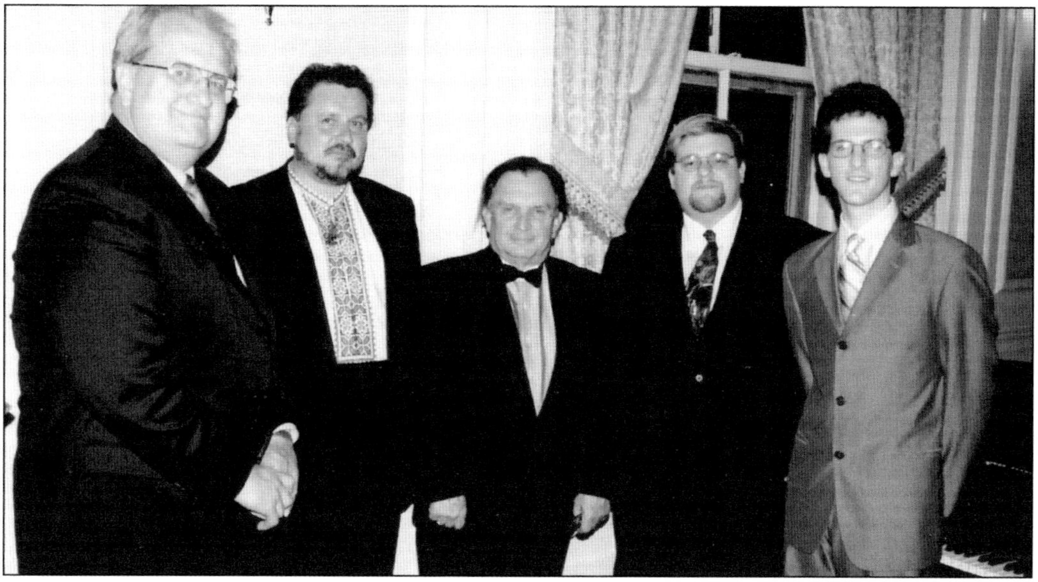

AN EVENING OF UKRAINIAN CLASSICAL MUSIC. Western Pennsylvania Ukrainian American and Pennsylvania state representative Nick Kotik stands on the left in this 2004 photograph with, from left to right, Kharkiv-born bass Vitaliy Lomakin, UCHI board member and violinist Jaropolk Lassowsky, pianist Michael Flohr, and UCHI president Stephen Haluszczak following the organization's fund-raiser held at the University Club in Oakland. Pieces by Ukrainian composers Mykola Lysenko and Mykhaylo Hayvoronsky were featured. (Courtesy of UCHI.)

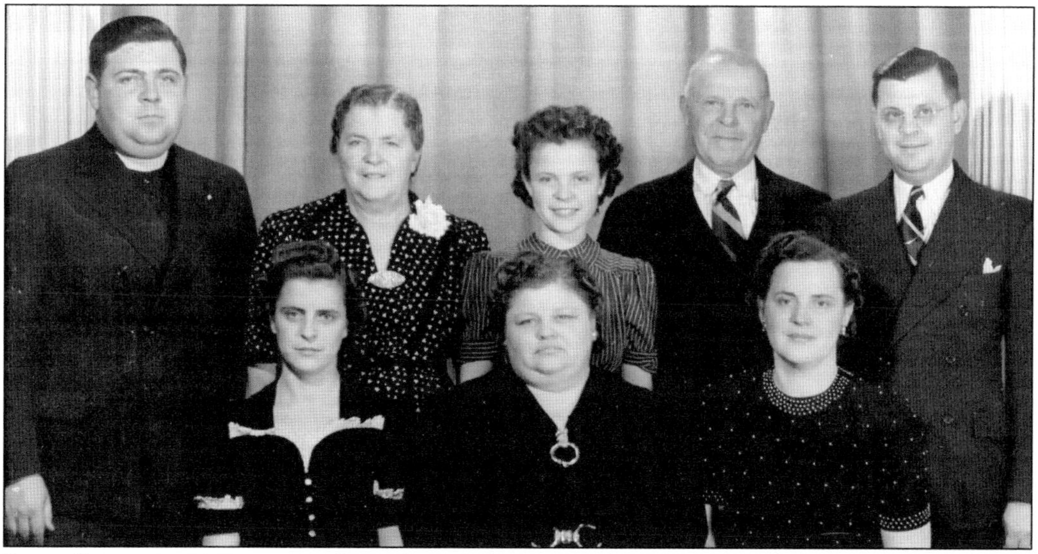

BECK SIBLINGS. At a time when the involvement of women in politics was a rarity, Ford City–born Mary Beck (first row, right) was elected to the city council of Detroit, Michigan, in 1950, serving for 20 years including a tenure as president. Recognized as the first Ukrainian woman in America to become an attorney, she was active in the establishment of several UNWLA chapters, was longtime editor of its journal *Zhinochiy Svit* (women's world), and was a well-known Ukrainian community activist throughout her life. Her brother Andrew (second row, left) became a Ukrainian Orthodox priest and served in parishes in Carnegie and Monessen and was the dean of its Western Pennsylvania deanery for a time. (Courtesy of Dorothy Korey.)

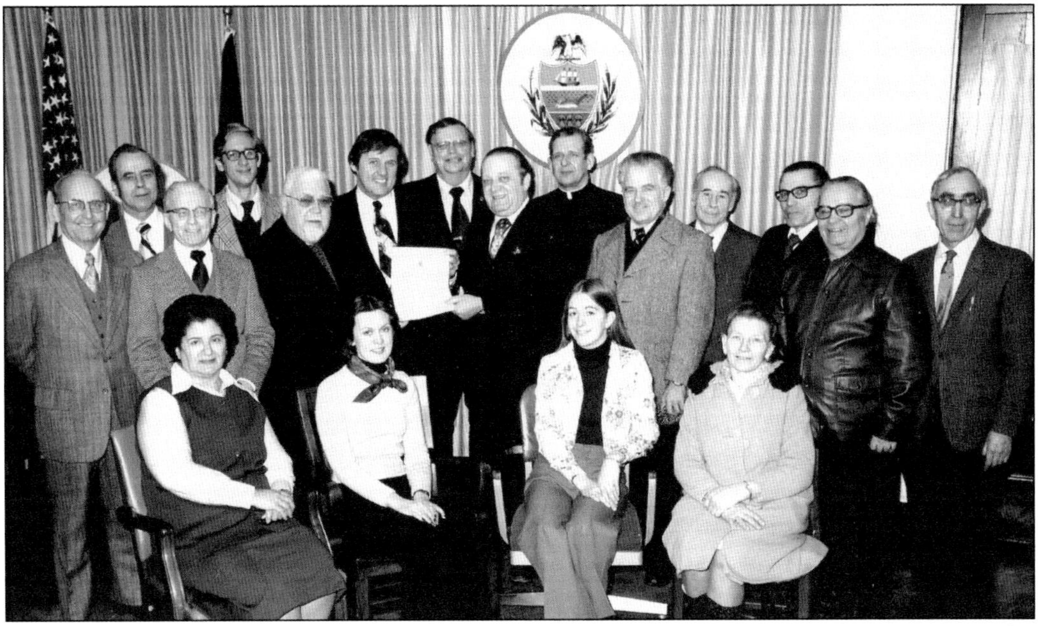

MEETING THE MAYOR AND THE ALLEGHENY COUNTY COMMISSIONERS. Members of the western Pennsylvania Ukrainian community are presented with proclamations commemorating Ukrainian Independence Day. The photograph above was taken with the county commissioners in 1977, and the one below shows Pittsburgh mayor Bob Barr with local Ukrainians around 1962. Civic proclamations recognizing important events in the life of the Ukrainian community were a popular way for Ukrainians to promote knowledge of their culture and community over the years. (Above, courtesy of MASPPUOGCCC; below, courtesy of Roman Kyshakevych.)

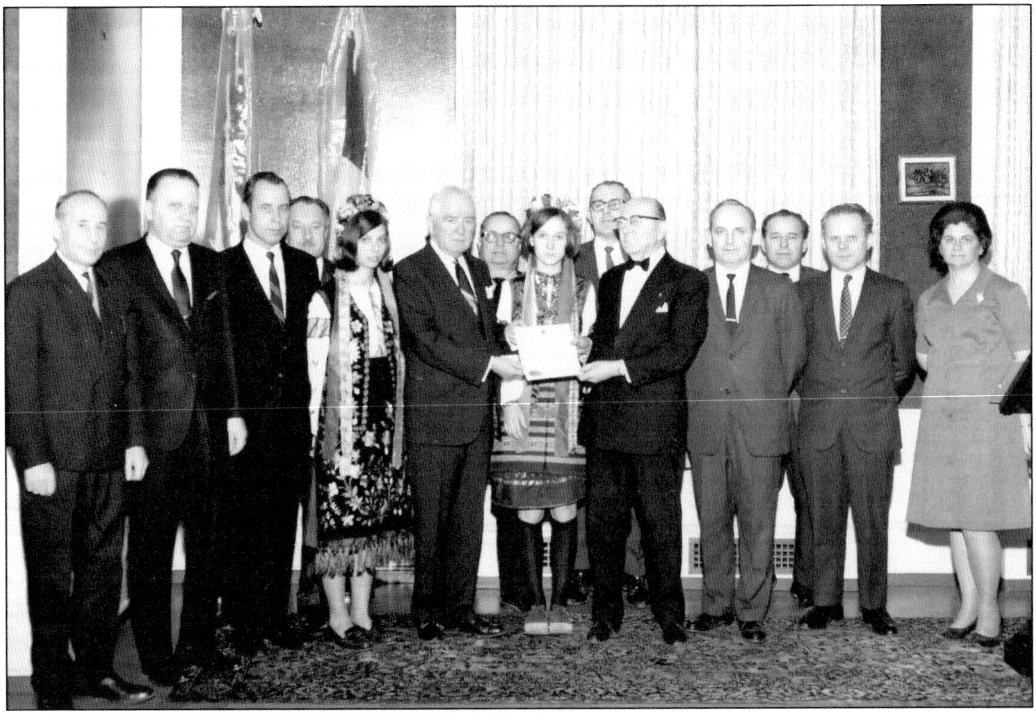

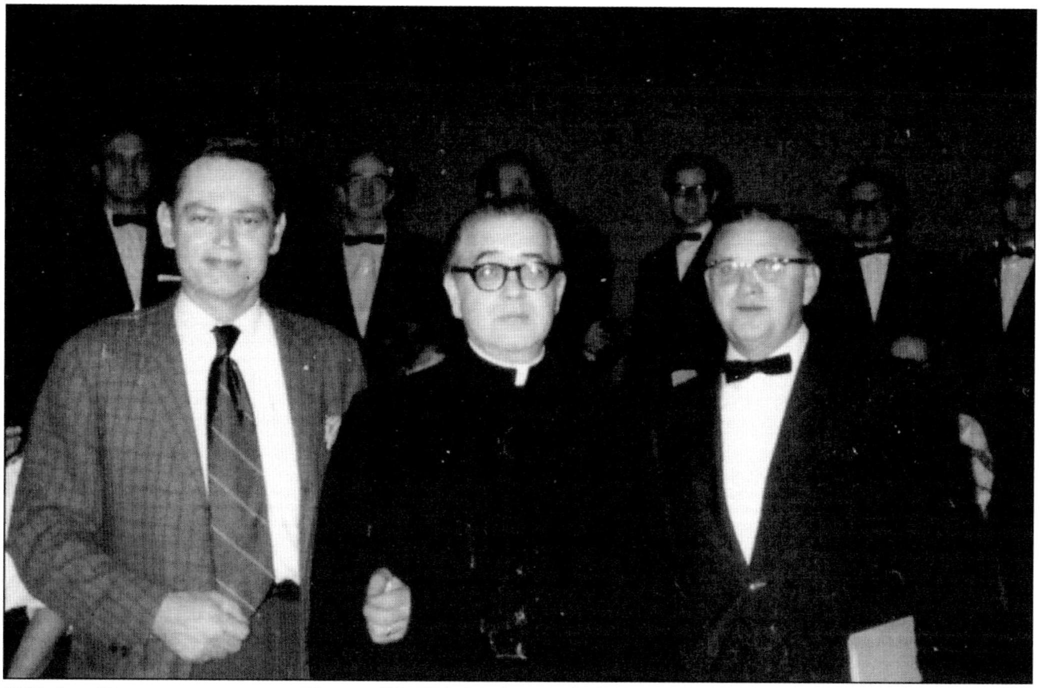

"We're Ready for our Close-Up." Members of the western Pennsylvania branch of the Ukrainian Orthodox League perform Ukrainian Christmas carols on the *Close Up* show hosted by Pittsburgh television personality Don Riggs in January 1971. (Courtesy of LAVRSHH.)

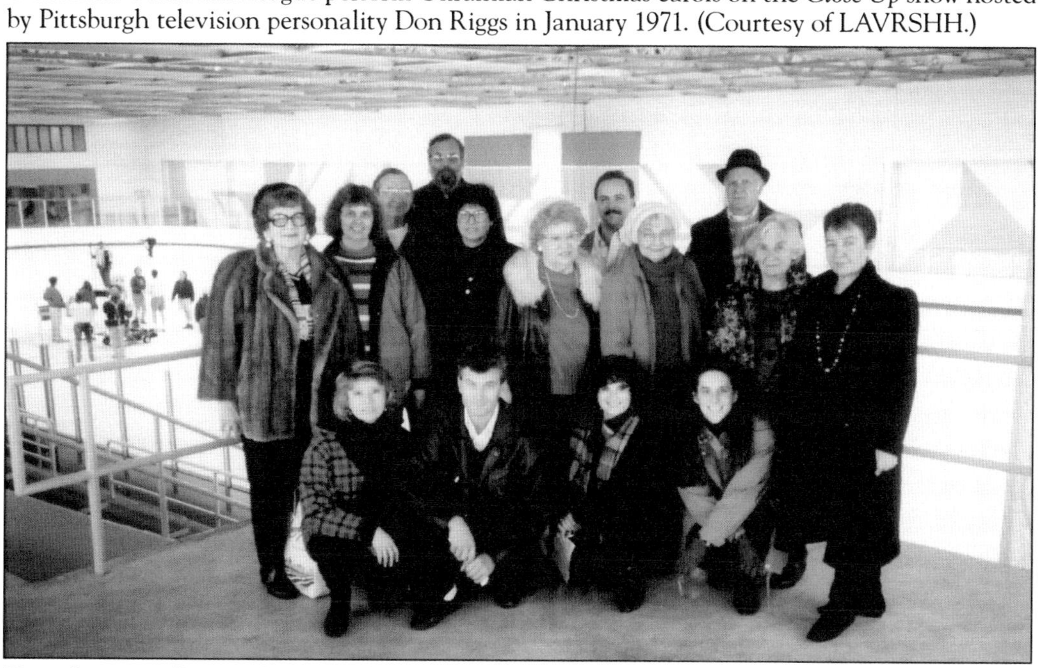

The Oksana Baiul Story. The 1994 Ukrainian Olympic gold medalist Oksana Baiul's life story was told in a Hallmark Hall of Fame movie, parts of which were filmed in western Pennsylvania. Local Ukrainians from Carnegie, McKees Rocks, and Pittsburgh played roles as extras in various movie scenes such as this one taken at Mount Lebanon ice-skating rink in 1995. (Courtesy of Oksana Byczkalo.)

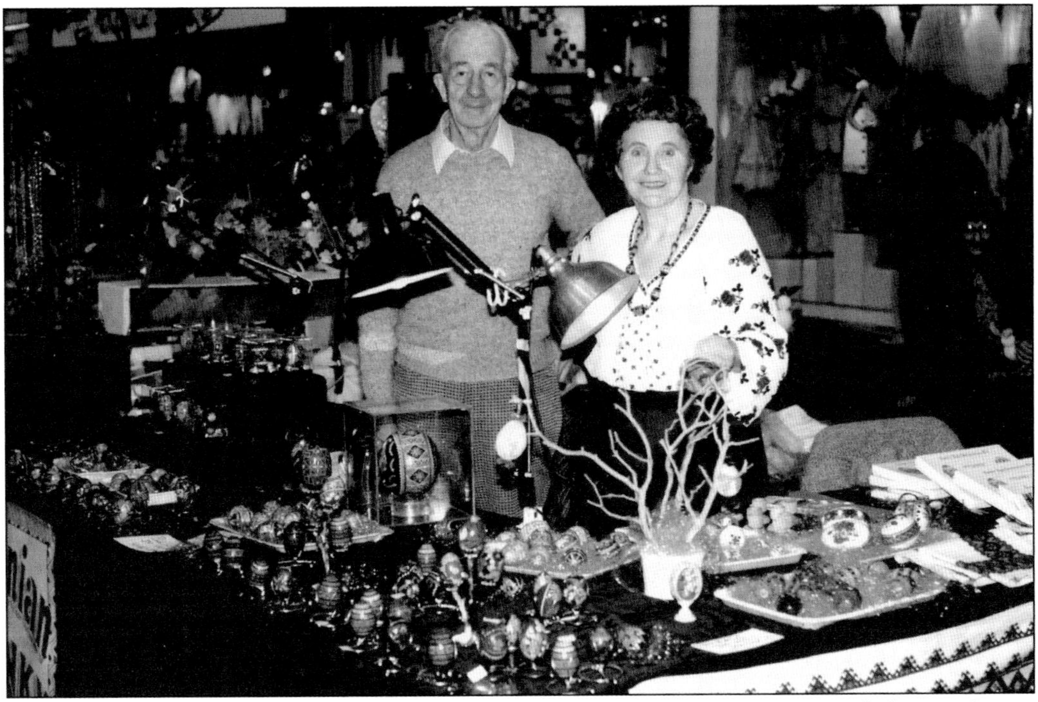

BRINGING UKRAINIAN CULTURE TO THE MALL. Metro and Joanne Staroschak met during Metro's service in the U.S. Army during World War II. Reunited after Joanne immigrated to the United States thanks to the Displaced Persons Act, they became tireless exponents of Ukrainian culture, hosting demonstrations and displays at places like the Washington Mall, PPG Plaza, and elsewhere. (Courtesy of Joanne Staroschak.)

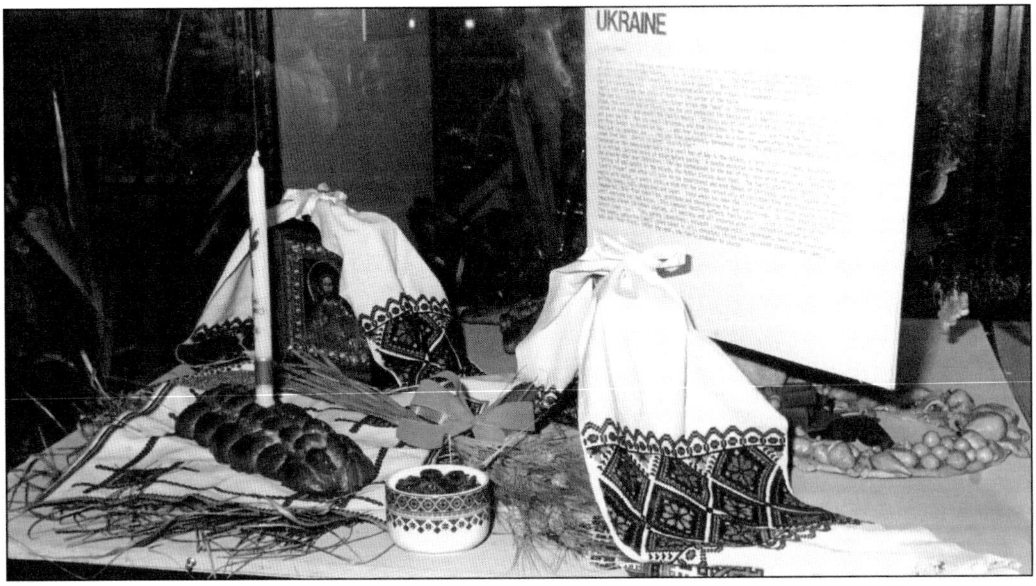

CULTURAL DISPLAY AT CITY-COUNTY BUILDING. Many of the most populous western Pennsylvania Ukrainian communities are located in Allegheny County, for which the city of Pittsburgh is the seat. This 1970s photograph shows the Ukrainian section of a display of ethnic Christmas customs. (Courtesy of MASPPUOGCCC.)

A Crafter's Delight. Crafters throughout western Pennsylvania have embraced the ancient and unique hand-craft of Ukrainian pysanky writing. Parishioners of SS. Peter and Paul Ukrainian Orthodox Greek Catholic Church in Carnegie have held an annual pysanky festival on (western) Palm Sunday since 1966. The event has received much attention in the press, and customers line up outside the church hall hours in advance of opening to get the best choice of eggs. (Courtesy of MASPPUOGCCC.)

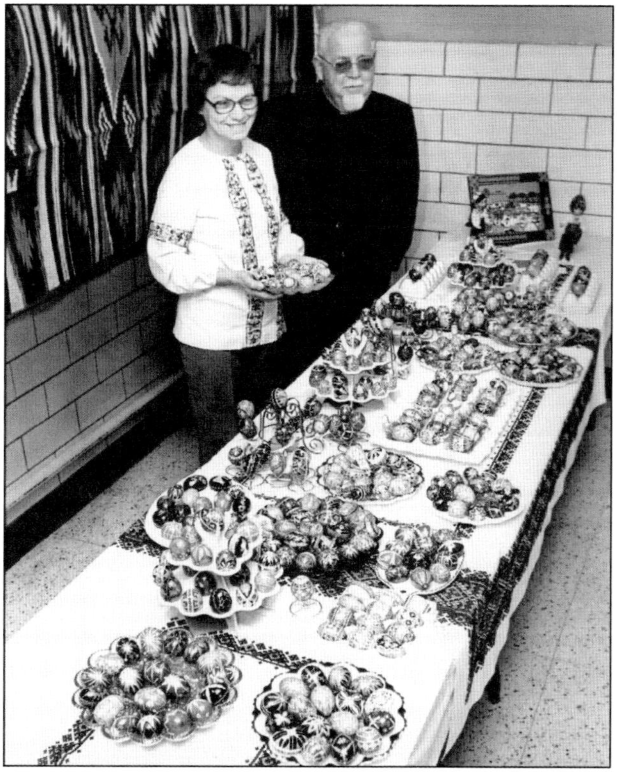

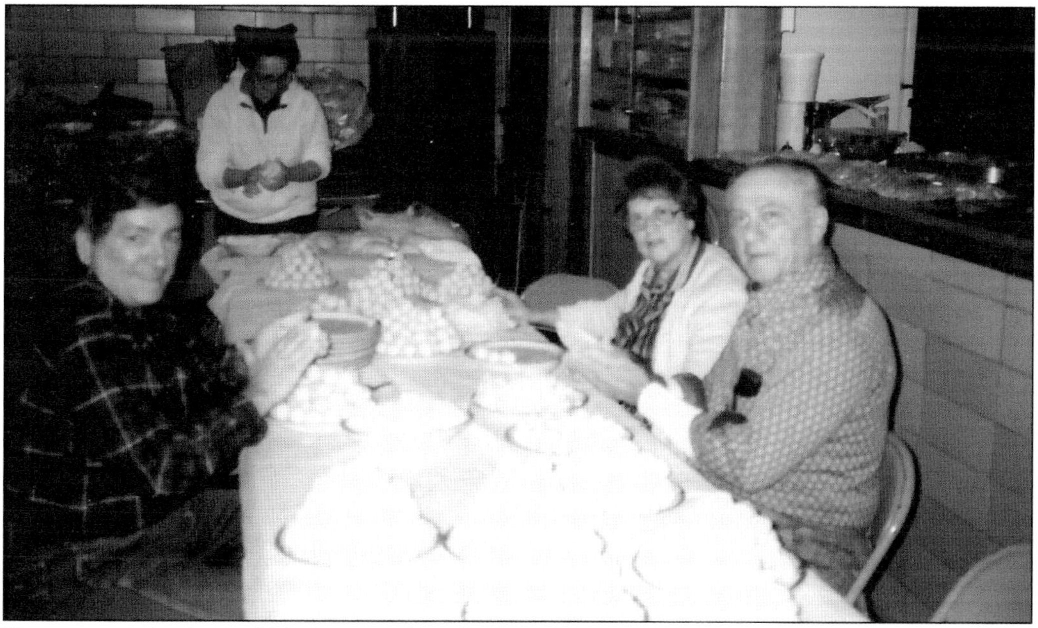

Varenyky. Members of SS. Peter and Paul Ukrainian Orthodox Church in Johnstown prepare potato balls, a key ingredient in the making of *varenyky*, also known as pierogies, *pyrohy*, *perohy*, or *pyrohi*. This staple of the Eastern European diet has become a western Pennsylvania favorite and is found on the menu of many area restaurants. Most Ukrainian churches sell varenyky to the public as a fund-raiser for church activities. (Courtesy of Peter Holubz Sr.)

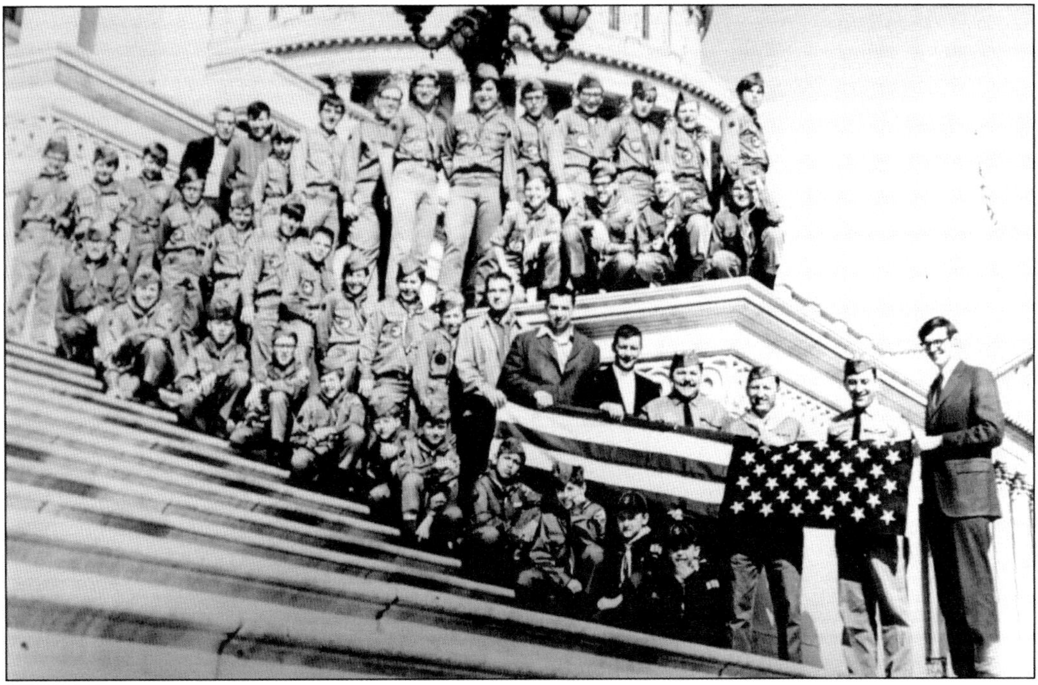

Scouts in Washington, D.C. Ukrainian churches were often the place where Boy Scout troops were sponsored. The troop based at SS. Peter and Paul Ukrainian Orthodox Greek Catholic Church in Carnegie traveled with other Scout troops from western Pennsylvania on this trip to Washington, D.C., in the late 1960s. (Courtesy of MASPPUOGCCC.)

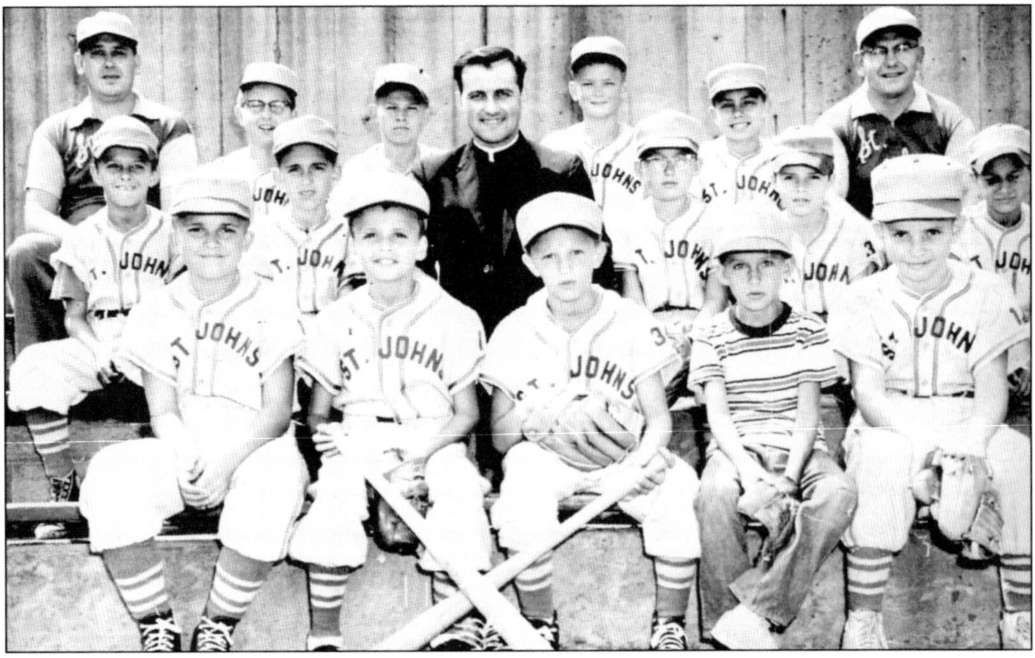

American Pastime. St. John the Baptist Ukrainian Catholic Church on Pittsburgh's South Side sponsored a Little League team in the 1960s. (Courtesy of St. John the Baptist Ukrainian Catholic Church.)

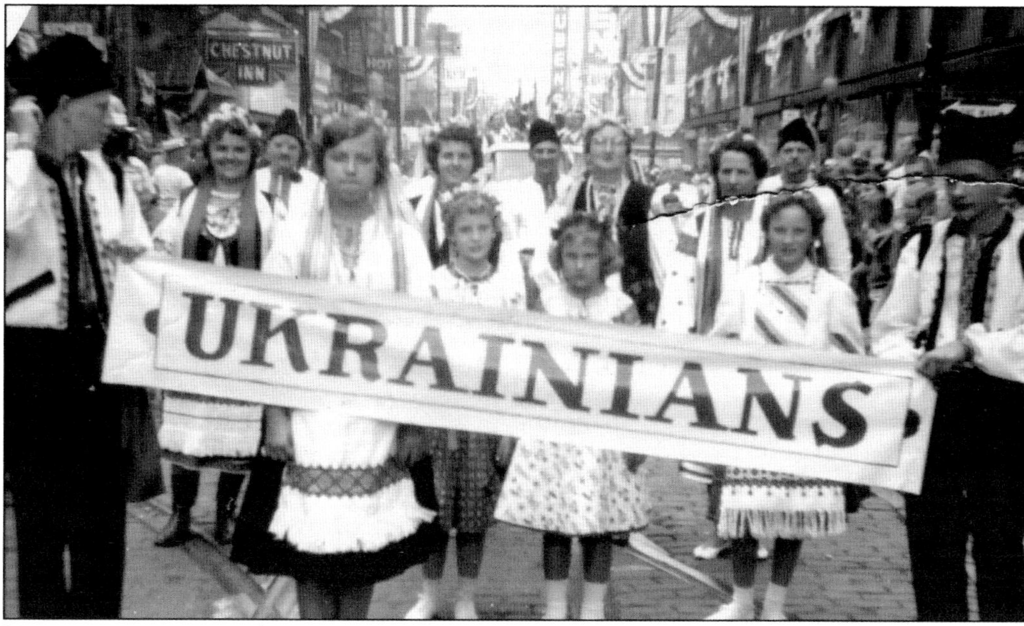

NATIONALITY DAYS. Ukrainians from McKeesport and the Mon Valley pose on the main street of the city during its first nationality days in 1959. Located at the confluence of the Monongahela and Youghiogheny Rivers, McKeesport was home to the National Tube Works, as well as the first location of the western Pennsylvania five and dime store G. C. Murphy. (Courtesy of Melanie Hutskow.)

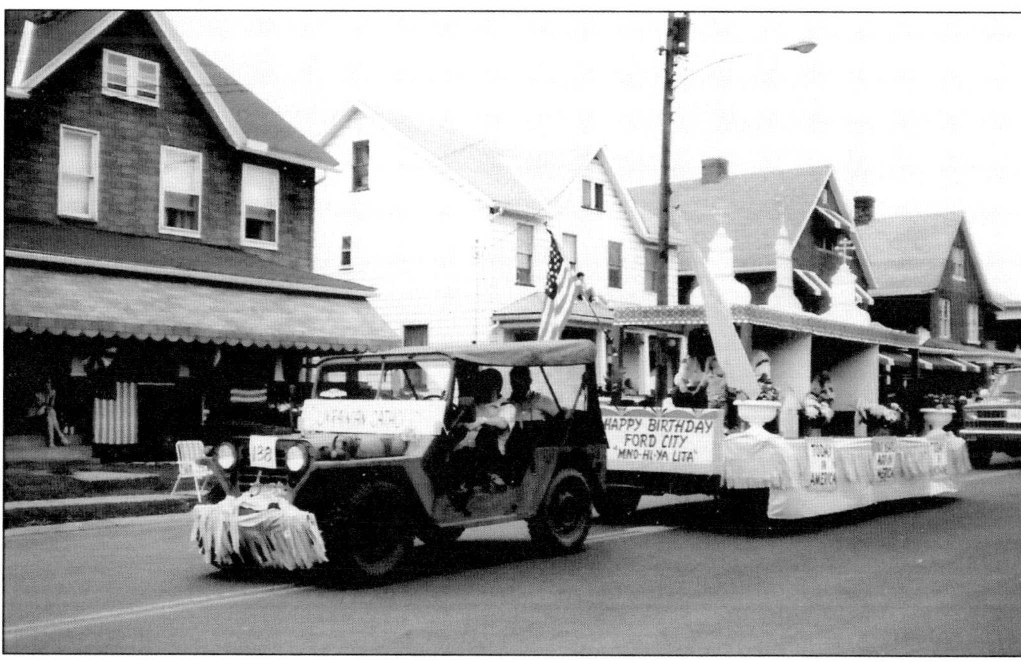

FORD CITY CENTENNIAL. The Ukrainian float travels down the streets of Ford City during its centennial celebration in 1987. Founded by Pittsburgh Plate Glass Company as a company town, it is located on the east bank of the Allegheny River in Armstrong County. (Courtesy of Pat Morovich.)

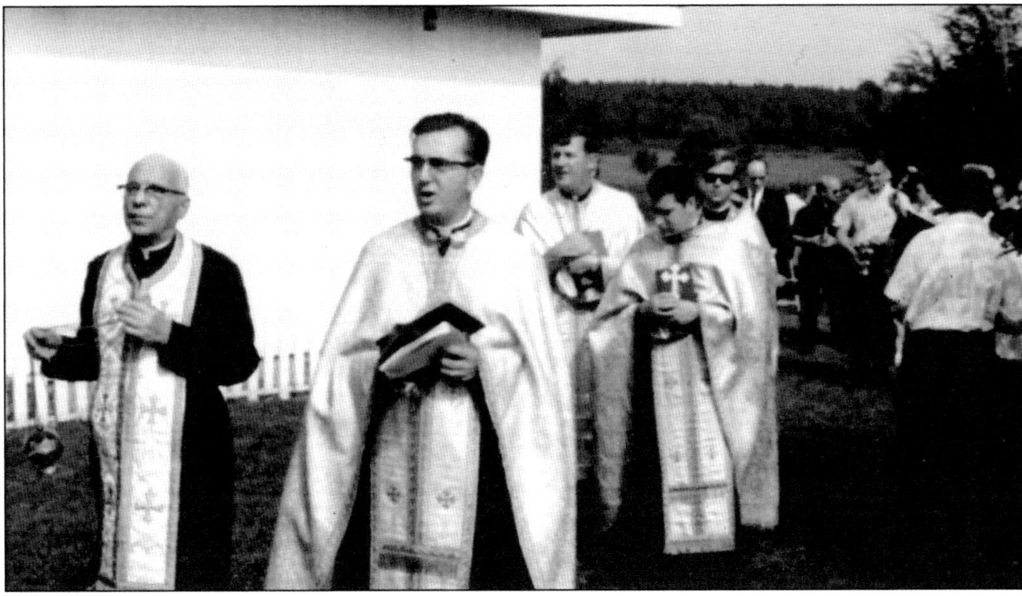

The Eastern Orthodox Foundation. Clergy and faithful of the Ukrainian Orthodox Church of the United States of America throughout western Pennsylvania and beyond have been actively involved in the Eastern Orthodox Foundation (EOF) located in Indiana County since its founding in 1966. In this 1969 photograph, EOF founder Fr. George Hnatko (third from left) is joined by Ukrainian clergy from Lyndora, Sharon, and Slickville at the foundation's annual festival. (Courtesy of LAVRSHH.)

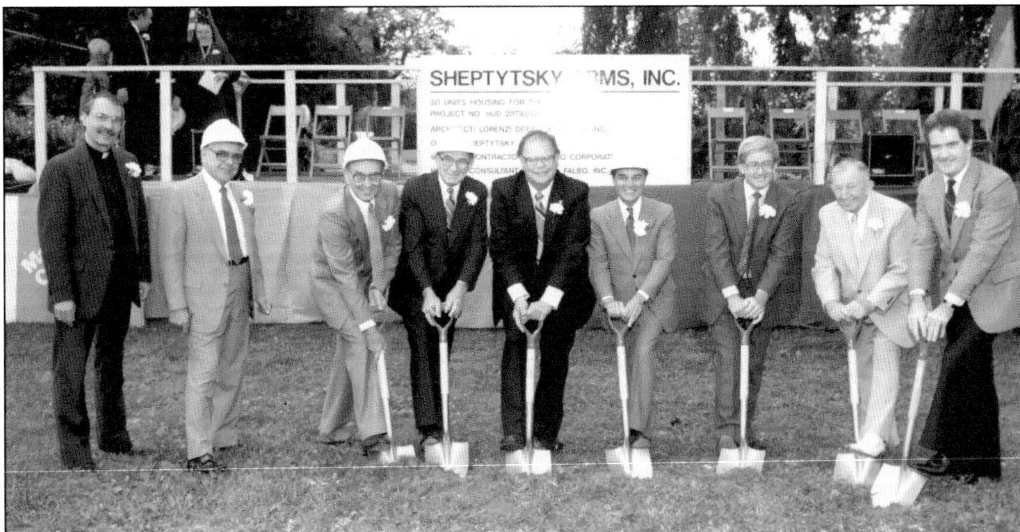

Sheptytsky Arms High-Rise for the Elderly. Opening in June 1987, this HUD facility serves the needs of low-income elderly and is located behind St. George Ukrainian Catholic Church in Pittsburgh's North Side neighborhood. It was named in honor of Metropolitan Andrew Sheptytsky, who when the Nazis invaded western Ukraine in the late spring of 1941 boldly condemned the treatment of the Jews in his pastoral letter "Thou Shalt Not Kill." He later hid thousands of Jews in his residence and in other Ukrainian Catholic church buildings. (Courtesy of Sheptytsky Arms, Inc.)

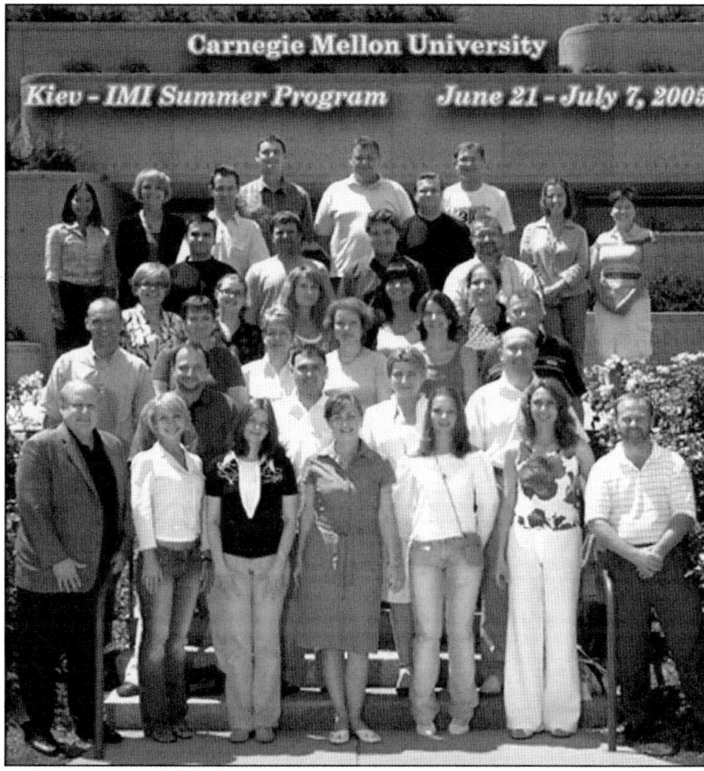

Carnegie Mellon University International Management Institute. Begun in 1996 with a United States Agency for International Development–funded grant, this summer internship program was designed to strengthen the long-term economic prospects of Ukraine. The program has brought between 60 and 90 students to the university's Pittsburgh campus almost every year since. (Courtesy of Michael Haritan.)

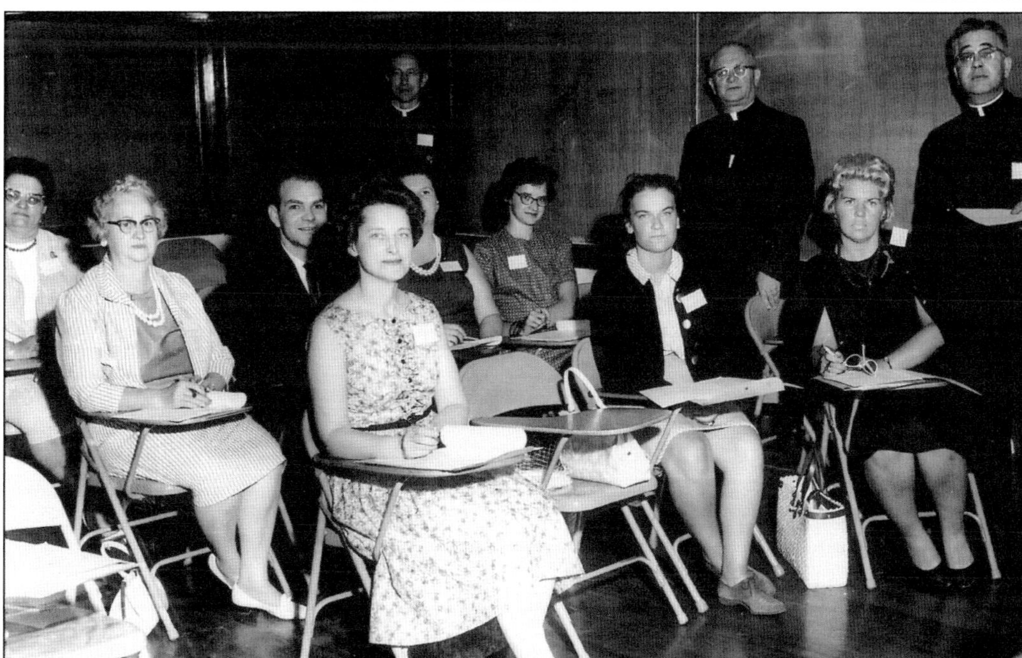

Thiel College. Local interest in church music was strong enough for Greenville-based Thiel College to sponsor a noncredited "Church Music Instruction Class" in 1963. (Courtesy of LAVRSHH.)

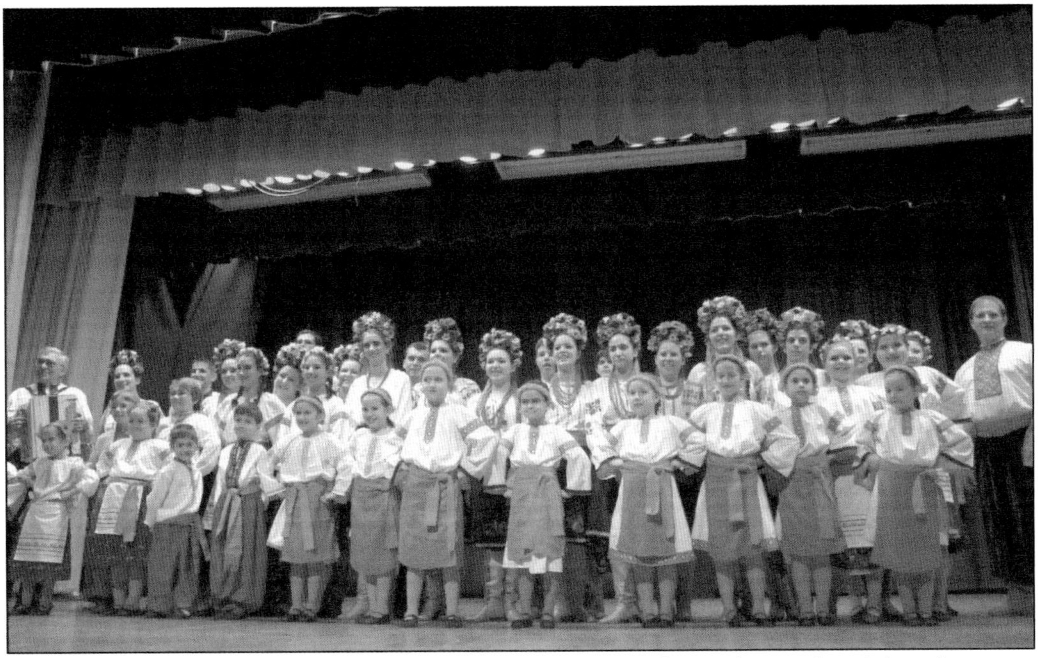

THE KYIV UKRAINIAN DANCE ENSEMBLE AND SCHOOL. Developing from a church-based group in Carnegie, the Kyiv Ukrainian Dance Ensemble has established a school of Ukrainian dance and attracts many students—a significant proportion of which are not of Ukrainian ancestry. This photograph was taken following the group's annual show in 2006. (Courtesy of MASPPUOGCCC.)

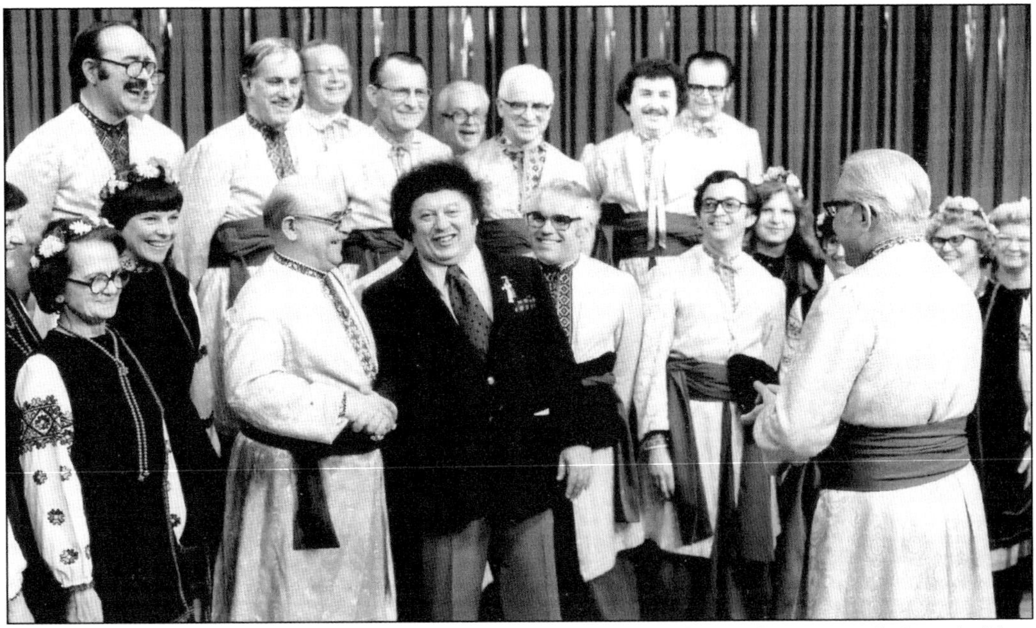

YUKKING IT UP WITH MARTY ALLEN. The LUC choir performs during a telethon held at WIIC-TV (now WPXI-TV) around 1980 to raise funds for a project of the Duquesne University Tamburitzans. The Tamburitzans are made up of full-time university students who perform and preserve the music, songs, and dances of Eastern Europe, including Ukraine. (Courtesy of Michael Haritan.)

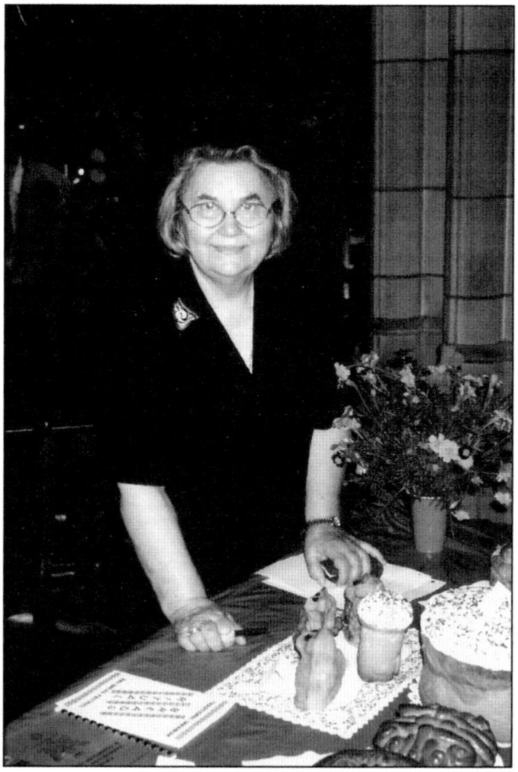

THE UKRAINIAN LANGUAGE PROGRAM AT THE UNIVERSITY OF PITTSBURGH. Kateryna Dowbenko began teaching Ukrainian language through the University of Pittsburgh's Department of Slavic Languages and Literatures in 1974. Accredited beginner, intermediate, and self-paced courses are offered, as well as independent study noncredit courses. She is also the advisor for the university's Ukrainian Students' Organization, which sponsors educational and cultural activities for interested students and also prepares events, such as this Ukrainian ritual breads display. (Courtesy of UCHI.)

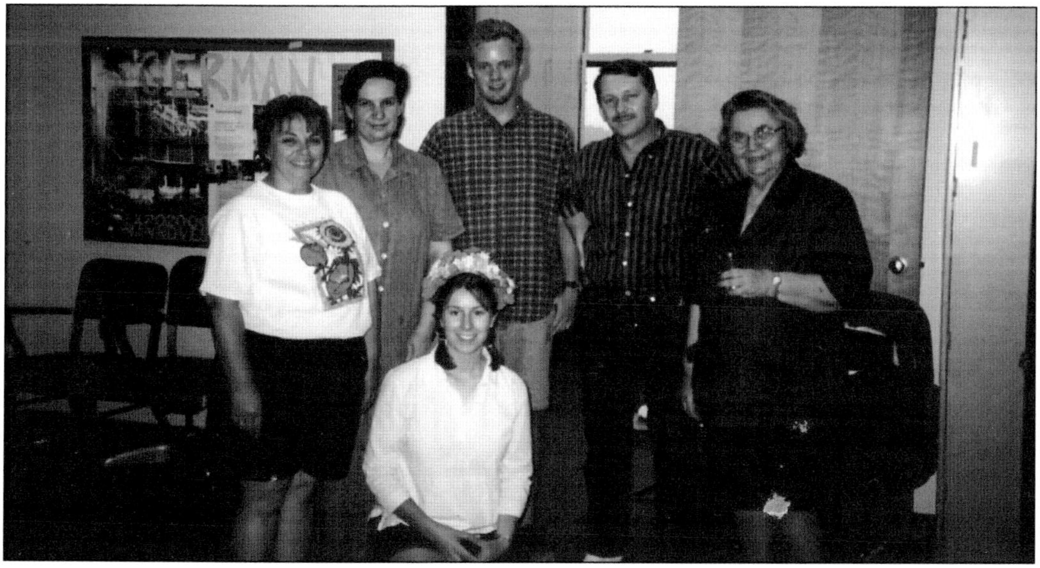

THE UKRAINIAN SUMMER LANGUAGE INSTITUTE AT THE UNIVERSITY OF PITTSBURGH. Using a mixture of funds from the university, Social Science Research Council, U.S. Department of Education, and tuition, the university's Department of Slavic Languages and Literatures has sponsored a six-week intensive course in Ukrainian language and culture most years since the mid-1990s. This 2000 photograph shows participants making a cultural presentation. The university also works with many Ukrainian exchange programs through its center for Russian and East European studies. (Courtesy of Hanna Chumachenko Lassowsky.)

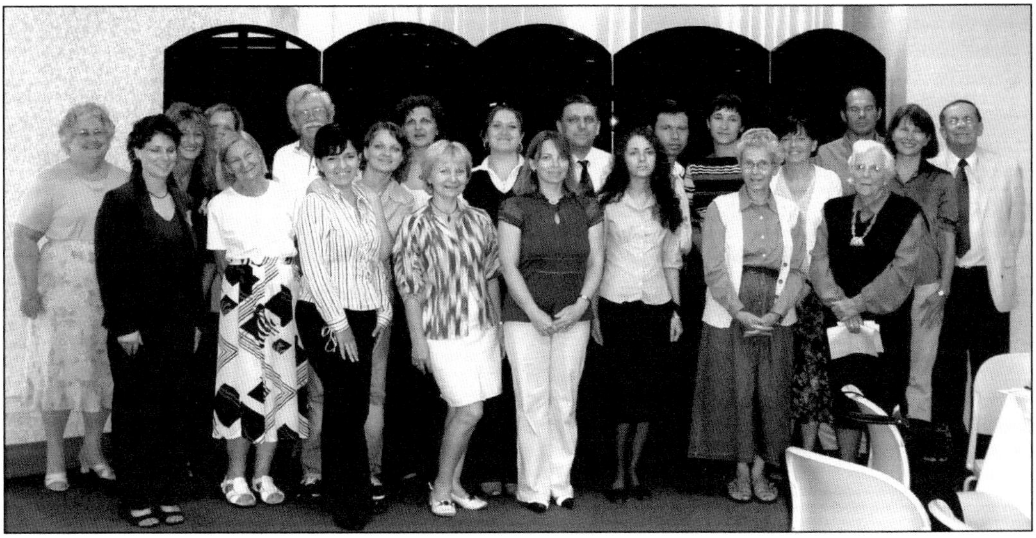

Magee WomanCare International. This international outreach arm of Pittsburgh's Magee Women's Hospital has hosted four training/exchange groups from Ukraine through the U.S. Library of Congress program Open World. Here home hosts, who come from both the local Ukrainian American community and the general populace, and professional hosts pose with guests and Magee WomanCare International (MWI) staff. Earlier, MWI established a primary health care program in Donets'k, Ukraine, in 2001 with an emphasis on preventive care including a community advisory board, as well as a miners' primary care health center, a family medicine center, and a women's wellness center. (Courtesy of MWI.)

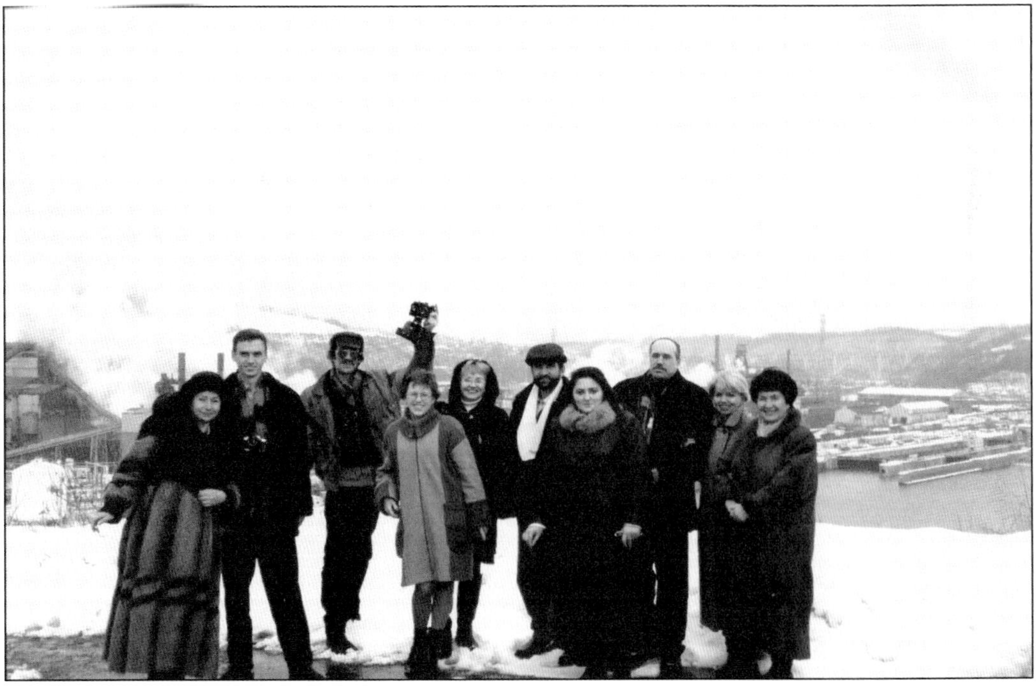

Reflections of the Homeland. A group of journalists hosted by the Pittsburgh Council for International Visitors (PCIV) visits U.S. Steel's Clairton Coke Works in February 2000. PCIV hosted 21 Ukrainian exchange groups from 1996 to 2003. (Courtesy of UCHI.)

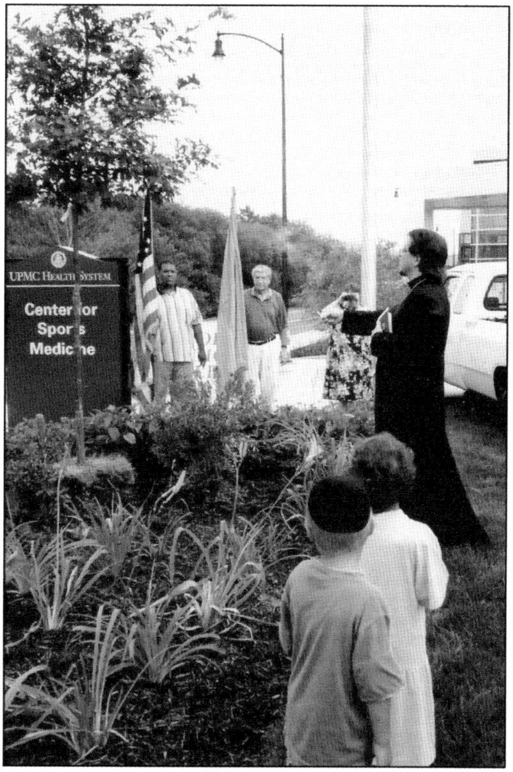

MAY THIS RELATIONSHIP BE AS LONG-LIVED AS THE MIGHTY OAK. Fr. John Haluszczak blesses an oak tree planted on the grounds of the University of Pittsburgh Medical Center (UPMC) Center for Sports Medicine at the South Side Works in Pittsburgh. The tree was planted on July 31, 2000, by the Pittsburgh-Donets'k Sister Cities Committee and a group of ecologists from Donets'k, Ukraine. The site was chosen to demonstrate Pittsburgh's transition from a reliance on heavy industry to a more diversified one featuring high technology, education, and health care. (Courtesy of UCHI.)

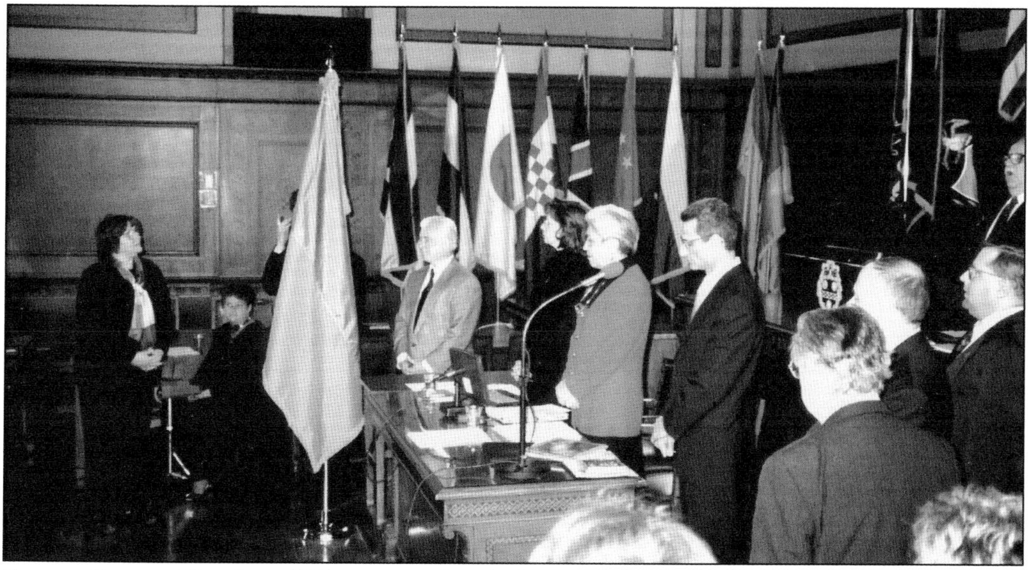

SISTER CITIES. The flag of Ukraine is placed alongside those of other countries in which the city of Pittsburgh has official sister city relationships in Pittsburgh City Council chambers. This February 15, 2000, photograph shows Ukrainian American city councilwoman Barbara Burns (left), city council president Bob O'Connor (second from left), and city councilman Eugene Ricciardi (fifth from left) during the ceremony following the ratification of the sister city agreement by council. Pittsburgh and Donets'k share a common industrial heritage and face similar challenges in a postindustrial environment. (Courtesy of UCHI.)

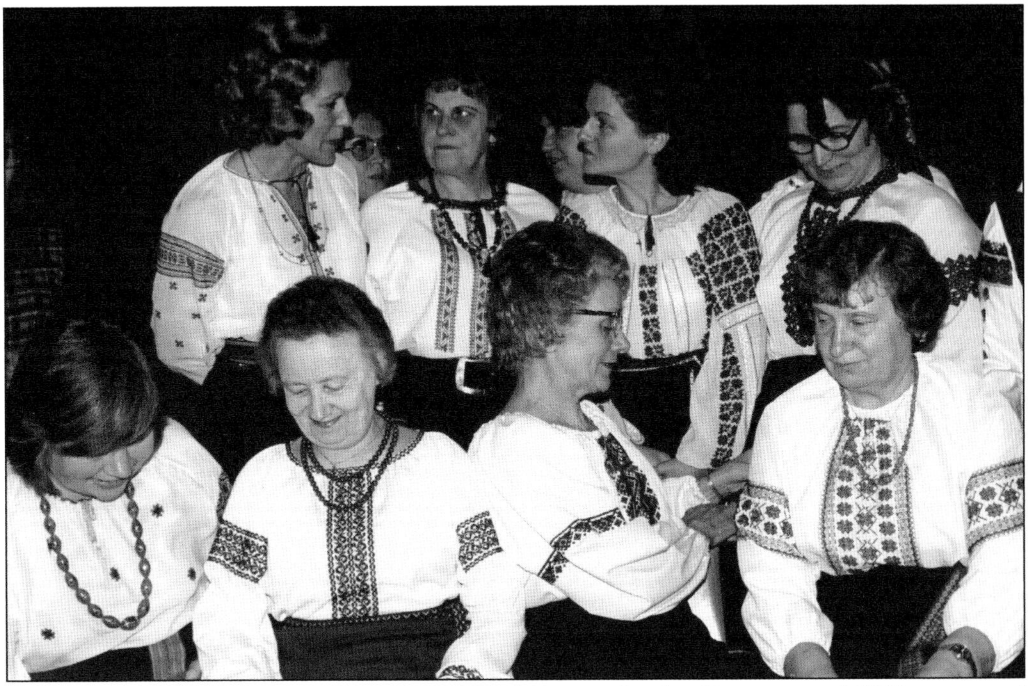

ERIE UKRAINIANS. In 1978, the National Endowment for the Humanities (NEH) sponsored a project to document ethnic groups in and around the city of Erie. Ukrainians were one of many groups included in this project, which produced 70 photographs for exhibit. Taken by photographers Gary Cardo and Thomas Volpe, these photographs show a Ukrainian women's group preparing for a performance as well as those attending the event. (Courtesy of Ethnic Impressions Collection, Erie County Historical Society.)

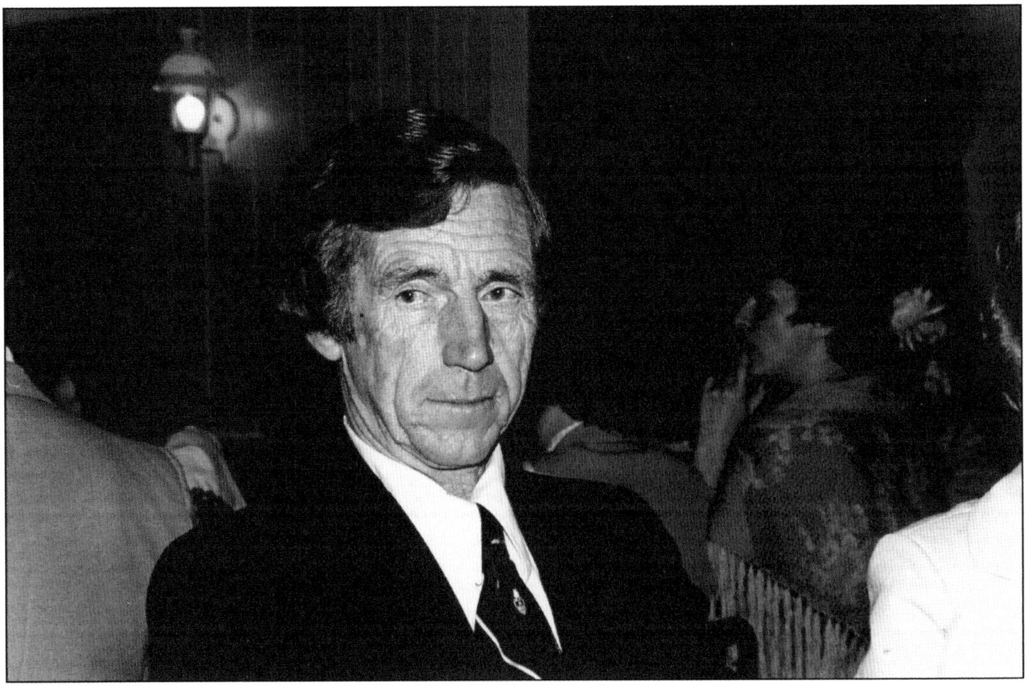

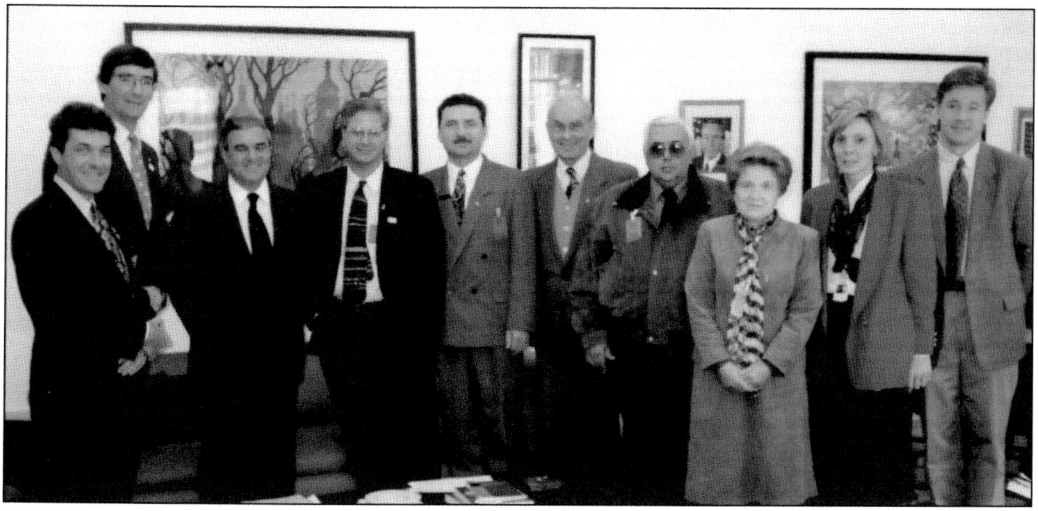

MEDICAL ASSISTANCE TO UKRAINE. By combining their strengths, the Tri-State Children of Chornobyl Relief Committee (TSCCRC) and the Norwin Rotary Club, have provided over $2.5 million in support to medical facilities in Ukraine since 1992. In addition to several medical exchanges, including training in bypass surgery by Dr. Michael Culig (fourth from left), the very first Poison Control Centers in Ukraine have been established—first in L'viv and then in Rivne. In this 1996 photograph, TSCCRC president S. Michael Tymiak (sixth from left), local Rotarians, and in-country partners discuss their program with U.S. ambassador to Ukraine William Green Miller (third from left). (Courtesy of Dennis Diffenderfer.)

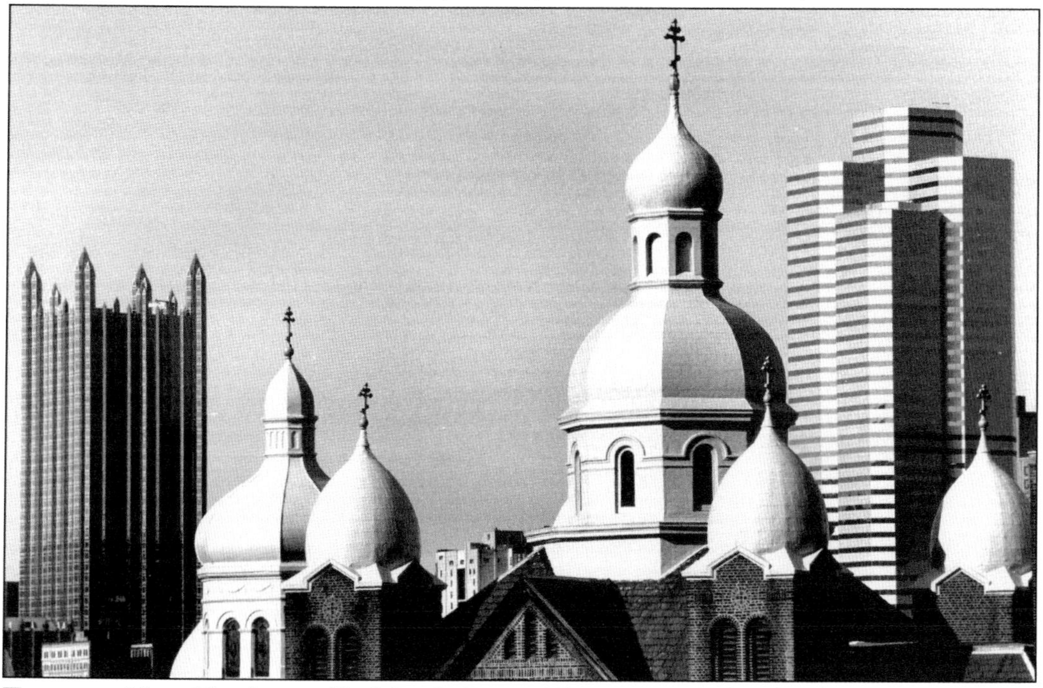

THEN AND NOW. The domes of St. John the Baptist Ukrainian Catholic Church stand in contrast to the modern skyscrapers of downtown Pittsburgh, most of which were built in the 1970s and 1980s. This scene is very popular among local photographers as it demonstrates that special western Pennsylvania quality of embracing the future while cherishing the past. (Courtesy of Michael Haritan.)

Discover Thousands of Local History Books Featuring Millions of Vintage Images

Arcadia Publishing, the leading local history publisher in the United States, is committed to making history accessible and meaningful through publishing books that celebrate and preserve the heritage of America's people and places.

Find more books like this at
www.arcadiapublishing.com

Search for your hometown history, your old stomping grounds, and even your favorite sports team.

Consistent with our mission to preserve history on a local level, this book was printed in South Carolina on American-made paper and manufactured entirely in the United States. Products carrying the accredited Forest Stewardship Council (FSC) label are printed on 100 percent FSC-certified paper.

MADE IN THE USA